PENGUIN CLASSICS

THREE AMERICAN P̶...
MELVILLE, TUC̶...
AND ROBIN̶...

HERMAN MELVILLE was born on 1 Aug̶... New York
City, the son of a merchant. Only twelve ... his father died
bankrupt, young Melville tried work as a bank clerk, as a cabin-boy
on a trip to Liverpool and as an elementary schoolteacher, before
shipping in January 1841 on the whaler *Acushnet*, bound for the
Pacific. Deserting ship the following year in the Marquesas, he
made his way to Tahiti and Honolulu, returning as ordinary sea-
man on the frigate *United States* to Boston, where he was dis-
charged in October 1844. Books based on these adventures won
him immediate success. By 1850 he was married, had acquired a
farm near Pittsfield, Massachusetts (where he was the impetuous
friend and neighbour of Nathaniel Hawthorne), and was hard at
work on his masterpiece *Moby-Dick*. But literary success soon
faded; his complexity increasingly alienated readers. After a visit
to the Holy Land in January 1857, he turned from writing prose
to poetry, including the long poem *Clarel* (1876) which grew
directly out of this journey and his search for religious faith. His
other verse includes *Battle-Pieces and Aspects of the War* (1866),
John Marr and Other Sailors (1888) and *Timoleon* (1891), which
contains poems based on his travels in Greece and Italy. In 1863,
during the Civil War, he moved back to New York City, where
from 1866 to 1885 he was a deputy inspector in the Customs
House, and where, on 28 September 1891, he died. A draft of
a final prose work, *Billy Budd, Sailor*, was left unfinished and
uncollated; packed tidily away by his widow, it was not redis-
covered and published until 1924.

FREDERICK TUCKERMAN (1821–73) was born in Boston. He
practised law for a short time, but spent the latter part of his life
living as a recluse in Greenfield, Massachusetts. Although his
collection *Poems* (1860) had its admirers, including Tennyson, he
achieved little recognition during his lifetime. His work was revised
by Witter Bynner and published as the *Sonnets of Frederick*

Goddard Tuckerman (1931). His most well-known poem, 'The Cricket', was not published until 1950.

EDWIN ARLINGTON ROBINSON (1869–1935) was born in Maine and studied at Harvard University before moving to New York to work. He made a name for himself with the poetry collection *The Children of the Night* (1897), which included some poems from his first, privately printed collection, *The Torrent and the Night Before* (1896). There followed *Captain Craig* (1902), *The Town down the River* (1910), *The Man Against the Sky* (1916) and his last work *King Jasper* (1935). He won the Pulitzer prize three times for *Collected Poems* (1922), *The Man Who Died Twice* (1925) and *Tristram* (1927).

JONATHAN BEAN received a BA from the University of Massachusetts and an MA from Boston University. A lifelong New Englander, he is a private scholar with a deep interest in the poets and writers of his native region. He lives near Concord, Massachusetts, the epicentre of Transcendentalism.

Three American Poets: Melville, Tuckerman and Robinson

Edited by JONATHAN BEAN

PENGUIN BOOKS

PENGUIN BOOKS

Published by the Penguin Group
Penguin Books Ltd, 80 Strand, London WC2R ORL, England
Penguin Putnam Inc., 375 Hudson Street, New York, New York 10014, USA
Penguin Books Australia Ltd, 250 Camberwell Road, Camberwell, Victoria 3124, Australia
Penguin Books Canada Ltd, 10 Alcorn Avenue, Toronto, Ontario, Canada M4V 3B2
Penguin Books India (P) Ltd, 11, Community Centre, Panchsheel Park, New Delhi – 110 017, India
Penguin Books (NZ) Ltd, Cnr Rosedale and Airborne Roads, Albany, Auckland, New Zealand
Penguin Books (South Africa) (Pty) Ltd, 24 Sturdee Avenue, Rosebank 2196, South Africa

Penguin Books Ltd, Registered Offices: 80 Strand, London WC2R ORL, England

www.penguin.com

This edition first published 2003
2

Introduction, Prefaces and Notes copyright © Jonathan Bean, 2003
All rights reserved

The moral right of the editor has been asserted

Set in 10.25/12.25 pt PostScript Adobe Sabon
Typeset by Rowland Phototypesetting Ltd, Bury St Edmunds, Suffolk
Printed in England by Clays Ltd, St Ives plc

Contents

Frederick Goddard Tuckerman

Edwin Arlington Robinson

Acknowledgements

The editor wishes to thank Christopher Ricks for his energy, his judgement and his friendship, and to thank the staff of the Houghton Library for their assistance. Publication of manuscript materials by Herman Melville and Frederick Tuckerman (MS Am 188[369], MS Am 188[386.B1], MS Am 1349[3] and MS Am 1349[4]) is by permission of the Houghton Library, Harvard University.

Introduction

This combination of Melville, Tuckerman and Robinson, three reclusive New England writers of the late nineteenth and early twentieth centuries, shows the great variety of American verse that was written in the shadow of the Civil War and during the reconstruction of an America that could never be the same. Their differences must be conceded, as each man went his way – Melville's travelled worldliness, ripening in his retirement into strange and sometimes bitter fruit; Tuckerman's one great journey, spending three days with the Poet Laureate Tennyson, then returning to his western Massachusetts reclusion with new confidence and inspiration, to be nearly racked with sorrow at the death of his young wife; and Robinson's inner journey, 'right through the forest, where none can see, / That's where I'm going, to Tilbury Town,' the grey-skied Maine home of his neo-transcendental imagination. To each his own, yet at the end of the long day each preferred the same company: none but himself. They make up a unique trio, joined in their solitariness, lending their voices in three distinct strains. From them we can hear what three Americans, independent Yankees beholden to no one, felt and thought during this turbulent era. *E pluribus unum*.

It was the Civil War, more than any other event, that set the tone of American life during this period. It is difficult now for us to imagine the turmoil – a large, semi-industrialized and progressive country, split utterly in half by bloody, newly mechanized warfare. The recent revival of religion and the abolition of Slavery gave the war its edges of morality and self-sacrifice – the assassination of the great Father, Lincoln, gave it a grand

martyr. The war seeped like blood through the fabric of the
rewoven union for decades afterwards, darkening, confusing
what had once seemed much purer, simpler.

And in its tumultuousness, the war caused a lot of different
reactions. Melville read the papers zealously, with a sailor's
interest in the naval engagements and with a deeply felt hu-
man interest in all. Perhaps the horribly detailed accounts of
the battles disinclined him to respond with prose – the scale
of suffering was too plainly painful and ugly to sustain for
page after page of novel or story – and so he took up writing
poems.

> I muse upon my country's ills –
> The tempest bursting from the waste of Time
> On the world's fairest hope linked with man's foulest crime.
> (from 'Misgivings (1860)')

In Melville, the war is expanded – it is not only North versus
South, or Abolition versus Slavery, or even simply Good versus
Evil, but also it is a mystery, a whirlwind, a state of eternal
struggle and restlessness, in which we all take part because we
are alive. But Melville managed to keep many details in, and
Battle Pieces and Aspects of the War brings new understanding
to any student of American history.

Tuckerman spent the Civil War in near-total seclusion at his
house in rural Greenfield, Massachusetts, like a Harvard-
educated druid, carefully observing the seasonal cycles of 'dear
New England nature'. He had already withdrawn from Boston,
from the world, mourning his young wife's death, and seeing to
the publication of his 1860 volume *Poems*. Some correspon-
dence exists to show that his seclusion was not complete by
about 1861, the year when the Civil War began. Precious little
worldly evidence of him can be found thereafter. The third,
fourth and fifth series of his sonnets were probably written
during this time. The first sonnet of series four ends:

> . . . Doubt contends with Hope, and Fear conspires
> To thwart them both: so that the Soul retires
> Even to her inmost keep and citadel;
> God views along the horizon darkening far,
> Vague tumult, lights of wo, and moving war.

The war is internal, and the national strife but an enlargement
of the real battles which are fought within the human breast.
'The Soul retires', and the soulful poet too – into the eternal
bastion of Nature – beyond the frail Unions among men and
the wars that attend upon their dissolution.

For Robinson too, child of the post-war years, life came to be
like nothing but a series of civil wars, waged in the heart.
His precise, short poems show us people who are struggling
internally with an idea, a sorrow or an unbreakable conflict.
Psychomachia becomes a way of life.

> There is one battle-field whereon we fall
> Triumphant and unconquered; but, alas!
> We are too fleshly fearful of ourselves
> To fight there till our days are whirled and blurred
> By sorrow, and the ministering wheels
> Of anguish take us eastward, where the clouds
> Of human gloom are lost against the gleam
> That shines on Thought's impenetrable mail.

So he wrote in 'Octaves', V. Note that anguish takes us east-
wards, in the direction of enlightenment. There, the clouds of
sorrow might dissipate in the light of reason. For Tuckerman
too, Thought wore armour:

> But Thought, like a mail'd warder helm'd and tall
> Treads ever on the outward battlement:
> Striving to pierce thro' embrasure and rent
> The secret of the gloom that girdleth all,
> The immeasurable gulf and interval!
>   (*Sonnets*, Part IV, 2)

What was it about life in this age of America that caused the feeling mind to so withdraw, away from the busy concourse of fellow men, behind the plate-mail of pure thought? These three solitary men bore witness to the rending agony and eventual rebuilding of a nation founded upon nothing firmer than ideas and ideals – the Constitution, no more solid than a collection of principles, to be interpreted and fought over to this very day – the country, and our human lives, no more substantial than a dream, and no less fragile or vast.

Table of Dates

1847 (February) Tuckerman buys a house in Greenfield, Massachusetts, from the father of Anna Jones, whom he soon marries. (March 30) Melville's novel *Omoo* published in London; in May it is published in New York.

1848 (June 29) Death of Tuckerman's infant daughter.

1849 (February 16) Birth of Melville's son Malcolm. (October–February 1850) Melville travels in Europe. (November) Tuckerman's first poem, 'November', published in the *Literary World*.

1850 (August 5) Melville begins friendship with Nathaniel Hawthorne. (September–October) Melville purchases a farm, which he names Arrowhead, near Pittsfield, Massachusetts.

1851 (Summer) Tuckerman travels widely in England and Scotland. (November 14) Melville's *Moby-Dick* published in New York. (October 22) Birth of Melville's son Stanwix.

1854 (July–February 1855) Tuckerman and his wife travel in Europe. During this trip (January 1855) Tuckerman spends three days as the guest of Tennyson at Farringford, Isle of Wight.

1855 Walt Whitman's *Leaves of Grass*.

1856 (October) With a loan from his father-in-law, Melville travels for his health, visiting Hawthorne at his consulship in Liverpool and sightseeing in Jerusalem, Greece and Italy. Returns to New York in May 1857.

1857 (May 12) Tuckerman's wife Anna dies of complications from the birth of their son Frederick, who survives.

1860 (May) Melville attempts (unsuccessfully) to publish his first collection of poems. Tuckerman's *Poems* printed privately in Boston.

1861 (April 12) Confederates bombard Fort Sumter, beginning the Civil War.

1863 (July 1–3) Battle of Gettysburg, the turning point of the Civil War. Tuckerman's *Poems* published in London. Melville sells Arrowhead to his brother Allan and returns to New York.

1864 Tuckerman's *Poems* published in Boston. (May 19) Hawthorne dies.

1865 (April 9) General Lee surrenders, ending the Civil War. (April 14) Lincoln assassinated.

1866 (August 23) Melville's *Battle Pieces and Aspects of the War* published in New York. (December 5) Melville takes a job as deputy inspector of customs at the Port of New York.

1867 (August) Tuckerman considers buying Hawthorne's house in Concord. (September 11) Melville's son Malcolm dies in his bed at the age of eighteen, from a self-inflicted gunshot wound.

1869 (December 22) Edwin Arlington Robinson born in Head Tide, Maine, to Edward and Mary Robinson.

1870 Tuckerman moves into a boarding house in Greenfield.

1871 (April) Tuckerman sells his house in Greenfield. He lives in the boarding house until his death.

1873 (February) Tuckerman sends three sonnets to the *Springfield Republican*, but they are not published. (May 9) Tuckerman dies of heart disease in Greenfield at the age of fifty-two.

1876 (June) Melville's poem *Clarel: A Poem and Pilgrimage in the Holy Land* published.

1878 Melville's wife's inheritance relieves his long-standing difficulty in supporting his family.

1885 (December 31) Melville retires from the customs house.

1886 (February 23) Melville's son Stanwix dies alone in San Francisco at the age of thirty-four.

1888 Melville's *John Marr and Other Sailors* privately printed in an edition of twenty-five copies.

1891 (May) Melville's *Timoleon, Etc.* privately printed in an edition of twenty-five copies. Robinson enters Harvard as a special student. (September 28) Melville dies in New York at the age of seventy-two.

1892 (October 6) Tennyson dies.

1893 Robinson leaves Harvard and returns to Gardiner, Maine.

1896 (November) Robinson's first book, *The Torrent and the Night Before*, privately printed.

1898 Robinson works in a clerical position at Harvard.

1899 Robinson moves to New York City, eventually finding work as a time-checker in the construction of the subway.

1902 Robinson publishes *Captain Craig*.

1905 President Roosevelt obtains for Robinson a sinecure as a Treasury agent. Robinson resigns after Roosevelt leaves office in 1909.

1909 (January) Twentieth-century rediscovery of Tuckerman begins with Walter Eaton's essay 'A Forgotten American Poet' in *Forum*.

1911 Robinson visits the MacDowell artist colony in New Hampshire, where he will spend all his remaining summers.

1917 T. S. Eliot's *Prufrock and Other Observations*. Robinson begins to turn away from short lyrical poetry towards longer, historical narratives with the publication of *Merlin*.

1921 Robinson's *Collected Poems* wins the first ever Pulitzer prize for poetry.

1923 (Spring) Robinson travels in England.

1924 Robinson's *The Man Who Died Twice* wins the Pulitzer prize.

1927 Robinson's long poem *Tristram* published. It becomes a best seller and wins Robinson a third Pulitzer prize.

1933 *The Sonnets of Frederick Goddard Tuckerman* published.

1935 (April 6) Robinson dies in New York City at the age of sixty-five.

1950 Tuckerman's 'The Cricket' first published.

Further Reading

HERMAN MELVILLE

Editions

The Works of Herman Melville (16 vols.; London, 1924); vol.
16 contains the poems

The Collected Poems of Herman Melville, ed. Howard Vincent
(Chicago, 1947)

The Battle-Pieces of Herman Melville, ed. Hennig Cohen (New
York, 1963)

Selected Poems of Herman Melville, ed. Robert Penn Warren
(New York, 1970)

Poems of Herman Melville, ed. Douglas Robillard (Albany,
1976)

Selected Poems of Herman Melville, ed. Hennig Cohen (New
York, 1991)

Biography

Howard, Leon, *Herman Melville, A Biography* (Berkeley and
Los Angeles, 1951)

The Melville Log: A Documentary Life of Herman Melville, ed.
Jay Leyda (2 vols.; New York, 1969)

Parker, Hershel, *Herman Melville: A Biography* (2 vols.; Balti-
more, 1996–2002)

Criticism

Donoghue, Denis, *Connoisseurs of Chaos: Ideas of Order in Modern American Poetry* (New York, 1965)

Spengemann, William, 'Melville the Poet', *American Literary History* (Autumn 1999)

Warren, Robert Penn, 'Melville the Poet', *Kenyon Review* 8 (1946); reprinted in Warren's *Selected Essays* (New York, 1958)

Warren, Rosanna, 'Dark Knowledge: Poems of the Civil War', *Raritan* (1999)

Weaver, Raymond, *Herman Melville, Mariner and Mystic* (New York, 1961)

FREDERICK GODDARD TUCKERMAN

Editions

The Sonnets of Frederick Goddard Tuckerman, ed. Witter Bynner (New York, 1931)

The Complete Poems of Frederick Goddard Tuckerman, ed. N. Scott Momaday (New York, 1965)

Criticism

Cady, E. H., 'Frederick Goddard Tuckerman', in *Essays on American Literature in Honor of Jay B. Hubbell* (Durham, North Carolina, 1967)

England, Eugene, *Beyond Romanticism: Tuckerman's Life and Poetry* (Provo, 1990)

Golden, Samuel A., *Frederick Goddard Tuckerman* (New York, 1966)

EDWIN ARLINGTON ROBINSON

Editions

Collected Poems of Edwin Arlington Robinson (New York, 1921–37); the edition of 1929 was the last published during Robinson's life

Tilbury Town: Selected Poems of Edwin Arlington Robinson, ed. Lawrance Thompson (New York, 1953)

Uncollected Poems and Prose of Edwin Arlington Robinson, ed. Richard Cary (Waterville, 1975)

Bibliography

Hogan, Charles Beecher, *A Bibliography of Edwin Arlington Robinson* (New Haven, 1936)

Biography

Hagedorn, Hermann, *Edwin Arlington Robinson: A Biography* (New York, 1938)

Correspondence

Untriangulated Stars: Letters of Edwin Arlington Robinson to Harry De Forest Smith, 1890–1905, ed. Denham Sutcliffe (Cambridge, Mass., 1947)

Edwin Arlington Robinson's Letters to Edith Brower, ed. Richard Cary (Cambridge, Mass., 1968)

Criticism

Anderson, Wallace, *Edwin Arlington Robinson: A Critical Introduction* (Cambridge, Mass., 1968)

Coxe, Louis, 'E. A. Robinson: The Lost Tradition', *Sewanee Review* 62 (Spring 1954)

Frost, Robert, 'Introduction' to Robinson's *King Jasper* (New York, 1935)

Fussell, Edwin S., *Edwin Arlington Robinson: The Literary Background of a Traditional Poet* (Berkeley and Los Angeles, 1954)

Winters, Yvor, *Edwin Arlington Robinson* (Norfolk, Conn., 1946)

HERMAN MELVILLE

Preface

This selection of Melville's poetry aims to show the range of his shorter verse: from Melville the public poet, intensely concerned with the Civil War and its meaning for the fate of humanity, to Melville the private poet, still deeply involved in mankind even as he withdrew from the eyes of the world. I have not sought especially to choose poems that shed light upon Melville the novelist; rather, the emphasis has been on giving the best of Melville's efforts in that form, poetry, in which he wrote almost exclusively for the last thirty years of his life.

In establishing the text I have used Melville's personal copy of the first edition of *Battle Pieces and Aspects of the War* (1866), and first editions of *John Marr and Other Sailors* (1888) and *Timoleon, Etc.* (1891). I have adopted changes that Melville inscribed in these volumes, and the lines as originally printed are given in the notes. For those pieces not published during Melville's lifetime, I have used the manuscripts in the Houghton Library at Harvard. For the text of 'Billy in the Darbies' I have consulted the text established by Harrison Hayford and Merton M. Sealts, Jr., for the University of Chicago Press edition of 1962. The manuscripts of 'Camoëns' and 'Pontoosuc' present the most significant textual difficulties; for details, see the notes to the poems.

I have excluded selections from the book-length poem *Clarel: A Poem and Pilgrimage in the Holy Land* (1876), since the preference of this series has been to include only whole poems and not to excerpt, and because distilling the essence of *Clarel's* 18,000 lines would be beyond the scope of this volume.

Interested readers are referred to Walter Bezanson's 1960 edition of that work.

I have also excluded songs that appear within prose works. Such pieces need the context of the fiction to shine fully. For the same reason are excluded poems from *John Marr and Other Sailors* that are accompanied by lengthy prose introductions. An exception is made for 'Billy in the Darbies' from *Billy Budd*, which stands on its own merits.

There is no definitive answer to the question 'Why did Melville stop writing novels?'. Poor health brought on by the strain of writing at length, despair at weak sales and the bad critical reception of his later novels, pressure from his family to give up a failed career and start earning money: all these have been offered in explanation. One should remember that Melville's public success did not increase during his career: *Typee* (1846) sold many more copies than *Moby-Dick* (1851), which was out of print by 1887. Melville quit writing fiction not at the height of fame but after a long struggle to bring a reluctant reading public along to an appreciation of the singularity of his art.

After the financial failure of *The Confidence Man* (1857), Melville turned to a new career as a lecturer. During three seasons speaking on topics such as Roman statuary and the South Sea islands, Melville began to write poetry with the intention of publishing it. In 1860, while preparing for a voyage to San Francisco, he left a list of memoranda for his brother 'concerning the publication of my verses'. The fifth item was: 'For God's sake don't have *By the author of "Typee" "Piddledee" &c* on the title-page.' The title was to be 'Poems, by Herman Melville'. He added dryly:

Of all human events, perhaps, the publication of a first volume of verses is the most insignificant; but though a matter of no moment to the world, it is still of some concern to the author.

Even as he made this defensive admission, Melville did not suppose that his verses would find no publisher. But that is exactly what happened. The contents of that first collection are not known, but it is reasonable to guess that it included poems on Greek and Italian subjects (such as 'Greek Architecture', which was not published until 1891 in *Timoleon*, his last book of poetry) that Melville had written while he was touring the Mediterranean in 1856–7. It could be, however, that Melville wrote the poems on Mediterranean subjects much later, using his journal of the tour as a memory aid while he worked on *Timoleon*.

After failing to find a publisher for the 1860 collection, Melville temporarily gave up writing. Several fruitless years trying to gain a position in a consulate (like that of his friend Hawthorne, who held the consulship at Liverpool) were spent under the burdens of illness and depression. It was not until the Civil War that he was stirred by subjects powerful enough to draw him back to publication. But when his *Battle Pieces and Aspects of the War* appeared in 1866, Melville's headnote implied that instinct, not intention, had guided his pen.

With few exceptions, the Pieces in this volume originated in an impulse imparted by the fall of Richmond. They were composed without reference to collective arrangement, but, being brought together in review, naturally fall into the order assumed ... Yielding instinctively, one after another, to feelings not inspired from any one source exclusively, and unmindful, without purposing to be, of consistency, I seem, in most of these verses, to have but placed a harp in a window, and noted the contrasted airs which wayward winds have played upon the strings.

As M. H. Abrams notes in *The Mirror and the Lamp*,[1] the Aeolian harp is conventionally used by the Romantic poets 'as a construct for the mind in perception as well as for the poetic mind in composition'. Though this deliberate use of the wind-harp topos (and he was to use it again in 'The Aeolian Harp' of *John Marr and Other Sailors*) suggests that Melville sees his connection to such poets as Coleridge, Wordsworth and Shelley, on its surface the headnote seems to deny that he seeks a triumphal return to the public eye in the laurels of a poet. If humility was a goal, the book achieved it: *Battle Pieces* did not cover its expenses, and Melville assumed half the debt of its losses. A few months later, he accepted a position as deputy inspector of customs in the Port of New York, and his days as a professional author were over.

But he did not stop writing. During the next several years, while most of his former readers forgot he was still living, he completed the 18,000 lines of *Clarel: A Poem and Pilgrimage in the Holy Land*, which describes a journey by a doubting student through Palestine. In the dialogue between Clarel and his companions the poem encounters many questions and problems of belief, sin and redemption. Published in 1876 by means of a gift from Melville's uncle Peter Gansevoort, *Clarel* perplexed critics while attracting little attention from readers. Melville's early fame as a writer of romances had shrunk so much by this time that the reviewer for *Lippincott's* magazine believed *Clarel* to be the first thing he had written since *Mardi* (1849).

John Marr and Other Sailors (1888) was printed privately in an edition of twenty-five copies, and attracted only one review. *Timoleon* (1891) was printed in the same number, but by then almost everyone had either completely forgotten Melville or assumed him to be dead.

Modern criticism, though paying Melville his due as a novelist since his rediscovery in the 1920s, has had difficulty making a direct assessment of his poetry. Usually it has been over-shadowed by his prose. 'Few of his poems reveal anything like the mastery of organic rhythm to be found in his best prose,' wrote F. O. Matthiessen in 'Melville as Poet'. Randall Jarrell echoes this: 'Melville is a great poet only in the prose of *Moby-Dick*.' Robert Penn Warren, in trying to get at a clear reading of the poet without the novelist, sees the connection between them as inextricable: 'If we are completely to understand Melville's poetry, we must see it against the backdrop of his defeat as a writer of fiction.'[2] For Walter Bezanson, in the introduction to his edition of *Clarel* (1960), the separation of the two Melvilles is a necessary step towards the fair appreciation of the poetry.

There is still, of course, the problem of how good a poet Melville was. It may well be that his poetic stature has been unduly overshadowed by his eminence as a prose romancer. We have not lived long enough with the idea that he was a poet at all to decide justly how good a poet he was. Fearing that claims for his verse would seem a generous illusion stemming from love of his prose, we may have sold the poetry short. Or we may have been unwittingly baffled by finding in the poetry many of the conceptual values of the novels expressed without that rich copiousness which is the hallmark of his best-known prose. Once we face up to the idea that Melville's poetry is not an extension of the lyric vein of his famous novels but is a wholly new mode of contracted discourse we will be more ready to judge his poetry.[3]

Melville entered that 'new mode' freely. If it is true, as Warren says, that we ought to read the poetry against 'the backdrop of his defeat as a writer of fiction', it does not follow that Melville was forced by that defeat into stooping to poetry. He failed as a poet too, but continued to write poetry for many years. Melville chose poetry in his artistic maturity, and this selection is made with the wish that more readers will choose to see him as a poet too.

NOTES

1. M. H. Abrams, *The Mirror and the Lamp* (Oxford, 1953), p. 61.
2. F. O. Matthiessen, Introduction to his edition of *Selected Poems of Herman Melville* (Norfolk, Conn., 1944); Randall Jarrell, *Poetry of the Age* (New York, 1953), p. 112; Robert Penn Warren, 'Melville's Poems', *Southern Review* 3 (1967), p. 800.
3. Walter Bezanson (ed.), *Clarel: A Poem and Pilgrimage to the Holy Land* (New York, 1960), p. x.

The Portent
(1859)

Hanging from the beam,
  Slowly swaying (such the law),
Gaunt the shadow on your green,
  Shenandoah!
The cut is on the crown
  (Lo, John Brown),
And the stabs shall heal no more.

Hidden in the cap
  Is the anguish none can draw;
So your future veils its face,   10
  Shenandoah!
But the streaming beard is shown
  (Weird John Brown),
The meteor of the war.

Misgivings
(1860)

When ocean-clouds over inland hills
  Sweep storming in late autumn brown,
And horror the sodden valley fills,
  And the spire falls crashing in the town,
I muse upon my country's ills –
The tempest bursting from the waste of Time
On the world's fairest hope linked with man's foulest
    crime.

Nature's dark side is heeded now –
  (Ah! optimist-cheer disheartened flown) –
A child may read the moody brow   10
  Of yon black mountain lone.

With shouts the torrents down the gorges go,
    And storms are formed behind the storm we feel:
The hemlock shakes in the rafter, the oak in the driving
        keel.

The Conflict of Convictions
(1860–61)

On starry heights
    A bugle wails the long recall;
Derision stirs the deep abyss,
    Heaven's ominous silence over all.
Return, return, O eager Hope,
    And face man's latter fall.
Events, they make the dreamers quail;
Satan's old age is strong and hale,
A disciplined captain, gray in skill,
And Raphael a white enthusiast still;
Dashed aims, whereat Christ's martyrs pale,
Shall Mammon's slaves fulfill?

        (Dismantle the fort,
        Cut down the fleet –
        Battle no more shall be!
        While the fields for fight in æons to come
        Congeal beneath the sea.)

The terrors of truth and dart of death
    To faith alike are vain;
Though comets, gone a thousand years,
    Return again,
Patient she stands – she can no more –
And waits, nor heeds she waxes hoar.

(At a stony gate,
A statue of stone,
Weed overgrown –
Long 'twill wait!)

But God His former mind retains,
   Confirms his old decree;
The generations are inured to pains,   30
   And strong Necessity
Surges, and heaps Time's strand with wrecks.
   The People spread like a weedy grass,
   The thing they will they bring to pass,
And prosper to the apoplex.
The rout it herds around the heart,
   The ghost is yielded in the gloom;
Kings wag their heads – Now save thyself
   Who wouldst rebuild the world in bloom.

(Tide-mark   40
And top of the ages' strife,
Verge where they called the world to come,
The last advance of life –
Ha ha, the rust on the Iron Dome!)

Nay, but revere the hid event;
   In the cloud a sword is girded on,
I mark a twinkling in the tent
   Of Michael the warrior one.
Senior wisdom suits not now,
The light is on the youthful brow.   50

(Ay, in caves the miner see:
His forehead bears a taper dim;
Darkness so he feebly braves –
Which foldeth him.)

But He who rules is old – is old;
Ah! faith is warm, but heaven with age is cold.

(Ho ho, ho ho,
The cloistered doubt
Of olden times
60   *Is blurted out!)*

The Ancient of Days forever is young,
    Forever the scheme of Nature thrives;
I know a wind in purpose strong –
    It spins *against* the way it drives.
What if the gulfs their slimed foundations bare?
So deep must the stones be hurled
Whereon the throes of ages rear
The final empire and the happier world.

(The poor old Past,
70   *The Future's slave,*
She drudged through pain and crime
To bring about the blissful Prime,
Then – perished. There's a grave!)

    Power unanointed may come –
Dominion (unsought by the free)
    And the Iron Dome,
Stronger for stress and strain,
Fling her huge shadow athwart the main;
But the Founders' dream shall flee.
80 Age after age shall be
As age after age has been,
(From man's changeless heart their way they win);
And death be busy with all who strive –
Death, with silent negative.

    YEA AND NAY –
    EACH HATH HIS SAY;
    BUT GOD HE KEEPS THE MIDDLE WAY.
    NONE WAS BY
    WHEN HE SPREAD THE SKY;
90 WISDOM IS VAIN, AND PROPHESY.

The March into Virginia,
Ending in the First Manassas
(July, 1861)

Did all the lets and bars appear
   To every just or larger end,
Whence should come the trust and cheer?
   Youth must its ignorant impulse lend –
Age finds place in the rear.
   All wars are boyish, and are fought by boys,
The champions and enthusiasts of the state:
   Turbid ardors and vain joys
    Not barrenly abate –
   Stimulants to the power mature,   10
    Preparatives of fate.

Who here forecasteth the event?
What heart but spurns at precedent
And warnings of the wise,
Contemned foreclosures of surprise?
The banners play, the bugles call,
The air is blue and prodigal.
   No berrying party, pleasure-wooed,
No picnic party in the May,
Ever went less loth than they   20
   Into that leafy neighborhood.
In Bacchic glee they file toward Fate,
Moloch's uninitiate;
Expectancy, and glad surmise
Of battle's unknown mysteries.
All they feel is this: 'tis glory,
A rapture sharp, though transitory,
Yet lasting in belaureled story.
So they gayly go to fight,
Chatting left and laughing right.   30

But some who this blithe mood present,
   As on in lightsome files they fare,
Shall die experienced ere three days are spent –
   Perish, enlightened by the vollied glare;
Or shame survive, and, like to adamant,
   The throe of Second Manassas share.

Ball's Bluff
A Reverie
(October, 1861)

One noonday, at my window in the town,
   I saw a sight – saddest that eyes can see –
   Young soldiers marching lustily
      Unto the wars,
With fifes, and flags in mottoed pageantry;
    While all the porches, walks, and doors
Were rich with ladies cheering royally.

They moved like Juny morning on the wave,
   Their hearts were fresh as clover in its prime
   (It was the breezy summer time),
      Life throbbed so strong,
How should they dream that Death in a rosy clime
    Would come to thin their shining throng?
Youth feels immortal, like the gods sublime.

Weeks passed; and at my window, leaving bed,
   By night I mused, of easeful sleep bereft,
   On those brave boys (Ah War! thy theft);
      Some marching feet
Found pause at last by cliffs Potomac cleft;
    Wakeful I mused, while on the street
Far footfalls died away till none were left.

A Utilitarian View of the Monitor's Fight

Plain be the phrase, yet apt the verse,
　　More ponderous than nimble;
For since grimed War here laid aside
His painted pomp, 'twould ill befit
　　　　Overmuch to ply
　　The rhyme's barbaric cymbal.

Hail to victory without the gaud
　　Of glory; zeal that needs no fans
Of banners; plain mechanic power
Plied cogently in War now placed –
　　　　Where War belongs –
　　Among the trades and artisans.

Yet this was battle, and intense –
　　Beyond the strife of fleets heroic;
Deadlier, closer, calm 'mid storm;
No passion; all went on by crank,
　　　　Pivot, and screw,
　　And calculations of caloric.

Needless to dwell; the story's known.
　　The ringing of those plates on plates
Still ringeth round the world –
The clangor of that blacksmiths' fray.
　　　　The anvil-din
　　Resounds this message from the Fates:

War shall yet be, and to the end;
　　But war-paint shows the streaks of weather;
War shall yet be, but warriors
Are now but operatives; War's made
　　　　Less grand than Peace,
　　And a singe runs through lace and feather.

Shiloh
A Requiem
(April, 1862)

Skimming lightly, wheeling still,
   The swallows fly low
Over the field in clouded days,
   The forest-field of Shiloh –
Over the field where April rain
Solaced the parched ones stretched in pain
Through the pause of night
That followed the Sunday fight
   Around the church of Shiloh –
The church so lone, the log-built one,
That echoed to many a parting groan
    And natural prayer
   Of dying foemen mingled there –
Foemen at morn, but friends at eve –
   Fame or country least their care:
(What like a bullet can undeceive!)
   But now they lie low,
While over them the swallows skim,
   And all is hushed at Shiloh.

Malvern Hill
(July, 1862)

Ye elms that wave on Malvern Hill
   In prime of morn and May,
Recall ye how McClellan's men
   Here stood at bay?
While deep within yon forest dim
   Our rigid comrades lay –

Some with the cartridge in their mouth,
Others with fixed arms lifted South –
   Invoking so
The cypress glades? Ah wilds of woe!   10

The spires of Richmond, late beheld
   Through rifts in musket-haze,
Were closed from view in clouds of dust
   On leaf-walled ways,
Where streamed our wagons in caravan;
   And the Seven Nights and Days
Of march and fast, retreat and fight,
Pinched our grimed faces to ghastly plight –
   Does the elm wood
Recall the haggard beards of blood?   20

The battle-smoked flag, with stars eclipsed,
   We followed (it never fell!) –
In silence husbanded our strength –
   Received their yell;
Till on this slope we patient turned
   With cannon ordered well;
Reverse we proved was not defeat;
But ah, the sod what thousands meet! –
   Does Malvern Wood
Bethink itself, and muse and brood?   30

   We elms of Malvern Hill
     Remember every thing;
   But sap the twig will fill:
   Wag the world how it will,
     Leaves must be green in Spring.

Stonewall Jackson
Mortally Wounded at Chancellorsville
(May, 1863)

The Man who fiercest charged in fight,
  Whose sword and prayer were long –
    Stonewall!
  Even him who stoutly stood for Wrong,
How can we praise? Yet coming days
  Shall not forget him with this song.

Dead is the Man whose Cause is dead,
  Vainly he died and set his seal –
    Stonewall!
  Earnest in error, as we feel;
True to the thing he deemed was due,
  True as John Brown or steel.

Relentlessly he routed us;
  But *we* relent, for he is low –
    Stonewall!
  Justly his fame we outlaw; so
We drop a tear on the bold Virginian's bier,
  Because no wreath we owe.

Gettysburg
(July, 1863)

O pride of the days in prime of the months
  Now trebled in great renown,
When before the ark of our holy cause
    Fell Dagon down –
Dagon foredoomed, who, armed and targed
Never his impious heart enlarged
Beyond that hour; God walled his power,
And there the last invader charged.

He charged, and in that charge condensed
   His all of hate and all of fire;   10
He sought to blast us in his scorn,
   And wither us in his ire.
Before him went the shriek of shells –
Aerial screamings, taunts and yells;
Then the three waves in flashed advance
   Surged, but were met, and back they set:
Pride was repelled by sterner pride,
   And Right is a strong-hold yet.

Before our lines it seemed a beach
   Which wild September gales have strown   20
With havoc on wreck, and dashed therewith
   Pale crews unknown –
Men, arms, and steeds. The evening sun
Died on the face of each lifeless one,
And died along the winding marge of fight
   And searching-parties lone.

Sloped on the hill the mounds were green,
   Our centre held that place of graves,
And some still hold it in their swoon,
   And over these a glory waves.   30
The warrior-monument, crashed in fight,
Shall soar transfigured in loftier light,
   A meaning ampler bear;
Soldier and priest with hymn and prayer
Have laid the stone, and every bone
   Shall rest in honor there.

The House-Top
A Night Piece
(July, 1863)

No sleep. The sultriness pervades the air
And binds the brain – a dense oppression, such
As tawny tigers feel in matted shades,
Vexing their blood and making apt for ravage.
Beneath the stars the roofy desert spreads
Vacant as Libya. All is hushed near by.
Yet fitfully from far breaks a mixed surf
Of muffled sound, the Atheist roar of riot.
Yonder, where parching Sirius set in drought,
Balefully glares red Arson – there – and there.
The Town is taken by its rats – ship-rats
And rats of the wharves. All civil charms
And priestly spells which late held hearts in awe –
Fear-bound, subjected to a better sway
Than sway of self; these like a dream dissolve,
And man rebounds whole æons back in nature.
Hail to the low dull rumble, dull and dead,
And ponderous drag that jars the wall.
Wise Draco comes, deep in the midnight roll
Of black artillery; he comes, though late;
In code corroborating Calvin's creed
And cynic tyrannies of honest kings;
He comes, nor parlies; and the Town, redeemed,
Gives thanks devout; nor, being thankful, heeds
The grimy slur on the Republic's faith implied,
Which holds that Man is naturally good,
And – more – is Nature's Roman, never to be scourged.

On the Photograph of a Corps Commander

Ay, man is manly. Here you see
   The warrior-carriage of the head,
And brave dilation of the frame;
   And lighting all, the soul that led
In Spottsylvania's charge to victory,
   Which justifies his fame.

A cheering picture. It is good
   To look upon a Chief like this,
In whom the spirit moulds the form.
   Here favoring nature, oft remiss,   10
With eagle mien expressive has endued
   A man to kindle strains that warm.

Trace back his lineage, and his sires,
   Yeoman or noble, you shall find
Enrolled with men of Agincourt,
   Heroes who shared great Harry's mind.
Down to us come the knightly Norman fires,
   And front the Templars bore.

Nothing can lift the heart of man
   Like manhood in a fellow-man.
The thought of heaven's great King afar   20
   But humbles us – too weak to scan;
But manly greatness men can span,
   And feel the bonds that draw.

The Swamp Angel

There is a coal-black Angel
   With a thick Afric lip,
And he dwells (like the hunted and harried)
   In a swamp where the green frogs dip.

But his face is against a City
   Which is over a bay of the sea,
And he breathes with a breath that is blastment,
   And dooms by a far decree.

By night there is fear in the City,
   Through the darkness a star soareth on;
There's a scream that screams up to the zenith,
   Then the poise of a meteor lone –
Lighting far the pale fright of the faces,
   And downward the coming is seen;
Then the rush, and the burst, and the havoc,
   And wails and shrieks between.

It comes like a thief in the gloaming;
   It comes, and none may foretell
The place of the coming – the glaring;
   They live in a sleepless spell
That wizens, and withers, and whitens;
   It ages the young, and the bloom
Of the maiden is ashes of roses –
   The Swamp Angel broods in his gloom.

Swift is his messengers' going,
   But slowly he saps their halls,
As if by delay deluding.
   They move from their crumbling walls
Farther and farther away;
   But the Angel sends after and after,
By night with the flame of his ray –
   By night with the voice of his screaming –
Sends after them, stone by stone,
   And farther walls fall, farther portals,
And weed follows weed through the Town.

Is this the proud City? the scorner
    Which never would yield the ground?
Which mocked at the coal-black Angel?
    The cup of despair goes round.

Vainly she calls upon Michael   40
    (The white man's seraph was he),
For Michael has fled from his tower
    To the Angel over the sea.

Who weeps for the woeful City
    Let him weep for our guilty kind;
Who joys at her wild despairing –
    Christ, the Forgiver, convert his mind.

The College Colonel

He rides at their head;
    A crutch by his saddle just slants in view,
One slung arm is in splints, you see,
    Yet he guides his strong steed – how coldly too.

He brings his regiment home –
    Not as they filed two years before,
But a remnant half-tattered, and battered, and
          worn,
Like castaway sailors, who – stunned
    By the surf's loud roar,
    Their mates dragged back and seen no more –   10
Again and again breast the surge,
    And at last crawl, spent, to shore.

A still rigidity and pale –
    An Indian aloofness lones his brow;
He has lived a thousand years
Compressed in battle's pains and prayers,
    Marches and watches slow.

There are welcoming shouts, and flags;
   Old men off hat to the Boy,
20   Wreaths from gay balconies fall at his feet,
   But to *him* – there comes alloy.

It is not that a leg is lost,
   It is not that an arm is maimed,
It is not that the fever has racked –
   Self he has long disclaimed.

But all through the Seven Days' Fight,
   And deep in the Wilderness grim,
And in the field-hospital tent,
   And Petersburg crater, and dim
30   Lean brooding in Libby, there came –
   Ah heaven! – what *truth* to him.

At the Cannon's Mouth
Destruction of the Ram Albemarle by the Torpedo-launch
(October, 1864)

Palely intent, he urged his keel
   Full on the guns, and touched the spring;
Himself involved in the bolt he drove
Timed with the armed hull's shot that stove
His shallop – die or do!
Into the flood his life he threw,
   Yet lives – unscathed – a breathing thing
To marvel at.

         He has his fame;
10   But that mad dash at death, how name?

Had Earth no charm to stay in the Boy
   The martyr-passion? Could he dare
Disdain the Paradise of opening joy
   Which beckons the fresh heart every where?

Life has more lures than any girl
    For youth and strength; puts forth a share
Of beauty, hinting of yet rarer store;
And ever with unfathomable eyes,
        Which bafflingly entice,
Still strangely does Adonis draw.
And life once over, who shall tell the rest?   20
Life is, of all we know, God's best.
What imps these eagles then, that they
Fling disrespect on life by that proud way
In which they soar above our lower clay.

Pretense of wonderment and doubt unblest:
    In Cushing's eager deed was shown
    A spirit which brave poets own –
That scorn of life which earns life's crown;
    Earns, but not always wins; but *he* –   30
    The star ascended in his nativity.

'The Coming Storm'
A Picture by S. R. Gifford, and owned by E. B.
Included in the N. A. Exhibition, April, 1865

All feeling hearts must feel for him
    Who felt this picture. Presage dim –
Dim inklings from the shadowy sphere
    Fixed him and fascinated here.

A demon-cloud like the mountain one
    Burst on a spirit as mild
As this urned lake, the home of shades,
    But Shakespeare's pensive child

Never the lines had lightly scanned,
    Steeped in fable, steeped in fate;   10
The Hamlet in his heart was 'ware,
    Such hearts can antedate.

No utter surprise can come to him
  Who reaches Shakespeare's core;
That which we seek and shun is there –
  Man's final lore.

The Released Rebel Prisoner
(June, 1865)

Armies he's seen – the herds of war,
  But never such swarms of men
As now in the Nineveh of the North –
  How mad the Rebellion then!

And yet but dimly he divines
  The depth of that deceit,
And superstition of vast pride
  Humbled to such defeat.

Seductive shone the Chiefs in arms –
  His steel the nearest magnet drew;
Wreathed with its kind, the Gulf-weed drives –
  'Tis Nature's wrong they rue.

His face is hidden in his beard,
  But his heart peers out at eye –
And such a heart! like a mountain-pool
  Where no man passes by.

He thinks of Hill – a brave soul gone;
  And Ashby dead in pale disdain;
And Stuart with the Rupert-plume,
  Whose blue eye never shall laugh again.

He hears the drum; he sees our boys
  From his wasted fields return;
Ladies feast them on strawberries,
  And even to kiss them yearn.

He marks them bronzed, in soldier-trim,
  The rifle proudly borne;
They bear it for an heir-loom home,
  And he – disarmed – jail-worn.

Home, home – his heart is full of it;
  But home he never shall see,   30
Even should he stand upon the spot:
  'Tis gone! – where his brothers be.

The cypress-moss from tree to tree
  Hangs in his Southern land;
As weird, from thought to thought of his
  Run memories hand in hand.

And so he lingers – lingers on
  In the City of the Foe –
His cousins and his countrymen
  Who see him listless go.   40

A Grave Near Petersburg, Virginia

Head-board and foot-board duly placed –
  Grassed is the mound between;
Daniel Drouth is the slumberer's name –
  Long may his grave be green!

Quick was his way – a flash and a blow,
  Full of his fire was he –
A fire of hell – 'tis burnt out now –
  Green may his grave long be!

May his grave be green, though he
  Was a rebel of iron mould;   10
Many a true heart – true to the Cause,
  Through the blaze of his wrath lies cold.

>   May his grave be green – still green
>   While happy years shall run;
>   May none come nigh to disinter
>   The – *Buried Gun*.

On the Slain Collegians

>   Youth is the time when hearts are large,
>   And stirring wars
>   Appeal to the spirit which appeals in turn
>   To the blade it draws.
>   If woman incite, and duty show
>   (Though made the mask of Cain),
>   Or whether it be Truth's sacred cause,
>   Who can aloof remain
>   That shares youth's ardor, uncooled by the snow
>   Of wisdom or sordid gain?

>   The liberal arts and nurture sweet
>   Which give his gentleness to man –
>   Train him to honor, lend him grace
>   Through bright examples meet –
>   That culture which makes never wan
>   With underminings deep, but holds
>   The surface still, its fitting place,
>   And so gives sunniness to the face
>   And bravery to the heart; what troops
>   Of generous boys in happiness thus bred –
>   Saturnians through life's Tempe led,
>   Went from the North and came from the South,
>   With golden mottoes in the mouth,
>   To lie down midway on a bloody bed.

>   Woe for the homes of the North,
>   And woe for the seats of the South:
>   All who felt life's spring in prime,
>   And were swept by the wind of their place and time –

10

20

All lavish hearts, on whichever side,
Of birth urbane or courage high,   30
Armed them for the stirring wars –
Armed them – some to die.
    Apollo-like in pride,
Each would slay his Python – caught
The maxims in his temple taught –
    Aflame with sympathies whose blaze
Perforce enwrapped him – social laws,
    Friendship and kin, and by-gone days –
Vows, kisses – every heart unmoors,
And launches into the seas of wars.   40
What could they else – North or South?
Each went forth with blessings given
By priests and mothers in the name of Heaven;
    And honor in all was chief.
Warred one for Right, and one for Wrong?
So put it; but they both were young –
Each grape to his cluster clung,
All their elegies are sung.

The anguish of maternal hearts
    Must search for balm divine;   50
But well the striplings bore their fated parts
    (The heavens all parts assign) –
Never felt life's care or cloy.
Each bloomed and died an unabated Boy;
Nor dreamed what death was – thought it mere
Sliding into some vernal sphere.
They knew the joy, but leaped the grief,
Like plants that flower ere comes the leaf –
Which storms lay low in kindly doom,
And kill them in their flush of bloom.   60

The Fortitude of the North
under the Disaster of the Second Manassas

No shame they take for dark defeat
    While prizing yet each victory won,
Who fight for the Right through all retreat,
    Nor pause until their work is done.
The Cape-of-Storms is proof to every throe;
    Vainly against that foreland beat
Wild winds aloft and wilder waves below:
    The black cliffs gleam through rents in sleet
When the livid Antarctic storm-clouds glow.

On the Men of Maine
Killed in the Victory of Baton Rouge, Louisiana

Afar they fell. It was the zone
    Of fig and orange, cane and lime
(A land how all unlike their own,
With the cold pine-grove overgrown),
    But still their Country's clime.
And there in youth they died for her –
    The Volunteers,
For her went up their dying prayers:
    So vast the Nation, yet so strong the tie.
What doubt shall come, then, to deter
    The Republic's earnest faith and courage high.

Inscription
For Marye's Heights, Fredericksburg

To them who crossed the flood
And climbed the hill, with eyes
   Upon the heavenly flag intent,
   And through the deathful tumult went
Even unto death: to them this Stone –
Erect, where they were overthrown –
   Of more than victory the monument.

On the Slain at Chickamauga

Happy are they and charmed in life
   Who through long wars arrive unscarred
At peace. To such the wreath be given,
If they unfalteringly have striven –
   In honor, as in limb, unmarred.
Let cheerful praise be rife,
   And let them live their years at ease,
Musing on brothers who victorious died –
   Loved mates whose memory shall ever please.

And yet mischance is honorable too –
   Seeming defeat in conflict justified
Whose end to closing eyes is hid from view.
The will, that never can relent –
The aim, survivor of the bafflement,
   Make this memorial due.

10

On Sherman's Men
Who Fell in the Assault of Kenesaw Mountain, Georgia

They said that Fame her clarion dropped
  Because great deeds were done no more –
That even Duty knew no shining ends,
And Glory – 'twas a fallen star!
  But battle can heroes and bards restore.
    Nay, look at Kenesaw:
Perils the mailed ones never knew
Are lightly braved by the ragged coats of blue,
And gentler hearts are bared to deadlier war.

Commemorative of a Naval Victory

Sailors there are of gentlest breed,
  Yet strong, like every goodly thing;
The discipline of arms refines,
  And the wave gives tempering.
  The damasked blade its beam can fling;
It lends the last grave grace:
The hawk, the hound, and sworded nobleman
  In Titian's picture for a king,
Are of hunter or warrior race.

10   In social halls a favored guest
  In years that follow victory won,
How sweet to feel your festal fame
  In woman's glance instinctive thrown:
  Repose is yours – your deed is known,
It musks the amber wine;
It lives, and sheds a light from storied days
  Rich as October sunsets brown,
Which make the barren place to shine.

But seldom the laurel wreath is seen
   Unmixed with pensive pansies dark;   20
There's a light and a shadow on every man
   Who at last attains his lifted mark –
   Nursing through night the ethereal spark.
Elate he never can be;
He feels that spirits which glad had hailed his
     worth,
   Sleep in oblivion. – The shark
Glides white through the phosphorus sea.

The Maldive Shark

About the Shark, phlegmatical one,
Pale sot of the Maldive sea,
The sleek little pilot-fish, azure and slim,
How alert in attendance be.
From his saw-pit of mouth, from his charnel of
     maw
They have nothing of harm to dread,
But liquidly glide on his ghastly flank
Or before his Gorgonian head;
Or lurk in the port of serrated teeth
In white triple tiers of glittering gates,   10
And there find a haven when peril's abroad,
An asylum in jaws of the Fates!
They are friends; and friendly they guide him to
     prey,
Yet never partake of the treat –
Eyes and brains to the dotard lethargic and dull,
Pale ravener of horrible meat.

The Berg
(A Dream)

I saw a ship of martial build
(Her standards set, her brave apparel on)
Directed as by madness mere
Against a stolid iceberg steer,
Nor budge it, though the infatuate ship went down.
The impact made huge ice-cubes fall
Sullen, in tons that crashed the deck;
But that one avalanche was all –
No other movement save the foundering wreck.

Along the spurs of ridges pale,
Not any slenderest shaft and frail,
A prism over glass-green gorges lone,
Topple; nor lace of traceries fine,
Nor pendant drops in grot or mine
Were jarred, when the stunned ship went down.
Nor sole the gulls in cloud that wheeled
Circling one snow-flanked peak afar,
But nearer fowl the floes that skimmed
And crystal beaches, felt no jar.
No thrill transmitted stirred the lock
Of jack-straw needle-ice at base;
Towers undermined by waves – the block
Atilt impending – kept their place.
Seals, dozing sleek on sliddery ledges
Slipt never, when by loftier edges
Through very inertia overthrown,
The impetuous ship in bafflement went down.

Hard Berg (methought), so cold, so vast,
With mortal damps self-overcast;
Exhaling still thy dankish breath –
Adrift dissolving, bound for death;

Though lumpish thou, a lumbering one –
A lumbering lubbard loitering slow,
Impingers rue thee and go down,
Sounding thy precipice below,
Nor stir the slimy slug that sprawls
Along thy dense stolidity of walls.

The Enviable Isles
(From 'Rammon')

Through storms you reach them and from storms are
    free.
    Afar descried, the foremost drear in hue,
But, nearer, green; and, on the marge, the sea
    Makes thunder low and mist of rainbowed dew.

But, inland, where the sleep that folds the hills
A dreamier sleep, the trance of God, instills –
    On uplands hazed, in wandering airs aswoon,
Slow-swaying palms salute love's cypress tree
    Adown in vale where pebbly runlets croon
A song to lull all sorrow and all glee.   10

Sweet-fern and moss in many a glade are here,
    Where, strown in flocks, what cheek-flushed myriads
        lie
Dimpling in dream – unconscious slumberers mere,
    While billows endless round the beaches die.

Billy in the Darbies

Good of the chaplain to enter Lone Bay
And down on his marrowbones here and pray
For the likes just o' me, Billy Budd. – But, look:
Through the port comes the moonshine astray!
It tips the guard's cutlass and silvers this nook;
But 'twill die in the dawning of Billy's last day.
A jewel-block they'll make of me tomorrow,
Pendant pearl from the yardarm-end
Like the eardrop I gave to Bristol Molly –
10   O, 'tis me, not the sentence they'll suspend.
Ay, ay, all is up; and I must up too,
Early in the morning, aloft from alow.
On an empty stomach now never it would do.
They'll give me a nibble – bit o' biscuit ere I go.
Sure, a messmate will reach me the last parting cup;
But, turning heads away from the hoist and the belay,
Heaven knows who will have the running of me up!
No pipe to those halyards. – But aren't it all a sham?
A blur's in my eyes; it is dreaming that I am.
20   A hatchet to my hawser? All adrift to go?
The drum roll to grog, and Billy never know?
But Donald he has promised to stand by the plank;
So I'll shake a friendly hand ere I sink.
But – no! It is dead then I'll be, come to think.
I remember Taff the Welshman when he sank.
And his cheek it was like the budding pink.
But me they'll lash in hammock, drop me deep.
Fathoms down, fathoms down, how I'll dream fast
        asleep.
I feel it stealing now. Sentry, are you there?
30   Just ease these darbies at the wrist,
And roll me over fair!
I am sleepy, and the oozy weeds about me twist.

Timoleon
(394 BC)

I

If more than once, as annals tell,
   Through blood without compunction spilt,
An egotist arch rule has snatched
And stamped the seizure with his sabre's hilt,
   And, legalized by lawyers, stood;
Shall the good heart whose patriot fire
Leaps to a deed of startling note,
Do it, then flinch? Shall good in weak expire?
   Needs goodness lack the evil grit
That stares down censorship and ban,   10
And dumfounds saintlier ones with this –
God's will avouched in each successful man?
   Or, put it, where dread stress inspires
A virtue beyond man's standard rate,
Seems virtue there a strain forbid –
Transcendence such as shares transgression's fate?
   If so, and wan eclipse ensue,
Yet glory await emergence won,
Is that high Providence, or Chance?
And proved it which with thee, Timoleon?   20
   O, crowned with laurel twined with thorn,
Not rash thy life's cross-tide I stem,
But reck the problem rolled in pang
And reach and dare to touch thy garment's hem.

II

   When Argos and Cleone strove
Against free Corinth's claim or right,
Two brothers battled for her well:
A footman one, and one a mounted knight.

Apart in place, each braved the brunt
30 Till the rash cavalryman, alone,
Was wrecked against the enemy's files,
His bayard crippled and he maimed and thrown.
    Timoleon, at Timophanes' need,
Makes for the rescue through the fray,
Covers him with his shield, and takes
The darts and furious odds and fights at bay;
    Till, wrought to palor of passion dumb,
Stark terrors of death around he throws,
Warding his brother from the field
40 Spite failing friends dispersed and rallying foes
    Here might he rest, in claim rest here,
Rest, and a Phidian form remain;
But life halts never, life must on,
And take with term prolonged some scar or stain.
    Yes, life must on. And latent germs
Time's seasons wake in mead and man;
And brothers, playfellows in youth,
Develop into variance wide in span.

III

Timophanes was his mother's pride –
50 Her pride, her pet, even all to her
Who slackly on Timoleon looked:
Scarce he (she mused) may proud affection stir.
    He saved my darling, gossips tell:
If so, 'twas service, yea, and fair;
But instinct ruled and duty bade,
In service such, a henchman e'en might share.
    When boys they were I helped the bent;
I made the junior feel his place,
Subserve the senior, love him, too;
60 And sooth he does, and that's his saving grace.
    But me the meek one never can serve,
Not he, he lacks the quality keen
To make the mother through the son
An envied dame of power, a social queen.

But thou, my first-born, thou art I
In sex translated; joyed, I scan
My features, mine, expressed in thee;
Thou art what I would be were I a man.
   My brave Timophanes, 'tis thou
Who yet the world's fore-front shalt win,   70
For thine the urgent resolute way,
Self pushing panoplied self through thick and thin.
   Nor here maternal insight erred:
Foresworn, with heart that did not wince
At slaying men who kept their vows,
Her darling strides to power, and reigns – a Prince.

IV

Because of just heart and humane,
Profound the hate Timoleon knew
For crimes of pride and men-of-prey
And impious deeds that perjurous upstarts do;   80
   And Corinth loved he, and in way
Old Scotia's clansman loved his clan,
Devotion one with ties how dear
And passion that late to make the rescue ran.
   But crime and kin – the terrorized town,
The silent, acquiescent mother –
Revulsion racks the filial heart,
The loyal son, the patriot true, the brother.
   In evil visions of the night
He sees the lictors of the gods,   90
Giant ministers of righteousness,
Their *fasces* threatened by the Furies' rods.
   But undeterred he wills to act,
Resolved thereon though Ate rise;
He heeds the voice whose mandate calls,
Or seems to call, peremptory from the skies.

V

Nor less but by approaches mild,
And trying each prudential art,
The just one first advances him
In parley with a flushed intemperate heart.
    The brother first he seeks – alone,
And pleads; but is with laughter met;
Then comes he, in accord with two,
And these adjure the tyrant and beset;
    Whose merriment gives place to rage:
'Go,' stamping, 'what to me is Right?
I am the Wrong, and lo, I reign,
And testily intolerant too in might:'
    And glooms on his mute brother pale,
Who goes aside; with muffled face
He sobs the predetermined word,
And Right in Corinth reassumes its place.

VI

But on his robe, ah, whose the blood?
And craven ones their eyes avert,
And heavy is a mother's ban,
And dismal faces of the fools can hurt.
    The whispering-gallery of the world,
Where each breathed slur runs wheeling wide
Eddies a false perverted truth,
Inveterate turning still on fratricide.
    The time was Plato's. Wandering lights
Confirmed the atheist's standing star;
As now, no sanction Virtue knew
For deeds that on prescriptive morals jar.
    Reaction took misgiving's tone,
Infecting conscience, till betrayed
To doubt the irrevocable doom
Herself had authorized when undismayed.

Within perturbed Timoleon here
Such deeps were bared as when the sea 130
Convulsed, vacates its shoreward bed,
And Nature's last reserves show nakedly.
    He falters, and from Hades' glens
By night insidious tones implore –
Why suffer? hither come and be
What Phocion is who feeleth man no more.
    But, won from that, his mood elects
To live – to live in wilding place;
For years self-outcast, he but meets
In shades his playfellow's reproachful face. 140
    Estranged through one transcendent deed
From common membership in mart,
In severance he is like a head
Pale after battle trunkless found apart.

VII

But flood-tide comes though long the ebb,
Nor patience bides with passion long;
Like sightless orbs his thoughts are rolled
Arraigning heaven as compromised in wrong:
    To second causes why appeal?
Vain parleying here with fellow clods. 150
To you, Arch Principals, I rear
My quarrel, for this quarrel is with gods.
    Shall just men long to quit your world?
It is aspersion of your reign;
Your marbles in the temple stand –
Yourselves as stony and invoked in vain?
    Ah, bear with one quite overborne,
Olympians, if he chide ye now;
Magnanimous be even though he rail
And hard against ye set the bleaching brow. 160
    If conscience doubt, she'll next recant.
What basis then? O, tell at last,
Are earnest natures staggering here
But fatherless shadows from no substance cast?

Yea, *are* ye, gods? Then ye, 'tis ye
Should show what touch of tie ye may,
Since ye, too, if not wrung are wronged
By grievous misconceptions of your sway.
But deign, some little sign be given –
170   Low thunder in your tranquil skies;
Me reassure, nor let me be
Like a lone dog that for a master cries.

VIII

Men's moods, as frames, must yield to years,
And turns the world in fickle ways;
Corinth recalls Timoleon – ay,
And plumes him forth, but yet with schooling phrase.
On Sicily's fields, through arduous wars,
A peace he won whose rainbow spanned
The isle redeemed; and he was hailed
180   Deliverer of that fair colonial land.
And Corinth clapt: Absolved, and more!
Justice in long arrears is thine:
Not slayer of thy brother, no,
But savior of the state, Jove's soldier, man divine.
Eager for thee thy City waits:
Return! with bays we dress your door.
But he, the Isle's loved guest, reposed,
And never for Corinth left the adopted shore.

The Ravaged Villa

In shards the sylvan vases lie,
    Their links of dance undone,
And brambles wither by thy brim,
    Choked fountain of the sun!
The spider in the laurel spins,
    The weed exiles the flower:
And, flung to kiln, Apollo's bust
    Makes lime for Mammon's tower.

Monody

To have known him, to have loved him
    After loneness long;
And then to be estranged in life,
    And neither in the wrong;
And now for death to set his seal –
    Ease me, a little ease, my song!

By wintry hills his hermit-mound
    The sheeted snow-drifts drape,
And houseless there the snow-bird flits
    Beneath the fir-trees' crape:
Glazed now with ice the cloistral vine
    That hid the shyest grape.

10

Lone Founts

Though fast youth's glorious fable flies,
View not the world with worldling's eyes;
Nor turn with weather of the time.
Foreclose the coming of surprise:
Stand where Posterity shall stand;
Stand where the Ancients stood before,
And, dipping in lone founts thy hand,
Drink of the never-varying lore:
Wise once, and wise thence evermore.

Art

In placid hours well-pleased we dream
Of many a brave unbodied scheme.
But form to lend, pulsed life create,
What unlike things must meet and mate:

A flame to melt – a wind to freeze;
Sad patience – joyous energies;
Humility – yet pride and scorn;
Instinct and study; love and hate;
Audacity – reverence. These must mate,
And fuse with Jacob's mystic heart,
To wrestle with the angel – Art.

10

Fragments of a Lost Gnostic Poem of the 12th Century

* * * *

Found a family, built a state,
The pledged event is still the same:
Matter in end will never abate
His ancient brutal claim.

* * * *

Indolence is heaven's ally here,
And energy the child of hell:
The Good Man pouring from his pitcher
    clear,
But brims the poisoned well.

In a Church of Padua

In vaulted place where shadows flit,
An upright sombre box you see:
A door, but fast, and lattice none,
But punctured holes minutely small
In lateral silver panel square
Above a kneeling-board without,
Suggest an aim if not declare.

Who bendeth here the tremulous knee
No glimpse may get of him within,
And he immured may hardly see   10
The soul confessing there the sin;
Nor yields the low-sieved voice a tone
Whereby the murmurer may be known.

Dread diving-bell! In thee inurned
What hollows the priest must sound,
Descending into consciences
    Where more is hid than found.

The Attic Landscape

Tourist, spare the avid glance
    That greedy roves the sight to see:
Little here of 'Old Romance',
    Or Picturesque of Tivoli.

No flushful tint the sense to warm –
Pure outline pale, a linear charm.
The clear-cut hills carved temples face,
Respond, and share their sculptural grace.

'Tis Art and Nature lodged together,
    Sister by sister, cheek to cheek;   10
Such Art, such Nature, and such weather
    The All-in-All seems here a Greek.

Greek Masonry

Joints were none that mortar sealed:
Together, scarce with line revealed,
The blocks in symmetry congealed.

Greek Architecture

Not magnitude, not lavishness,
But Form – the Site;
Not innovating wilfulness,
But reverence for the Archetype.

Immolated

Children of my happier prime,
When One yet lived with me, and threw
Her rainbow over life and time,
Even Hope, my bride, and mother to you!
O, nurtured in sweet pastoral air,
And fed on flowers and light, and dew
Of morning meadows – spare, ah, spare
Reproach; spare, and upbraid me not
That, yielding scarce to reckless mood
10   But jealous of your future lot,
I sealed you in a fate subdued.
Have I not saved you from the drear
Theft and ignoring which need be
The triumph of the insincere
Unanimous Mediocrity?
Rest therefore, free from all despite,
Snugged in the arms of comfortable night.

When Forth the Shepherd Leads the Flock

When forth the shepherd leads the flock,
White lamb and dingy ewe,
And there's dibbling in the garden,
Then the world begins anew.

When Buttercups make bright
The meadows up and down,
The Golden Age returns to fields
If never to the town.

When stir the freshening airs
    Forerunning showers to meads,   10
And Dandelions prance,
Then Heart-Free shares the dance –
    A Wilding with the Weeds!

    But alack and alas
For things of wilding feature!
    Since hearsed was Pan
Ill befalls each profitless creature –
    Profitless to man!

Buttercup and Dandelion,
    Wildings, and the rest,   20
Commoners and holiday-makers,
    Note them in one test.

    The farmers scout them,
Yea, and would rout them,
Hay is better without them –
    Tares in the grass!
The florists pooh-pooh them;
Few but children do woo them,
Love them, reprieve them,
Retrieve and inweave them,   30
    Never sighing – *Alas!*

Trophies of Peace
Illinois in 1840

Files on files of Prairie Maize:
On hosts of spears the morning plays!
Aloft the rustling streamers show:
The floss embrowned is rich below.

When Asia scarfed in silks came on
Against the Greek at Marathon,
Did each plume and pennon dance
Sun-lit thus on helm and lance
Mindless of War's sickle so?

For them, a tasseled dance of death:
For these – the reapers reap them low.
Reap them low, and stack the plain
With Ceres' trophies, golden grain.

Such monuments, and only such,
O Prairie! termless yield,
Though trooper Mars disdainful flout
Nor Annals fame the field.

Field Asters

Like the stars in commons blue
Peep their namesakes, Asters here,
Wild ones every autumn seen –
Seen of all, arresting few.

Seen indeed. But who their cheer
Interpret may, or what they mean
When so inscrutably their eyes
Us star-gazers scrutinize.

The Avatar

Bloom or repute for graft or seed
In flowers the flower-gods never heed.
The rose-god once came down and took –
Form in a rose? Nay, but indeed
The meeker form and humbler look
Of Sweet-Briar, a wilding or weed.

The American Aloe on Exhibition

*It is but a floral superstition, as everybody knows, that this
plant flowers only once in a century. When in any instance
the flowering is for decades delayed beyond the normal period
(eight or ten years at furthest), it is owing to something
retarding in the environment or soil.*

But few they were who came to see
    The Century-Plant in flower:
Ten cents admission – price you pay
    For bon-bons of the hour.

In strange inert blank unconcern
    Of wild things at the Zoo,
The patriarch let the sight-seers stare –
    Nor recked who came to view.

But lone at night the garland sighed
    While moaned the aged stem:
'At last, at last! but joy and pride
    What part have I with them?'

Let be the dearth that kept me back
    Now long from wreath decreed;
But, ah, ye Roses that have passed
    Accounting me a weed!

10

Inscription
For a Boulder near the spot
Where the last Hardhack was laid low
By the new proprietor
Of the Hill of Arrowhead.

A weed grew here. – Exempt from use,
   Weeds turn no wheel, nor run;
Radiance pure or redolence
   Some have, but this had none.
And yet heaven gave it leave to live
   And idle it in the sun.

Rose Window

The preacher took from *Solomon's Song*
Four words for text with mystery rife –
The Rose of Sharon – figuring Him
The Resurrection and the Life;
And, pointing many an urn in view,
How honied a homily he drew.

There, in the slumberous afternoon,
Through minister gray, in lullaby rolled
The brimmed metheglin charged with swoon.
Drowsy, my decorous hands I fold
Till sleep overtakes with dream for boon.

I saw an Angel with a Rose
Come out of Morning's garden-gate,
And lamp-like hold the Rose aloft.
He entered a sepulchral Strait.
I followed. And I saw the Rose
Shed dappled down upon the dead;
The shrouds and mort-cloths all were lit
To plaids and chequered tartans red.

I woke. The great Rose Window high,   20
A mullioned wheel in gable set,
Suffused with rich and soft in dye
Where Iris and Aurora met;
Aslant in sheaf of rays it threw
From all its foliate round of panes
Transfiguring light on dingy stains,
While danced the motes in dusty pew.

Thy Aim, Thy Aim?

Thy aim, thy aim?
'Mid the dust dearth and din,
An exception wouldst win
By some deed shall ignite the acclaim?
Then beware, and prepare thee
Lest Envy ensnare thee,
And yearning be sequelled by shame.
But strive bravely on, yet on and yet on,
Let the goal be won;
Then if, living, you kindle a flame,   10
Your guerdon will be but a flower,
Only a flower,
The flower of repute,
A flower cut down in an hour.

But repute, if this be too tame,
And, dying, you truly ennoble a name –

Again but a flower!
Only a flower,
A funeral flower,
A blossom of Dis from Proserpine's bower –   20
The belated funeral flower of fame.

Camoëns
I
(Before)

Forever must I fan this fire?
Forever in flame on flame aspire?
Restless, restless, craving rest –
The Imperfect toward Perfection pressed!
Yea, for the God demands thy best.
The world with endless beauty teems,
And thought evokes new worlds of dreams:
Hunt then the flying herds of themes!
And fan, yet fan thy fervid fire,
10   Until the crucibled gold shall show
That fire can purge, as well as glow.
In ordered ardor, nobly strong,
Flame to the height of epic song.

Camoëns in the Hospital
2
(After)

What now avails the pageant verse,
Trophies and arms with music borne?
Base is the world; and some rehearse
How noblest meet ignoble scorn.
Vain now thy ardor, vain thy fire,
Delirium mere, unsound desire:
Fate's knife hath ripped the chorded lyre.
Exhausted by the exacting lay,
I do but fall a surer prey
10   To wile and guile ill understood;
While they who work them, fair in face,
Still keep their strength in prudent place,
And claim they worthier run life's race,
Serving high God with useful good.

A Spirit Appeared to Me

A Spirit appeared to me, and said
'Where now would you choose to dwell?
In the Paradise of the Fool,
Or in wise Solomon's hell?' –

Never he asked me twice:
'Give me the fool's Paradise.'

Pontoosuc

Crowning a bluff where gleams the lake below,
Some pillared pines in well-spaced order stand
And like an open temple show.
And here in best of seasons bland,
Autumnal noon-tide, I look out
From dusk arcades on sunshine all about.

Beyond the Lake, in upland cheer
Fields, pastoral fields and barns appear,
They skirt the hills where lonely roads
Revealed in links thro' tiers of woods   10
Wind up to indistinct abodes
And faery-peopled neighborhoods;
While further fainter mountains keep
Hazed in romance impenetrably deep.

Look, corn in stacks, on many a farm,
And orchards ripe in languorous charm,
As dreamy Nature, feeling sure
Of all her genial labor done,
And the last mellow fruitage won,
Would idle out her term mature;   20
Reposing like a thing reclined
In kinship with man's meditative mind.

For me, within the brown arcade –
Rich life, methought; sweet here in shade
And pleasant abroad in air! – But, nay,
A counter thought intrusive played,
A thought as old as thought itself,
And who shall lay it on the shelf! –
I felt the beauty bless the day
In opulence of autumn's dower;
But evanescence will not stay!
A year ago was such an hour,
As this, which but foreruns the blast
Shall sweep these live leaves to the dead leaves past.

All dies! –

    I stood in revery long.
Then, to forget death's ancient wrong,
I turned me in the deep arcade,
And there by chance in lateral glade
I saw low tawny mounds in lines,
Relics of trunks of stately pines
Ranked erst in colonnades where, lo!
Erect succeeding pillars show!

    All dies! and not alone
The aspiring trees and men and grass;
The poet's forms of beauty pass,
And noblest deeds they are undone
Even truth itself decays, and lo,
From truth's sad ashes fraud and falsehood grow.

All dies!

The workman dies, and after him, the work;
Like to these pines whose graves I trace,
Statue and statuary fall upon their face:
In very amaranths the worm doth lurk,

Even stars, Chaldæans say, have left their place.
Andes and Apalachee tell
Of havoc ere our Adam fell,
And present Nature as a moss doth show
On the ruins of the Nature of the æons of long ago.

But look – and hark!   60

    Adown the glade,
Where light and shadow sport at will,
Who cometh vocal, and arrayed
As in the first pale tints of morn –
So pure, rose-clear, and fresh and chill!
Some ground-pine sprigs her brow adorn,
The earthy rootlets tangled clinging.
Over tufts of moss which dead things made,
Under vital twigs which danced or swayed,
Along she floats, and lightly singing: 70

'Dies, all dies!
The grass it dies, but in vernal rain
Up it springs and it lives again;
Over and over, again and again
It lives, it dies and it lives again.
Who sighs that all dies?
Summer and winter, and pleasure and pain
And everything everywhere in God's reign,
They end, and anon they begin again:
Wane and wax, wax and wane: 80
Over and over and over amain
End, ever end, and begin again –
End, ever end, and forever and ever begin again!'

She ceased, and nearer slid, and hung
In dewy guise; then softlier sung:
'Since light and shade are equal set
And all revolves, nor more ye know;
Ah, why should tears the pale cheek fret

For aught that waneth here below.
Let go, let go!'

With that, her warm lips thrilled me through,
She kissed me, while her chaplet cold
Its rootlets brushed against my brow,
With all their humid clinging mould.
She vanished, leaving fragrant breath
And warmth and chill of wedded life and death.

FREDERICK GODDARD
TUCKERMAN

Preface

In choosing the poems for this edition, an underlying principle has been the conviction that Tuckerman deserves more notice. The endeavour to present the best of his work has required that I follow my own taste, since criticism has not reached any consensus as to which Tuckerman poems are most rewarding (with perhaps the single exception of 'The Cricket'). I have also been guided by a desire to show Tuckerman's breadth: from the grieving personal sonnets to the lightsome historical narrative 'Rhotruda'. It is my belief that a reader with little or no knowledge of Tuckerman will come away from this selection with ample reason to admit him among the true poets of the nineteenth century.

This is the largest selected edition of Tuckerman to date. His appearance in anthologies usually totals no more than ten sonnets and 'The Cricket'. John Hollander's *American Poetry: The Nineteenth Century* is a recent exception, containing about twice that many poems.[1] Perhaps this represents the start of a trend, an acknowledgement of this discriminating poet.

The history of Tuckerman in print is easily summarized. *Poems by Frederick Goddard Tuckerman* was privately printed in 1860, then published in London in 1863 and Boston in 1864. A reprint in 1869 was the last publication during the poet's lifetime, and the book went out of print. After Ralph Waldo Emerson included Tuckerman's 'Rhotruda' in his 1874 anthology *Parnassus*, it was thirty-five years before Tuckerman's poetry appeared again. In January 1909 the critic Walter Prichard Eaton published a piece on Tuckerman in *Forum* magazine.[2] Eaton had heard of Tuckerman from his friend Louis How, who was assembling a (never published) anthology of American poetry that was to contain two Tuckerman sonnets. Eaton obtained an old copy of Tuckerman's book, and praised and quoted the poetry in his essay. Witter Bynner saw Eaton's article, and his interest led him to discover, in the keeping of Tuckerman's family, the manuscripts of Tuckerman's three remaining sonnet series and 'The Cricket'. In 1931 Bynner published all five series in *The Sonnets of Frederick Goddard Tuckerman*. Some of the sonnets made appearances in anthologies, beginning with the *Oxford Anthology of American Literature* in 1938. 'The Cricket' remained unpublished until the Cummington Press put it out in 1950. *The Complete Poems of Frederick Goddard Tuckerman*, edited by N. Scott Momaday, appeared in 1965.

There is as yet no authoritative edition of Tuckerman. Momaday's edition (though an indispensable resource as the only complete collection) lacks annotation, and several critics have objected to flaws in Momaday's text. My corrections to Momaday's occasional misreadings of the manuscripts are made plain in the notes. In giving primacy to the manuscripts, Momaday was led to ignore the likelihood that Tuckerman communicated changes to his editors during and after the printing of the first edition. Because of its combination of close attention to the last version of the published poems and careful reading of Tuckerman's manuscript, it is my belief that the text of this edition constitutes an advance.

In establishing the text, I have used the 1864 edition of Tuckerman's *Poems*, making the changes demanded by the errata list included with that edition. I have not adopted the changes pencilled by Tuckerman into the 'author's copy' of the 1860 *Poems* in the Houghton Library (unless those changes are reflected in the 1864 edition), since we cannot be sure that these changes were his last words on the matter. (It is likely that there was communication between Tuckerman and the London editors of the 1863 edition upon which the 1864 is based.) Those of Tuckerman's pencilled changes in the Houghton's 'author's copy' not adopted in the 1864 edition (and therefore not in mine) are recorded in the notes. In establishing the text for those poems which were not published during Tuckerman's lifetime (that is, Sonnet series III–V and 'The Cricket'), I have mainly relied upon Houghton MSS Am 1349(3) and 1349(4). I have sometimes had to choose between two or more manuscript readings of apparently equal authority, but I have not introduced any words that do not appear in the author's own hand.

It is impossible to date most Tuckerman poems with accuracy. Internal evidence within the sonnets and certain other poems (such as 'Again, again, ye part in stormy grief' and 'I took from its glass a flower') suggests that they were written after the death of Tuckerman's wife, Anna, in 1857. An autograph ink draft of the 1860 collection (probably the one used by the printers) exists in a notebook inscribed 'F G Tuckerman, Litchfield [sic], Eng., 1854', which was perhaps purchased there as a convenient showcase for the poems Tuckerman brought with him on his second trip to England. But because several poems in the notebook refer to the death of his wife, Tuckerman must have continued adding poems to the notebook for several years after it was purchased in 1854.

This selection presents the poems in order of publication. The first two series of sonnets, which were published in *Poems* (1860), are followed here by the third, fourth and fifth series, which were not published during Tuckerman's lifetime. 'The Cricket', also never published by Tuckerman, is placed last.

The text of 'The Cricket' challenges editors, who are faced with an array of five distinct manuscript versions. Discussions of these can be found in appendices to Momaday's and England's books; see Further Reading. I agree with England that the so-called 'Cricket 2' (Houghton MS Am 1349[4]) is probably the last written of the five. In ink, with pencilled corrections, it is found in a notebook that contains a few other late poems. On the page with one of these is a pencilled note in Tuckerman's hand: 'This poem was sent to the Springfield Rep. Feb 7th/73 but has not appeared.' Tuckerman died about two months later. While I have relied upon 'Cricket 2', I have kept an eye on the other versions, exercising my judgement when the manuscripts contradict each other. Line 58 is one example, where the various manuscripts offer 'closing tears', 'final tears' and 'perfect tears'.

I concur with Momaday and England that the last provides the best phrasing.

One contextual fact of importance to readers is Tuckerman's admiration for and friendship with Alfred, Lord Tennyson. Tuckerman's esteem led him to carry a copy of Tennyson's *Poems* (1842) on a journey to England in 1851, where he noted his visits to places mentioned by Tennyson. For example, next to 'Godiva', which begins, 'I waited for the train at Coventry', Tuckerman inscribed, 'Railroad Station – Coventry July 14th 1851.' Other notes show the vast breadth of Tuckerman's reading, drawing parallels with the works of many other poets. Tuckerman also recorded some of his own emotional responses to Tennyson's poetry, writing at the end of 'The Departure' (from 'The Day Dream'):

I can scarce ever read or recite these two lines without a sensation of tears, partly from their exquisite expression; but chiefly from an association, undefinable but utterly pathetic which the imagery always brings up.

This volume Tuckerman probably carried with him when he visited Tennyson at his home in Farringford, Isle of Wight, in January 1855. There Tuckerman impressed Tennyson with his ability to quote lengths of the Laureate's work from memory. The two sat in the 'smoking attic' at Farringford and discussed poetry over a three-day weekend that was to shine in Tuckerman's memory. Upon his departure, Tennyson presented him with the manuscript of 'Locksley Hall', which was, as Tuckerman later wrote, 'a favour of which I may be justly proud as he says he never did such a thing in his life before, for anybody'.

Perhaps the greatest boon for Tuckerman in their friendship was an increased confidence in his own worth as a judge of poetry and as a poet. He was moved to continue his writing, although his life suffered devastation with the death in childbirth of Anna in 1857. Intense grief enhanced the seclusive tendency of this man who had retired from practising law in Boston to the rural village of Greenfield at the age of twenty-six. The loss of his wife and the almost overwhelming sorrow are evoked repeatedly in the poetry written thereafter. Tuckerman's self-doubt as a poet mingled with his despair:

> What though indeed a joyless verse I turn?
> The flowers are fair, and give their glimmering heaps
> To grace her rest. And so to-night I pass
> To that low mound, gone over now with grass,
> And find her stirless still . . .

The urge to write through and with his sadness, coupled with the bolstering (if long-distance) friendship of his great contemporary Tennyson, culminated in the printing of Tuckerman's *Poems* of 1860. A careful list among Tuckerman's papers reveals that he sent copies to famous men of letters such as Emerson and Hawthorne, Longfellow, Bryant, and of course Tennyson. Emerson replied with praise of Tuckerman's 'love of native flowers, the skill to name them, and delight in words that are melodies'. Hawthorne, with kindness and foresight, wrote back:

I question whether the poems will obtain a very early or wide acceptance from the public either in England or America because their merit does not lie upon the surface, but must be looked for with faith and sympathy, and a kind of insight as when you look into a carbuncle to discover its hidden fire.

It is hoped that this selection of his poetry displays Tuckerman for what he truly is: a gem.

NOTES

1. John Hollander, *American Poetry: The Nineteenth Century* (New York, 1993).
2. Walter Prichard Eaton, 'A Forgotten American Poet', *Forum*, vol. 41 (New York, 1909).

November

Oh! who is there of us that has not felt
The sad decadence of the failing year,
And marked the lesson still with grief and fear
Writ in the rolled leaf, and widely dealt?
When now no longer burns yon woodland belt
Bright with disease; no tree in glowing death
Leans forth a cheek of flame to fade and melt
In the warm current of the west wind's breath;
Nor yet through low blue mist, on slope and plain,
Droops the red sunlight in a dream of day;   10
But, from that lull, the winds of change have burst
And dashed the drowsy leaf with shattering rain,
And swung the groves, and roared, and wreaked their
    worst,
Till all the world is harsh, and cold, and gray.

April

The first of April! yet November's haze
Hangs on the wood, and blurs the hill's blue tip:
The light of noon rests wanly on the strip
Of sandy road; recalling leaf-laid ways,
Shades stilled in death, and tender twilight days
Ere Winter lifts the wind-trump to his lip.
No moss is shyly seen a tuft to raise,
Nor under grass a gold-eyed flower to dip;
Nor sound is breathed, but haply the south-west
Faint rippling in the brushes of the pine,   10
Or of the shrunken leaf, dry-fluttering.
Compact the village lies, a whitened line
Gathered in smoke. What holds this brooding rest?
Is it dead Autumn? or the dreaming Spring?

Inspiration

The common paths by which we walk and wind
Unheedful, but perhaps to wish them done,
Though edged with brier and clotbur, bear behind
Such leaves as Milton wears, or Shakespeare won.
Still could we look with clear poetic faith,
No day so desert but a footway hath,
Which still explored, though dimly traced it turn,
May yet arrive where gates of glory burn;
Nay, scarce an hour, of all the shining twelve
10   But to the inmost sight may ope a valve
On those hid gardens, where the great of old
Walked from the world, and their sick hearts consoled
Mid bowers that fall not, wells which never waste,
And gathered flowers, the fruit whereof we taste:
While, of the silent hours that mourn the day,
Not one but bears a poet's crown away;
Regardless, or unconscious, how he might
Collect an import from the fires of night,
Which, when the hand is still, and fixed the head,
20   Shall tremble, starlike, o'er the undying dead;

And, with a tearful glory,
    Through the darkness shadowing then,
Still light the sleeper's story,
    In the memories of men.

And such are mine; for me these scenes decay, –
For me, in hues of change, are ever born:
The faded crimson of a wasted day,
The gold and purple braveries of the Morn;
The life of Spring, the strength that Summer gains,
30   The dying foliage sad September stains;
By latter Autumn shattered on the plain,
Massed by the wind, blent by the rotting rain;

Till belts of snow from cliff to cliff appear,
And whitely link the dead and new-born year.
All these, to music deep, for me unfold,
Yet vaguely die: their sense I cannot hold, –
But shudder darkly as the years drop by
And leave me, lifting still a darkened eye.
Or if from these despondingly I go
To look for light where clear examples glow,   40
Though names constellate glitter overhead,
To prompt the path, and guide the failing tread,
I linger, watching for a warmer gleam,
While still my spirit shivers, and I seem

    Like one constrained to wander
      Alone, till morning light,
    Beneath the hopeless grandeur
      Of a star-filled winter's night.

Sonnet

Again, again, ye part in stormy grief
From these bare hills, and bowers so built in vain,
And lips and hearts that will not move again, –
Pathetic Autumn, and the writhled leaf;
Dropping away in tears with warning brief;
The wind reiterates a wailful strain,
And on the skylight beats the restless rain,
And vapour drowns the mountain, base and brow.
I watch the wet black roofs through mist defined,
I watch the raindrops strung along the blind,   10
And my heart bleeds, and all my senses bow
In grief; as one mild face, with suffering lined,
Comes up in thought: oh wildly, rain and wind,
Mourn on! she sleeps, nor heeds your angry sorrow
    now.

Sic Itur Ad Astra

I

The starry flower, the flower-like stars that fade
And brighten with the daylight and the dark, –
The bluet in the green I faintly mark,
And glimmering crags with laurel overlaid,
Even to the Lord of light, the Lamp of shade,
Shine one to me, – the least, still glorious made
As crowned moon, or heaven's great hierarch.
And, so, dim grassy flower, and night-lit spark,
Still move me on and upward for the True;
Seeking through change, growth, death, in new and old,
The full in few, the statelier in the less,
With patient pain; always remembering this, –
His hand, who touched the sod with showers of gold,
Stippled Orion on the midnight blue.

II

And so, as this great sphere (now turning slow
Up to the light from that abyss of stars,
Now wheeling into gloom through sunset bars) –
With all its elements of form and flow,
And life in life; where crowned, yet blind, must go
The sensible king, – is but a Unity
Compressed of motes impossible to know;
Which worldlike yet in deep analogy,
Have distance, march, dimension, and degree;
So the round earth – which we the world do call –
Is but a grain in that that mightiest swells,
Whereof the stars of light are particles,
As ultimate atoms of one infinite Ball,
On which God moves, and treads beneath his feet the
        All!

Twilight

In the darkening silence, –
When the hilltops dusk and fail,
And the purple damps of evening now
No longer edge the vale;
When the faint flesh-tinted clouds have parted
To the westward, one by one, –
In the glimmering silence,
I love to steal alone
By river and by runside,
Through knots of aspens gray,   10
And hearken for the voices
Of a music ceased away.

About the winding water,
And among the bulrush-spears,
Like the wind of empty Autumn, comes
Their sorrow in my ears;
Like the wind of hollow Autumn, blowing
From swamp and shallow dim,
Comes the sorrow of the voices;
Whilst along the weedy brim   20
I follow in the evenfall,
And darkly reason why
Those whispers breathe so mournfully
From depths of days gone by.

Is it that, in the stealing
Of the tender, tearful tones,
The knowledge stirs, that bowers and homes
Are dust and fallen stones,
Where once they sang? – that on lips so loving
Settled a still gray sleep,   30
With tears, though mindful memory
Still brings them from the deep?
Is it that Conscience muses,

' ''Twas for thee their high hearts heaved?'
Or is it so, that I am not
What those best hearts believed?

O falling stream! O voices!
O grief! O gaining night!
Ye bring no comfort to the heart:
Ye but again unite
In a brooding gloom, and a windy wail;
And a sorrow, cold like Death,
Steals from the river-border,
Falls in the dampening breath
Of the unavailing night-wind, –
Falls with the strength of tears,
And an unreal bitterness
On the life of latter years.

I see the flags of the River,
And the moss-green alder bark,
While faintly the far-set village lights
Flash through the rainy dark;
And the willow drops to the dipping water, –
But why, from shelf and shore,
Comes the trouble of the voices
Of the loved of heretofore?
They never knew these shadows,
And the river's sighing flow
Swept not their ears in those dim days,
Nor lulled them long ago.

Sunk are the ships, or shattered, –
Yet, as 'mid the burying foam,
On the wild sea-bar, beat here and there,
As the surges go and come,
Pieces and parts of a broken vessel;
So, to this stranger stream
And its still woods, come drifting in,
Thought, memory, doubt, and dream,

Of the noble hearts that sailed with me:
Here to this desert spot   70
Come their dim ghosts, where they, indeed
Were known and nurtured not.

'Tis the heart, the heart, remembers,
And with wild and passionate will
Peoples the woods and vales, and pours
Its cry round stream and hill.
I look o'er the hills to the mournful morning,
And it whispers still of home, –
And, in the darkening of the day,
Impels me forth to roam,   80
With a desolate and vague desire,
Like the evil spirit's quest;
Who walketh through dry places,
Seeking still, nor finding rest.

Yet, in the gathering silence,
When the hilltops faint and fail,
And the tearful tints of twilight now
No longer edge the vale;
When the crimson-faded clouds have parted
To the westward, one by one, –   90
In the passionate silence,
I love to steal alone
By river and by runside,
Through knots of aspens gray,
And hearken for the voices
Of a music ceased away.

The Stranger

Ere the first red-orange glimmer
Touched the dial on the lawn,
In the earliest shade, and shimmer
Of the dawn;

When the dark was growing dimmer,
And the moon, 'mid wavy clouds
Struggling for the horizon-land,
Had vanished like a worn-out swimmer: –
Feeding on the misty shrouds,
Nature's grief to grief suborning,
Stood a man alone in sorrow
On a lifted ledge of pines;
Over mounted woods, and sand,
Valley, and rolling mountain-lines,
Watching for the morrow; –
   Watching for the daylight,
   In the weeping twilight,
   In the anguish of the morning.

When first I paused upon these barren bluffs
Of westland Massachusetts, and looked off
From mountain-roofs thatched by the dropping pine
With his loose leaf, – a natural water-shed; –
Upon the hamlet twinkling through the growth,
The river-silver scattered in the grass,
And all the Tyrian hills! there seemed to me
No spot so fair in all the fair Estate.
And He believed it too; for when the hours
Had, field by field, unlinked the folded vale,
And led me softly by the mountain paths,
And up the hollow rivers; – teaching still
New names and natures in their thoughtful round:
And I had followed all the groves that go
From Shaking-Acres, to the Neighbour's Hole!
Still, with each deep-blue gap, or piece of pines,
Or upland farm-field lovely and apart,
I found him there, the Stranger. Vague and dim
The wind stirs through these mountain-terraces
In the burning day; and such his motion seemed:
Yet, like the ailing wind, went everywhere
With a faint, fluttering step; and, when he stood,

He stood as one about to fall, as now
Sick Autumn stands, with weak-blue vapour crowned.
A man who seemed to have walked through life alone:
Feeble he was, and something stepped in years,
Yet sought no succour save of sun and shade;
But ever went apart, and held his face
Deep in the shadow. But most he loved to lie
By poplar-shafts, or where yon maple-stock
Bears on his fork a ball of umbrage up,
And waits for Autumn's wain: in the deep day,   50
At morning's edge, or night, his place was there.

Skirting the valley, north by needle runs
A sapling coppice, scrags and second-growth,
With sucker-brush and seedlings intermixed,
And a wood-path thrids through from end to end:
There breathes the scented pyrola, and there
The perfect fragrance of the partridge-flower,
'Mid moss, and maiden-hair, and damp dead leaves; –
A poet's cloister for a hidden hour.
And there I found him murmuring to himself   60
Like a low brook, but could not come to drink
His words; for still the bond that should have drawn
Held us apart, – that love of lonely Nature,
And quick impatience of human neighbourhood.
And I believed he was some natural poet,
With a great sorrow hard against his heart,
And shunned to tread too close: yet while I gazed
On the sad, patient brow, and the fixed lip
Where silence brooded, I longed to look within
On the completed story of his life;   70
So easy still it seemed to lift the hand,
And open it, as I would a disused door
Locked with a dusty web. But he passed out;
And, if he had a grief, it went with him,
And all the treasure of his untold love; –
A love that carried him forward with the cloud,

Drew him with river-currents, and at night
Impelled him to the mountain's edge and fall
Among the crowding woods and cataracts.

So
80
The Summer parted: but ere Autumn's cold
Bade the fall-cricket cease his mournful hymn,
By steps and rests of rock, I once again,
Half-seeking him I shunned, one still fair day
And in the sunshine of the afternoon,
Climbed upward to the overlooking ledge,
And stood in thought beneath the dropping pine.
There shook the shining River, and there glimpsed
The village sunk in foliage at my feet,
90
And one vast pine leaned outward to the gulf.
On a great root that held the tree to the hill,
I saw him sitting, till the late red light
Fell wearing westward, and still he sat, and looked
Toward the dim remainder of the day;
And in his hand a bunch of blazing leaves,
Torn from the sumach as he passed along;
While round his feet gathered the mountain flower,
Dry asters, hardhack, and the withering fern.
The night came dark between us on the hill,
100
And nevermore have I beheld his face;
Yet often since, when I have walked with Sorrow,
In solitude, and hopelessness of heart,
Have I recalled that time, and wondered whether
The old man still went weary on the earth,
And if my dreams of his high gift were true:
But I have waited long indeed to hear
These rivers break in song, or, bluely dark,
Behold these mountains rank in rolling verse,
Or our red forests light the landscape line.
110
Something I still have learned, – respect of patience,
And that mysterious Will that proves the heart,
Breaking away the blossoms of its joy,

And, for our latest love, restoring grief;
A swifter sympathy for human pain;
And knowledge of myself, grown out of this,
Unguessed before; a humbler, higher belief
In God and Nature; and more surrendered love.
Still clings the pine-root clamped into the crag;
But the dead top is dry, beneath whose boughs
He sat, and watched the West; and, in my walks,   120
So changed I feel as I approach the place,
So old in heart and step, it almost seems
As if the Wanderer left his life for mine,
When night came dark between us on the hill:
A double interchange, as if indeed
'Twas my old self that disappeared with him,
And he in me still walks the weary earth.
But these are fancies, and so indeed is most
That I have dreamed or uttered in this regard,
Worthless of utterance may be at the best,   130
Since first the Stranger came among these rocks:
A common man perhaps, with common cares;
Guiltless of grief, or high romantic love
Of natural beauty; a common life at last,
Though strangely set and shrined in circumstance.

Ah! did the brook sob hoarse, the dark tree pine
With all its branches, when first I missed him hence? –
And found him not, whether my erring feet
Followed the waste flowers up the upland side,
Or dipped in grass, or scaled the Poet's Rock,   140
Or slid beneath the pines in Wells's woods:
Did Nature bid me mourn? or was it but
The restless beating in my own vague mind
That drove me on? I know not this; but he
Had passed away for ever from the hills.
No more for him, 'mid fallen waves of grass,
Mower or harvest-hand shall mop his brows,
And look across the sunshine; nevermore

Gruff village cur, or even the patient yoke
That after them draw the furrow in the field,
Shall seem to watch those footsteps.
                                        Years have gone,
And, but with me, his memory must be dead;
Yet oft I see a Figure in the fields,
And scarce less real than his personal self,
Which ever faded as the foot drew near.
I often see the figure in the fields,
And hear low verses wailing in the wind,
And I have mourned for him and for his grief;
Yet never heard his name, and never knew
Word of his history, or why he came
Into this outskirt of the wilder land;
And know not now, whether among the roofs
He parted fair, or, as the people say,
Went off between two days, and left the woods
And wilds to mourn him, with the sighing stream.

The School-Girl, An Idyll

The wind, that all the day had scarcely clashed
The cornstalks in the sun, as the sun sank
Came rolling up the valley like a wave,
Broke in the beech, and washed among the pine,
And ebbed to silence; but at the welcome sound, –
Leaving my lazy book without a mark,
In hopes to lose among the blowing fern
The dregs of a headache brought from yesternight,
And stepping lightly lest the children hear, –
I from a side-door slipped, and crossed a lane
With bitter Mayweed lined, and over a field
Snapping with grasshoppers, until I came
Down where an interrupted brook held way
Among the alders. There, on a strutting branch
Leaving my straw, I sat and wooed the west,
With breast and palms outspread as to a fire.

The breeze had faded, and the day had died;
And twilight, rosy-dark, had ceased to climb
Above the borders; when through the alder-thicks
A school-girl fair came up against the brook;   20
From dell and gurgling hollow, where she had
    stopped
To pull sweet-flag. And she had been below,
Where the brook doubles, – for well I knew each
    knot,
Angle, and alnage of the weedy stream, –
For those pale amber bell-worts wet with shade:
A girl whom the girl-mother's desperate love
Had clung to, through the years when, one on one,
All of her blood had blushed to drop away;
And she was left the last, with this one tie
To hang her to the earth. So her young life,   30
Above the gulf, detached, and yet detained,
Suspended swung; as o'er a fresh-fallen pool
A laurel-blossom, loosened by the rain,
Hangs at its pistil-thread – hangs, shakes, and falls.

I saw her crossing through the alder-thicks
And flowerless spoonwood: but, when she stopped to
    speak,
I seemed to lift my head out of a dream
To gaze upon her; for the ceaseless chime
Of insect-voices singing in the grass, –
Ticking and thrilling in the seeded grass, –   40
Had sent me dreaming. I mused; and consciously,
In a half-darkness, so would sink away.
But ever and again the soft wind rose,
And from my eyelids blew the skimming sleep.
I looked upon her, and her eyes were wet;
While something of her mother's colour burned
Gay in her cheek: too like her mother there,
She stood, and called me from the land of dreams.

The land of visions! But she, lingering, seemed
Most like a vision, standing in her tears,   50
Speaking unreal words: but, when I sought
Their import, she said again in clearer tone
Her salutation, and asked, 'Did I not fear
The night's unwholesome dew?' and offered flowers.
And as we wandered homeward, by the slopes,
And through the sugar-orchard to the hill,
She told me of her griefs: her music-lesson –
She could not play the notes, nor count aright.
And she had sung before she broke her fast
That morning, and needs must weep before she slept;   60
And so throughout the day: until at night,
As she was winding upward by the brook,
The thought of her dead mother crossed her heart,
And with it came the fear that she herself
Would die, too, young.
                         I spoke some soothing words,
For her frank sorrow yielding sympathy;
And, as we rose the hill, stood for a breath,
And told an Indian story of the place, –
Of Wassahoale and the fair Quaker maid,   70
Who left the log-hut for a chieftain's lodge,
Until her face grew clear again and calm,
Yet like a sky that cleareth in the night,
Presaging rain to follow. We wandered down;
But, ere we reached the village, she said farewell,
Nearing the house in which her father dwelt, –
Her father, and his brother, and herself.
But I passed on until she left me there
At her own garden-gate, with a half-smile,
And eyelashes fresh-pointed with her tears.   80

Two brothers were they, dwelling in this place
When first I knew their names and history,
And held for heirs upon the village street;
Yet trained to work from starlight until dusk
For their old father. But he now was old,

Reputed rich, and like the bark to the tree;
Tougher perhaps, but tight enough for that.
And so they toiled and waited, stretched and scrimped,
With one maid-sister fitted to reserve,
Early and late, until their hands were hard   90
And their youth left them. Still the promised day
Drew nearer, – the day of rest and competence;
And years went round, and still they rose and slept,
Not for themselves, but him who harder held,
Like a man drowning, his remorseless gripe
As his strength went. At length, when hope was o'er,
The very doorstones at the door worn out,
And they themselves grown old, the old man died;
And left them poor at last, with a great house
That fed upon their substance like a moth.   100
Bond-debt and meadow-mortgage had the rest,
All but the house, – a sorry patrimony.
To-day I saw it, staring, lacking paint,
With a new suit of shingles to the sky;
Spruce-pine perhaps, but sapwood at the best,
Good for three years, and warranted to rot.

Regardless this; but she of whom I spoke,
The elder brother's child, was like a light
In the blank house: not practical, in truth,
Nor like the father's side, as oftentimes   110
The child is more the mother's than the man's;
But dearer far for this: and in the porch, –
Where, for a mortal lifetime certainly,
Was seen the old man sitting like a stone, –
Gathered young footsteps, and light laughter ran,
And sweet-girl voices. Once, indeed, I saw
An awkward youth in the dark angle there,
Dangling and flapping like a maple-key
Hung in a cobweb; but she still was kind,
Gentle with all, and, as she seemed for me   120
Beside the brook, thoughtful beyond her years.

That night, I scarcely slept, before I dreamed
Of softly stepping in the meadow grass
With moccason on foot: and like indeed,
The Indian of the story that I told;
While she who wandered with me in the day,
Still went beside; yet changing in her turn,
Became the truant daughter of the woods!
Now seemed herself, now Phœbe Bellflower,
130   And neither now, – but on I passed alone,
And like myself, thro' dewless bent and reed,
Brooding again the School-girl's simple griefs,
And her sweet farewell face, and murmuring soft
These words: –

   'Sleep, sister! let thy faint head fall,
      Weary with day's long-fading gleam;
   And blessed Gloom, in interval
      Of daylight, bind thine eyes, and seem
   To lead thee on through dim-lit dells,
140   Trembling with tiny harps and bells.
      The flowers you found along the day,
   While balmy stars of midnight shine,
      May those forgetting fingers sway;
      And so, until the morning stream,
   May all of fair and good be thine, –
      Gathered from daylight, or dim hours
   When balmy stars of midnight shine!

   'Rest, maiden! let thy sorrows rest, –
      Nor tearful on the future look, –
150   The sinless secrets of thy breast;
      And close the record like a book.
   And thus aside for ever lay
   The disappointments of the day:
      Nor note nor number bid thee weep;
   But lie, lie on, and let thy dream
      Dim off to slumber dark and deep.' –

I heard the whisper of the brook;
While the dry fields across the stream,
With myriad-music of the night,
Still shook and jingled in my dream.   160

Rhotruda

In the golden reign of Charlemaign the king,
The three and thirtieth year, or thereabout,
Young Eginardus, bred about the court,
(Left mother-naked at a postern-door,)
Had thence by slow degrees ascended up; –
First page, then pensioner, lastly the king's knight
And secretary; yet held these steps for naught
Save as they led him to the Princess' feet,
Eldest and loveliest of the regal three,
Most gracious too, and liable to love: 10
For Bertha was betrothed; and she, the third,
Giselia, would not look upon a man.
So, bending his whole heart unto this end,
He watched and waited, trusting to stir to fire
The indolent interest in those large eyes,
And feel the languid hands beat in his own,
Ere the new spring. And well he played his part;
Slipping no chance to bribe, or brush aside,
All that would stand between him and the light;
Making fast foes in sooth, but feeble friends.   20
But what cared he, who had read of ladies' love,
And how young Launcelot gained his Guenovere;
A foundling too, or of uncertain strain?
And when one morning, coming from the bath,
He crossed the Princess on the palace-stair,
And kissed her there in her sweet disarray,
Nor met the death he dreamed of, in her eyes, –
He knew himself a hero of old romance;
Not seconding, but surpassing, what had been.

30 And so they loved; if that tumultuous pain
Be love, – disquietude of deep delight,
And sharpest sadness; nor, though he knew her heart
His very own, – gained on the instant too,
And like a waterfall that at one leap
Plunges from pines to palms, – shattered at once
To wreaths of mist, and broken spray bows bright,
He loved not less, nor wearied of her smile;
But through the daytime held aloof and strange
His walk; mingling with knightly mirth and game;
40 Solicitous but to avoid alone
Aught that might make against him in her mind;
Yet strong in this, – that, let the world have end,
He had pledged his own, and held Rhotruda's troth.

But Love, who had led these lovers thus along,
Played them a trick one windy night and cold:
For Eginardus, as his wont had been,
Crossing the quadrangle, and under dark, –
No faint moonshine, nor sign of any star, –
Seeking the Princess' door, such welcome found,
50 The knight forgot his prudence in his love;
For lying at her feet, her hands in his,
And telling tales of knightship and emprise,
And ringing war; while up the smooth white arm
His fingers slid insatiable of touch,
The night grew old: still of the hero-deeds
That he had seen, he spoke; and bitter blows
Where all the land seemed driven into dust!
Beneath fair Pavia's wall, where Loup beat down
The Longobard, and Charlemaign laid on,
60 Cleaving horse and rider; then, for dusty drought
Of the fierce tale, he drew her lips to his,
And silence locked the lovers fast and long,
Till the great bell crashed One into their dream.

The castle-bell! and Eginard not away!
With tremulous haste she led him to the door,

When, lo! the courtyard white with fallen snow,
While clear the night hung over it with stars.
A dozen steps, scarce that, to his own door:
A dozen steps? a gulf impassable!
What to be done? Their secret must not lie   70
Bare to the sneering eye with the first light;
She could not have his footsteps at her door!
Discovery and destruction were at hand:
And, with the thought, they kissed, and kissed again;
When suddenly the lady, bending, drew
Her lover towards her half-unwillingly,
And on her shoulders fairly took him there, –
Who held his breath to lighten all his weight, –
And lightly carried him the courtyard's length
To his own door; then, like a frightened hare,   80
Fled back in her own tracks unto her bower,
To pant awhile, and rest that all was safe.

But Charlemaign the king, who had risen by night
To look upon memorials, or at ease
To read and sign an ordinance of the realm, –
The Fanolehen, or Cunigosteura
For tithing corn, so to confirm the same
And stamp it with the pommel of his sword, –
Hearing their voices in the court below,
Looked from his window, and beheld the pair.   90

Angry, the king; yet laughing half to view
The strangeness and vagary of the feat;
Laughing indeed! with twenty minds to call
From his inner bed-chamber the Forty forth,
Who watched all night beside their monarch's bed,
With naked swords and torches in their hands,
And test this lover's-knot with steel and fire;
But with a thought, 'To-morrow yet will serve
To greet these mummers,' softly the window closed,
And so went back to his corn-tax again.   100

But, with the morn, the king a meeting called
Of all his lords, courtiers and kindred too,
And squire and dame, – in the great Audience Hall
Gathered; where sat the king, with the high crown
Upon his brow; beneath a drapery
That fell around him like a cataract!
With flecks of colour crossed and cancellate;
And over this, like trees about a stream,
Rich carven-work, heavy with wreath and rose,
110 Palm and palmirah, fruit and frondage, hung.

And more the high Hall held of rare and strange;
For on the king's right hand Leœna bowed
In cloudlike marble, and beside her crouched
The tongueless lioness; on the other side,
And poising this, the second Sappho stood, –
Young Erexcea, with her head discrowned,
The anadema on the horn of her lyre;
And by the walls there hung in sequence long
Merlin himself, and Uterpendragon,
120 With all their mighty deeds; down to the day
When all the world seemed lost in wreck and rout,
A wrath of crashing steeds and men; and, in
The broken battle fighting hopelessly,
King Arthur, with the ten wounds on his head!

But not to gaze on these, appeared the peers.
Stern looked the king, and, when the court was met, –
The lady and her lover in the midst, –
Spoke to his lords, demanding them of this:
What merits he, the servant of the king,
130 Forgetful of his place, his trust, his oath,
Who, for his own bad end, to hide his fault,
Makes use of her, a Princess of the realm,
As of a mule; – a beast of burthen! – borne
Upon her shoulders through the winter's night,
And wind and snow? 'Death!' said the angry lords;

And knight and squire and minion murmured,
   'Death!'
Not one discordant voice. But Charlemaign –
Though to his foes a circulating sword,
Yet, as a king, mild, gracious, exorable,
Blest in his children too, with but one born   140
To vex his flesh like an ingrowing nail –
Looked kindly on the trembling pair, and said:
'Yes, Eginardus, well hast thou deserved
Death for this thing; for, hadst thou loved her so,
Thou shouldst have sought her Father's will in this, –
Protector and disposer of his child, –
And asked her hand of him, her lord and thine.
Thy life is forfeit here; but take it, thou! –
Take even two lives for this forfeit one;
And thy fair portress – wed her; honour God,   150
Love one another, and obey the king.'

Thus far the legend; but of Rhotrude's smile,
Or of the lords' applause, as truly they
Would have applauded their first judgment too,
We nothing learn: yet still the story lives;
Shines like a light across those dark old days,
Wonderful glimpse of woman's wit and love;
And worthy to be chronicled with hers
Who to her lover dear threw down her hair,
When all the garden glanced with angry blades!   160
Or like a picture framed in battle-pikes
And bristling swords, it hangs before our view; –
The palace-court white with the fallen snow,
The good king leaning out into the night,
And Rhotrude bearing Eginard on her back.

    I took from its glass a flower,
To lay on her grave with dull accusing tears;
But the heart of the flower fell out as I handled the rose,
And my heart is shattered, and soon will wither away.

    I watch the changing shadows,
And the patch of windy sunshine upon the hill,
And the long blue woods; and a grief no tongue can tell,
Breaks at my eyes in drops of bitter rain.

    I hear her baby-wagon,
10 And the little wheels go over my heart:
Oh! when will the light of the darkened house return?
Oh! when will she come who made the hills so fair?

    I sit by the parlour-window
When twilight deepens, and winds get cold without;
But the blessed feet no more come up the walk,
And my little girl and I cry softly together.

Sidney

    Have you forgotten that still afternoon,
How fair the fields were, and the brooks how full?
The hills how happy in their hanging green?
The fields were green; and here, in spots and holes
Where the rich rain had settled, greener green.
We sat beside a window to the south,
Talking of nothing, or in silence sat,
Till, weary of the summer-darkened room,
I in an impulse spoke, you smiled; and so
10 In this consent we wandered forth together
Across the fields to entertain the time.

Shall I retrace those steps until we reach
Again the crossing River? Yes; for so
Again I seem to tread those paths with you:
Here are the garden-beds, the shrubbery,
And moody murmur of the poising bee;
And here the hedge that to the River runs.
Beside me still you mov'd thro' meadow-flowers;
Beside, yet unapproached; cold as a star
On the morning's purple brink; and seemingly   20
Unconscious of the world beneath your feet.
Yet as I plucked up handfuls from the grass,
With here and there a flower, telling their names
And talking ignorant words of why they were,
You paused to gather berries from the hedge;
And I despaired to reach you with my words,
Believed you cold, nor wished to find myself
Calling your face back, and as in a dream
Lingering about the places where you were;
And would not if I might, or so it seemed,   30
Attain unto the property of your love:
Knowing full well that I must soon awake,
Gaze blankly round, and, with a bottomless sigh,
Relapse into my life; – the life I knew
Before I saw your fair hair softly put
From off your temples, and the parted mouth, –
More beautiful indeed, than any flower,
Half-open, and expectant of the rain.
O youth and loveliness! are ye less dear
Placed at impracticable height, or where   40
Not wholly clear, but touched with shades and
     spots
Of coldness and caprice? or do such make
The bright more bright, as sometimes we may see
In the old pictures? Is the knight's brow held
Not noble for its scar? or she less fair,
The lady with the lozenge on her lip?
So may your very failings grace you more;

And I, most foolish in my wisdom, find
The grapes alone are sour we cannot gain.
But, Sidney, look! the River runs below, –
Dark-channelled Deerfield, here beneath our feet,
Unfordable, – a natural bar and stay.
Yet, ere you turn, let us look off together,
As travellers from a hill; not separate yet,
But being to be divided, let us look
Upon the mountains and the summer sky;
The meadow with the herd in its green heart;
The ripple, and the rye-grass on the bank,
As what we ne'er may so behold again.
And, do me right in this, the eye, that saw
These accidents and adjuncts, could not fail
To mark you, loveliest of the place and time;
A separate beauty, which was yet akin
To all soft graces of the earth and sky,
While wanting naught that human warmth could
        give.
So, lady, take the bitter from my words:
Let us go onward now; and should you prize
In any way the homage of a heart
Most desolate of love, that finds in all
Still the salt taste of tears, receive it here,
With aught that I can give, or you retain.
Let me, though turning backward with dim eyes,
Recover from the past one golden look,
Remembering this valley of the stream;
And the sweet presence that gave light on all,
And my injustice, and indeed your scorn,
Refusing me the half-stripped clover-stalk
Your fingers picked to pieces as we walked.
Yet, ere we part, take from my lips this wish, –
Not from my lips alone, from my heart's midst, –
That your young life may be undimmed with storms,
Nor the wind beat, nor wild rain lash it out,
But over change and sorrow rise and ride!
Lending o'er all a tranquil, lenient light;

And, when your evening comes, around that beam
No tragic twilight brood, but late and long
Your crystal beauty linger like a star, –
Like a pure poignant star in the fleecy pink.

But give your poet now one perfect flower:
For here we reach again the garden's bound, –   90
Sweet as yourself, and of one lustre too;
Yet not the red dark bud Damascus yields,
Nor York-and-Lancaster, nor white, nor yellow,
But a rose-coloured rose.

Paulo to Francesca*

When weary Summer had laid down her leaves,
And all the autumn fields were brown and bleak,
How often did we, wandering cheek to cheek,
Tread these deserted ways! On those sad eves,
You – clinging to my side how fearfully! –
Would scarcely dare to speak or breathe aloud;
While every gust seemed like a voice to rise,
And Nature's self to mourn. How often we,
Low in the westward, where they stood like eyes,
Saw the Gemelli under brows of cloud;   10
Or, through dim pine-boughs, – now the quick tears
        start, –
Watched the red beating of the Scorpion's heart,
While winged with love and fear the hours fled by!
O stolen hours of danger and delight!
O lamp of erring passion burned to waste!
O true false heart! even now I seem to taste
The bitter of the kisses that you gave.
You were the traitor, – yes; and more than I,
You were the tempter. Ah! that autumn night,

*See the 'Story of Rimini' [Tuckerman's note]

20 The hour that seemed a wavering line to mark
'Twixt early sunset and determined dark,
Found us together. Menacing and grave,
The night sank down; no lingering gleam allowed,
But in the west one fiery cupreous cloud.
Do you remember, desperate in my mood,
Of all things, of myself, and most of you,
Half-careless, too, whether the worst were known,
So that the storm might split on me alone,
I laughed to think how far we had got from good!
30 Then, with a quick revulsion, wept to view
The misery of our lives! for cruel hands
Had digged a gulf between, a gulf of sin
We could not cross, nor dared to plunge within,
And yet, – as, musing on our fate and fall,
I spoke as one who surely understands,
Of that deep peace that had been found by some,
And good from evil; reasoning, like Paul,
Of temperance, judgment, and the life to come;
Deeming it better here to weep and fast,
40 Than mourn with those who shall mourn at the last;
And we had wept as ne'er till then before,
And half-resolved that we would meet no more, –
In the pine-hollow, under the bare skies,
While darker yet the Shadow closed and clung,
You, pausing, turned, (do you remember this?)
With clinging arms, and die-away sweet eyes,
And kissed me in the mouth, with such a kiss
As that Apollo gave Cassandra young;
Sealing her prophet-lips, alas! with serpent-tongue.

Margites

I neither plough the field, nor sow,
  Nor hold the spade, nor drive the cart,
Nor spread the heap, nor hill nor hoe,
  To keep the barren land in heart.

And tide and term, and full and change,
  Find me at one with ridge and plain;
And labour's round, and sorrow's range,
  Press lightly, like regardless rain.

Pleasure and peril, want and waste,
  Knock at the door with equal stress,   10
And flit beyond; nor aught I taste
  Disrelishing of bitterness.

And tide and term, and full and change,
  Crown me no cup with flowers above;
Nor reck I of embraces strange,
  Nor honey-month of lawful love.

The seasons pass upon the mould
  With counter-change of cloud and clear;
Occasion sure of heat and cold,
  And all the usage of the year.   20

But, leaning from my window, chief
  I mark the Autumn's mellow signs, –
The frosty air, the yellow leaf,
  The ladder leaning on the vines.

The maple from his brood of boughs
  Puts northward out a reddening limb;
The mist draws faintly round the house;
  And all the headland heights are dim.

And yet it is the same, as when
    I looked across the chestnut woods,
And saw the barren landscape then
    O'er the red bunch of lilac-buds;

And all things seem the same. – 'Tis one,
    To lie in sleep, or toil as they
Who rise beforetime with the sun,
    And so keep footstep with their day;

For aimless oaf, and wiser fool,
    Work to one end by differing deeds; –
The weeds rot in the standing pool;
    The water stagnates in the weeds;

And all by waste or warfare falls,
    Has gone to wreck, or crumbling goes,
Since Nero planned his golden walls,
    Or the Cham Cublai built his house.

But naught I reck of change and fray;
    Watching the clouds at morning driven,
The still declension of the day;
    And, when the moon is just in heaven,

I walk, unknowing where or why;
    Or idly lie beneath the pine,
And bite the dry brown threads, and lie
    And think a life well-lost is mine.

from *Sonnets, Part I*

I

Sometimes, when winding slow by brook and bower,
Beating the idle grass, – of what avail,
I ask, are these dim fancies, cares, and fears?
What though from every bank I drew a flower, –
Bloodroot, king-orchis, or the pearlwort pale, –
And set it in my verse with thoughtful tears?
What would it count, though I should sing my death,
And muse and mourn with as poetic breath
As, in damp garden walks, the autumn gale
Sighs o'er the fallen floriage? What avail   10
Is the swan's voice, if all the hearers fail?
Or his great flight, that no eye gathereth,
In the blending blue? And yet, depending so,
God were not God, whom knowledge cannot know.

II

Wherefore, with this belief, held like a blade, –
Gathering my strength and purpose, fair and slow,
I wait; resolved to carry it to the heart
Of that dark doubt in one collected blow;
And stand at guard with spirit undismayed,
Nor fear the Opposer's anger, arms, or art;
When, from a hiding near, behold him start
With a fresh weapon of my weakness made;
And goad me with myself, and urge the attack,
While I strike short, and still give back and back   10
While the foe rages. Then from that disgrace
He points to where they sit that have won the race,
Laurel by laurel wreathing, face o'er face,
And leaves me lower still; for, ranked in place,

III

And borne with theirs, my proudest thoughts do seem
Bald at the best, and dim; a barren gleam
Among the immortal stars, and faint and brief
As north-light flitting in the dreary north.
'What have thy dreams, – a vague, prospective worth?
An import imminent? or dost thou deem
Thy life so fair, that thou wouldst set it forth
Before the day? or art thou wise in grief,
Has fruitful Sorrow swept thee with her wing?'
10   To-day I heard a sweet voice carolling
In the wood-land paths, with laugh and careless cry,
Leading her happy mates. Apart I stept;
And, while the laugh and song went lightly by,
In the wild bushes I sat down and wept.

IV

Nor looks that backward life so bare to me,
My later youth, and ways I've wandered through;
But touched with innocent grace, – the early bee
On the maple log, the white-heaped cherry-tree
That hummed all day in the sun, the April blue!
Yet hardly now one ray the Forward hath
To show where sorrow rests, and rest begins;
Although I check my feet, nor walk to wrath
Through days of crime, and grosser shadowings
10   Of evil done in the dark; but fearfully,
Mid unfulfilled yet unrelinquished sins
That hedge me in, and press about my path,
Like purple-poison flowers of stramony,
With their dull opiate-breath, and dragon-wings.

V

And so the day drops by; the horizon draws
The fading sun, and we stand struck in grief;
Failing to find our haven of relief, –
Wide of the way, nor sure to turn or pause;
And weep to view how fast the splendour wanes,
And scarcely heed, that yet some share remains
Of the red after-light, some time to mark,
Some space between the sundown and the dark.
But not for him those golden calms succeed,
Who, while the day is high, and glory reigns,   10
Sees it go by, – as the dim Pampas plain,
Hoary with salt, and gray with bitter weed,
Sees the vault blacken, feels the dark wind strain,
Hears the dry thunder roll, and knows no rain.

VI

Not sometimes, but, to him that heeds the whole,
And in the Ample reads his personal page,
Labouring to reconcile, content, assuage,
The vexed conditions of his heritage,
For ever waits an angel at the goal;
And ills seem but as food for spirits sage,
And grief becomes a dim apparelage,
The weed and wearing of the sacred soul.
Might I but count, but here, one watchlight spark!
But vain, oh vain! this turning for the light, –   10
Vain as a groping hand to rend the dark.
I call, entangled in the night, – a night
Of wind and voices! but the gusty roll
Is vague, nor comes there cheer of pilotage.

VII

Dank fens of cedar; hemlock-branches gray
With tress and trail of mosses wringing-wet;
Beds of the black pitch-pine in dead leaves set
Whose wasted red has wasted to white away;
Remnants of rain, and droppings of decay, –
Why hold ye so my heart, nor dimly let
Through your deep leaves the light of yesterday,
The faded glimmer of a sunshine set?
Is it that in your blindness, shut from strife,
The bread of tears becomes the bread of life?
Far from the roar of day, beneath your boughs
Fresh griefs beat tranquilly, and loves and vows
Grow green in your gray shadows, dearer far
Even than all lovely lights, and roses, are?

VIII

As when, down some broad River dropping, we,
Day after day, behold the assuming shores
Sink and grow dim, as the great Water-course
Pushes his banks apart and seeks the sea;
Benches of pines, high shelf and balcony,
To flats of willow and low sycamores
Subsiding, till, where'er the wave we see,
Himself is his horizon utterly:
So fades the portion of our early world.
Still on the ambit hangs the purple air;
Yet, while we lean to read the secret there,
The stream that by green shore-sides plashed and
　　　purled
Expands; the mountains melt to vapors rare,
And life alone circles out flat and bare.

IX

Yet wear we on; the deep light disallowed
That lit our youth, – in years no longer young,
We wander silently, and brood among
Dead graves, and tease the sun-break and the cloud
For import. Were it not better yet to fly,
To follow those who go before the throng,
Reasoning from stone to star, and easily
Exampling this existence? or shall I –
Who yield slow reverence where I cannot see,
And gather gleams, where'er by chance or choice   10
My footsteps draw, – though brokenly dispensed, –
Come into light at last? or suddenly,
Struck to the knees like Saul, one arm against
The overbearing brightness, hear – a Voice?

X

An upper chamber in a darkened house,
Where, ere his footsteps reached ripe manhood's brink,
Terror and anguish were his cup to drink, –
I cannot rid the thought, nor hold it close;
But dimly dream upon that man alone; –
Now though the autumn clouds most softly pass;
The cricket chides beneath the doorstep stone,
And greener than the season grows the grass.
Nor can I drop my lids, nor shade my brows,
But there he stands beside the lifted sash;   10
And, with a swooning of the heart, I think
Where the black shingles slope to meet the boughs,
And – shattered on the roof like smallest snows –
The tiny petals of the mountain-ash.

XI

What profits it to me, though here allowed
Life, sunlight, leisure, if they fail to urge
Me to due motion, or myself to merge
With the onward stream, too humble, or too proud?
That find myself not with the popular surge
Washed off and on, or up to higher reefs
Flung with the foremost, when the rolling crowd
Hoists like a wave, nor strong to speak aloud;
But standing here, gazing on my own griefs,
Strange household woe, and wounds that bleed and
10   smart;
With still lips, and an outcry in the heart! –
Or now, from day to day, I coldly creep
By summer farms and fields, by stream and steep,
Dull, and like one exhausted with deep sleep.

XIV

Not proud of station, nor in worldly pelf
Immoderately rich, nor rudely gay;
Gentle he was, and generous in a way,
And with a wise direction ruled himself.
Large Nature spread his table every day;
And so he lived, – to all the blasts that woo,
Responsible, as yon long locust spray
That waves and washes in the windy blue.
Nor wanted he a power to reach and reap
10   From hardest things a consequence and use;
And yet this friend of mine, in one small hour
Fell from himself, and was content to weep
For eyes love-dark, red lips, and cheeks in hues
Not red, but rose-dim, like the jacinth-flower!

XVII

All men, – the Preacher saith, – whate'er or whence
Their increase, walking thro' this world has been;
Both those that gather out, or after-glean,
Or hold in simple fee of harvests dense;
Or but perhaps a flowerless barren green,
Barren with spots of sorrel, knot-grass, spurge: –
See to one end their differing paths converge,
And all must render answer, here or hence.
'Lo! Death is at the doors,' he crieth, 'with blows!'
But what to him, unto whose feverish sense   10
The stars tick audibly, and the wind's low surge
In the pine, attended, tolls, and throngs, and grows
On the dread ear, – a thunder too profound
For bearing, – a Niagara of sound!

XXV

By this low fire I often sit to woo
Memory to bring the days for ever done;
And call the mountains, where our love begun,
And the dear happy woodlands dipped in dew;
And pore upon the landscape, like a book,
But cannot find her: or there rise to me
Gardens and groves in light and shadow outspread:
Or, on a headland far away, I see
Men marching slow in orderly review;
And bayonets flash, as, wheeling from the sun,   10
Rank after rank give fire: or, sad, I look
On miles of moonlit brine, with many a bed
Of wave-weed heaving, – there, the wet sands shine,
And just awash, the low reef lifts its line.

XXVI

For Nature daily through her grand design
Breathes contradiction where she seems most clear:
For I have held of her the gift to hear;
And felt, indeed, endowed of sense divine,
When I have found, by guarded insight fine,
Cold April flowers in the green end of June;
And thought myself possessed of Nature's ear,
When, by the lonely mill-brook, into mine,
Seated on slab, or trunk asunder sawn,
10   The night-hawk blew his horn at sunny noon;
And in the rainy midnight I have heard
The ground-sparrow's long twitter from the pine,
And the cat-bird's silver song, – the wakeful bird
That to the lighted window sings for dawn.

XXVII

So, to the mind long brooding but on it –
A haunting theme for anger, joy, or tears, –
With ardent eyes, not what we think, appears,
But, hunted home, behold its opposite!
Worn Sorrow breaking in disastrous mirth,
And wild tears wept of laughter, like the drops
Shook by the trampling thunder to the earth;
And each seems either, or but a counterfeit
Of that it would dissemble: hopes are fears,
10   And love is woe. Nor here the discord stops;
But through all human life runs the account, –
Born into pain, and ending bitterly;
Yet sweet perchance, between-time, like a fount,
That rises salt, and freshens to the sea.

XXVIII

Not the round natural world, not the deep mind,
The reconcilement holds: the blue abyss
Collects it not; our arrows sink amiss;
And but in Him may we our import find.
The agony to know, the grief, the bliss
Of toil, is vain and vain! clots of the sod
Gathered in heat and haste, and flung behind
To blind ourselves and others, – what but this,
Still grasping dust, and sowing toward the wind?
No more thy meaning seek, thine anguish plead;   10
But, leaving straining thought, and stammering word,
Across the barren azure pass to God;
Shooting the void in silence, like a bird, –
A bird that shuts his wings for better speed!

Sonnets, Part II

I

'That boy,' – the farmer said, with hazel wand
Pointing him out, half by the haycock hid, –
'Though bare sixteen, can work at what he's bid,
From sun till set, – to cradle, reap, or band.'
I heard the words, but scarce could understand
Whether they claimed a smile, or gave me pain;
Or was it aught to me, in that green lane,
That all day yesterday, the briers amid,
He held the plough against the jarring land
Steady, or kept his place among the mowers;   10
Whilst other fingers, sweeping for the flowers,
Brought from the forest back a crimson stain?
Was it a thorn that touched the flesh? or did
The poke-berry spit purple on my hand?

II

Nor idle all, though naught he sees in thine –
But dallying with the day to make it brief;
And thinks it braver far to tramp the leaf
With dog and gun, thro' tamerac, birch, and pine;
Or lounge the day beneath a tavern-sign:
Yet in *his* labour can I well discern
Great workings moving, both in his, and mine.
What though indeed a joyless verse I turn?
The flowers are fair, and give their glimmering heaps
10 To grace her rest. And so to-night I pass
To that low mound, gone over now with grass,
And find her stirless still; whilst overhead
Creation moveth, and the farm-boy sleeps
A still strong sleep, till but the east is red.

III

Yes: though the brine may from the desert deep
Run itself sweet before it finds the foam,
Oh! what for him – the deep heart once a home
For love and light – is left? – to walk and weep;
Still, with astonished sorrow, watch to keep
On his dead day: he weeps, and knows his doom,
Yet standeth stunned; as one who climbs a steep,
And dreaming softly of the cottage-room,
The faces round the porch, the rose in showers, –
10 Gains the last height between his heart and it;
And, from the windows where his children sleep,
Sees the red fire fork; or, later come,
Finds, where he left his home, a smouldering pit, –
Blackness and scalding stench, for love and flowers!

IV

But Grief finds solace faint in others' ills,
And but in her own shadow loves to go:
For her, the mountain-side may flower or flow;
Alike to that dull eye, the wild brook fills
With mist the chasm, or feeds the fields below;
Alike the latter rain, with sure return,
Breaks in the barren pine, or thick distils
On the pond-lily and the green brook-flags
Or rises softly up to flood the fern.
What though the world were water-drowned? or
    though   10
The sun, from his high place descending slow,
Should over the autumn landscapes brood and burn,
Till all the vales were tinder, and their crags,
Apt to the touch of fire, Hephæstian hills?

V

No shame dissuades his thought, no scorn despoils
Of beauty, who, the daily heaven beneath,
Gathers his bread by run-sides, rocks, and groves.
He drinks from rivers of a thousand soils;
And, where broad Nature blows, he takes his breath:
For so his thought stands like the things he loves,
In thunderous purple like Cascadnac peak,
Or glimpses faint with grass and cinquefoils.
The friend may listen with a sneering cheek,
Concede the matter good, and wish good luck;   10
Or plainly say, 'Your brain is planet-struck!' –
And drop your hoarded thought as vague and vain,
Like bypast flowers, to redden again in rain,
Flung to the offal-heap with shard and shuck!

VI

No! cover not the fault. The wise revere
The judgment of the simple: harshly flow
The words of counsel; but the end may show
Matter and music to the unwilling ear.
But perfect grief, like love, should cast out fear,
And, like an o'er-brimmed river, moaning go.
Yet shrinks it from the senseless chaff and chat
Of those who smile, and insolently bestow
Their ignorant praise; or those who stoop and peer
10   To pick with sharpened fingers for a flaw;
Nor ever touch the quick, nor rub the raw.
Better than this, were surgery rough as that,
Which, hammer and chisel in hand, at one sharp blow
Strikes out the wild tooth from a horse's jaw!

VII

His heart was in his garden; but his brain
Wandered at will among the fiery stars:
Bards, heroes, prophets, Homers, Hamilcars,
With many angels, stood, his eye to gain;
The devils, too, were his familiars.
And yet the cunning florist held his eyes
Close to the ground, – a tulip-bulb his prize, –
And talked of tan and bone-dust, cutworms, grubs,
As though all Nature held no higher strain;
10   Or, if he spoke of Art, he made the theme
Flow through box-borders, turf, and flower-tubs;
Or, like a garden-engine's, steered the stream, –
Now spouted rainbows to the silent skies;
Now kept it flat, and raked the walks and shrubs.

VIII

Companions were we in the grove and glen!
Through belts of summer wandered hour on hour,
Ransacking sward and swamp to deck his bower, –
River, and reservoir of mountain rain;
Nor sought for hard-named herb, or plant of power,
But Whippoorwill-shoe, and quaint Sidesaddle-flower.
And still he talked, asserting, thought is free;
And wisest souls by their own action shine:
'For beauty,' he said, 'is seen where'er we look,
Growing alike in waste and guarded ground;   10
And, like the May-flower, gathered equally
On desolate hills, where scantily the pine
Drops his dry wisps about the barren rock,
And in the angles of the fences found.'

IX

But unto him came swift calamity,
In the sweet spring-time, when his beds were green;
And my heart waited, trustfully serene,
For the new blossom on my household-tree.
But flowers, and gods, and quaint Philosophy,
Are poor, in truth, to fill the empty place;
Nor any joy, nor season's jollity,
Can aught, indeed, avail to grace our grief.
Can spring return to him a brother's face?
Or bring my darling back to me, – to me?   10
Undimmed the May went on with bird and bower;
The summer filled and faded like a flower:
But rainy Autumn and the red-turned leaf
Found us at tears, and wept for company.

X

Thy baby, too, the child that was to be,
Thro' happier days, – a brightening sun above, –
Held to thy heart with more forgetful love, –
So proud a portion of thyself and me:
We talked it o'er, – the bliss that was to bless;
The birth, the baby-robes, the christening,
And all our hearts were carried in this thing.
Cold, cold she lies where houseless tempests blow;
The baby's face is here, almost a woe;
And I, so seared in soul, so sapped and shrunk,
Gaze hopeless, – careless, in my changed estate
To fall at once, or in the wilderness
Stand like a charred and fire-hardened trunk,
To break the axe's edge of Time and Fate!

XI

Still pressing through these weeping solitudes,
Perchance I snatch a beam of comfort bright, –
And pause, to fix the gleam, or lose it quite,
That darkens as I move, or but intrudes
To baffle and forelay: as sometimes here,
When late at night the wearied engineer
Driving his engine up through Whately woods,
Sees on the track a glimmering lantern-light
And checks his crashing speed, – with hasty hand
Reversing and retarding. But, again!
Look where it burns, a furlong on before! –
The witchlight of the reedy river-shore,
The pilot of the forest and the fen,
Not to be left, but with the waste woodland.

XII

How most unworthy, echoing in mine ears,
The verse sounds on! – Life, Love, Experience, Art,
Fused into grief; and like a grief-filled heart,
Where all emotion tends and turns to tears,
Broken by its own strength of passion and need:
Unworthy, though the bitter waters start
In these dim eyes, reviewing thought and word;
The high desire, the faint accomplished deed;
Unuttered love and loss, – and feverish
Beatings against a gate for ever barred.   10
Yet over and again I range and read
The blotted page, re-turning leaf and leaf;
And half-believe the words are what I wish,
And pore upon my verse, and court my grief, –

XIII

Even as a lover, dreaming, unaware,
Calls o'er his mistress' features hour by hour,
Nor thinks of simple dress, and humble dower;
But pictures to himself her graces rare, –
Dark eyes, dark lashes, and harmonious hair
Caught lightly up with amaryllis flower,
Hæmanthus, eardrop, or auricula:
And deems within wide Nature's bound and law
All to beseem her beauty but designed –
Of pure or proud; nor counts himself too bold   10
To fit her forehead with the perfect gold;
Or round her girlish temples belt and bind
Some lamp of jewels, lovelier than the whole, –
Green diamond, or gem of girasol!

XIV

The breeze is sharp, the sky is hard and blue, –
Blue with white tails of cloud. On such a day,
Upon a neck of sand o'erblown with spray,
We stood in silence the great sea to view;
And marked the bathers at their shuddering play
Run in and out with the succeeding wave,
While from our footsteps broke the trembling turf.
Again I hear the drenching of the wave;
The rocks rise dim, with wall and weedy cave;
Her voice is in mine ears, her answer yet:
Again I see, above the froth and fret,
The blue loft standing like eternity!
And white feet flying from the surging surf
And simmering suds of the sea!

XV

Gertrude and Gulielma, sister-twins,
Dwelt in the valley, at the farm-house old;
Nor grief had touched their locks of dark and gold,
Nor dimmed the fragrant whiteness of their skins:
Both beautiful, and one in height and mould;
Yet one had loveliness which the spirit wins
To other worlds, – eyes, forehead, smile, and all,
More softly serious than the twilight's fall.
The other – can I e'er forget the day,
When, stealing from a laughing group away,
To muse with absent eye, and motion slow,
Her beauty fell upon me like a blow? –
Gertrude! with red flowerlip, and silk black hair!
Yet Gulielma was by far more fair!

XVI

Under the mountain, as when first I knew
Its low black roof, and chimney creeper-twined,
The red house stands; and yet my footsteps find
Vague in the walks, waste balm and feverfew.
But they are gone: no soft-eyed sisters trip
Across the porch or lintels; where, behind,
The mother sat, – sat knitting with pursed lip.
The house stands vacant in its green recess,
Absent of beauty as a broken heart;
The wild rain enters; and the sunset wind   10
Sighs in the chambers of their loveliness,
Or shakes the pane; and in the silent noons,
The glass falls from the window, part by part,
And ringeth faintly in the grassy stones.

XVII

Roll on, sad world! not Mercury or Mars
Could swifter speed, or slower, round the sun,
Than in this year of variance thou hast done
For me. Yet pain, fear, heart-break, woes, and wars
Have natural limit; from his dread eclipse
The swift sun hastens, and the night debars
The day, but to bring in the day more bright;
The flowers renew their odorous fellowships;
The moon runs round and round; the slow earth dips,
True to her poise, and lifts; the planet-stars   10
Roll and return from circle to ellipse;
The day is dull and soft, the eave-trough drips;
And yet I know the splendour of the light
Will break anon: look! where the gray is white!

XVIII

And Change, with hurried hand, has swept these scenes:
The woods have fallen; across the meadow-lot
The hunter's trail and trap-path is forgot;
And fire has drunk the swamps of evergreens!
Yet for a moment let my fancy plant
These autumn hills again, – the wild dove's haunt,
The wild deer's walk. In golden umbrage shut,
The Indian river runs, Quonecktacut!
Here, but a lifetime back, where falls to-night
Behind the curtained pane a sheltered light
On buds of rose, or vase of violet
Aloft upon the marble mantel set, –
Here, in the forest-heart, hung blackening
The wolf-bait on the bush beside the spring.

XIX

And faces, forms, and phantoms, numbered not,
Gather and pass like mist upon the breeze;
Jading the eye with uncouth images, –
Women with muskets, children dropping shot;
By fields half-harvested, or left, in fear
Of Indian inroad, or the Hessian near;
Disaster, poverty, and dire disease.
Or from the burning village, through the trees,
I see the smoke in reddening volumes roll;
The Indian file in shadowy silence pass,
While the last man sets up the trampled grass;
The Tory priest declaiming, fierce and fat;
The Shay's-man, with the green branch in his hat;
Or silent sagamore, Shaug, or Wassahoale!

XX

O hard endeavour, to blend in with these –
Deep shadings of the past, a deeper grief
Or blur with stranger woes a wound so chief, –
Though the great world turn slow with agonies!
What though the forest wind-flowers fell and died,
And Gertrude sleeps at Gulielma's side?
They have their tears, nor turn to us their eyes:
But we pursue our dead with groans, and cries,
And bitter reclamations, to the term
Of undiscerning darkness and the worm;   10
Then sit in silence down, and brooding dwell,
Through the slow years, on all we loved, and tell
Each tone, each look of love, each syllable,
With lips that work, with eyes that overwell!

XXI

Last night I dreamed we parted once again;
That all was over. From the outward shore,
I saw a dark bark lessen more and more,
That bore her from me o'er the boundless main;
And yearned to follow: no sense of mystery
Fell on me, nor the old fear of the sea;
Only I thought, 'Knowledge must bring relief;' –
Nor feared the sunless gulfs, the tempest's breath,
Nor drowning, nor the bitterness of death!
Yet while, as one who sees his hope decay,   10
And scarcely weeping, vacant in my grief,
I on the jetty stood, and watched the ship, –
The wave broke fresher, flinging on my lip
Some drops of salt: I shuddered, and turned away.

XXII

Put off thy bark from shore, tho' near the night;
And, leaving home, and friends, and hope, behind, –
Sail down the lights! Thou scarce canst fail to find,
O desolate one! the morning breaking white;
Some shore of rest beyond the labouring wave:
Ah! 'tis for this I mourn: too long I have
Wandered in tears along Life's stormy way,
Where, day to day, no haven or hope reveals.
Yet on the bound my weary sight I keep,
As one who sails, a landsman on the deep,
And, longing for the land, day after day
Sees the horizon rise and fall, and feels
His heart die out, – still riding restlessly
Between the sailing cloud, and the seasick sea.

XXIII

Some truths may pierce the spirit's deeper gloom,
Yet shine unapprehended: grand, remote,
We bow before their strength, yet feel them not;
When some low promise of the life to come,
Blessing the mourner, holds the heart indeed,
A leading lamp that all may reach and read!
Nor reck those lights, so distant over us,
Sublime, but helpless to the spirit's need
As the night-stars in heaven's vault! yet, thus,
Though the great asterisms mount and burn
In inaccessible glory, – this, its height
Has reached; but lingers on till light return,
Low in the sky, like frosty Sirius,
To snap and sparkle through the winter's night.

XXIV

Each common object, too, – the house, the grove,
The street, the face, the ware in the window, – seems
Alien and sad, the wreck of perished dreams;
Painfully present, yet remote in love.
The day goes down in rain, the winds blow wide.
I leave the town; I climb the mountain-side,
Striving from stumps and stones to wring relief;
And in the senseless anger of my grief,
I rave and weep; I roar to the unmoved skies;
But the wild tempest carries away my cries! –   10
Then back I turn to hide my face in sleep,
Again with dawn the same dull round to sweep,
And buy, and sell, and prate, and laugh, and chide,
As if she had not lived, or had not died.

XXV

Small gossip, whispering at the window-pane,
Finds reason still, for aught beneath the sun:
Answers itself ere answer shall be none,
And in the personal field delights to reign, –
Meting to this, his grief; to that, his gain;
And busy to detract, to head or hang!
Oh! wiser far, for him who lieth hid
Within himself, – secure, like him to stay,
Icesius' son; who, when the city rang,
Knew there was news abroad, nor wondered what! –   10
If these conspire, why should I counterplot?
Or vex my heart with guessing whether or not
John went to church, or what my neighbour did
The day before, day before yesterday?

XXVI

Yet from indifference may we hope for peace?
Or in inaction lose the sense of pain?
Joyless I stand, with vacant heart and brain,
And scarce would turn the hand, to be, or cease.
No onward purpose in my life seems plain:
To-day may end it, or to-morrow will;
Life still to be preserved, though worthless still,
A tear-dimmed face glassed in a gilded locket.
But Conscience, starting, with a reddening cheek,
Loud on the ear her homely message sends!
'Ere the sun plunge, determine; up! awake!
And for thy sordid being make amends:
Truth is not found by feeling in the pocket,
Nor Wisdom sucked from out the fingers' end!'

XXVII

But the heart murmurs at so harsh a tone, –
So sunk in tears it lies, so gone in grief,
With its own blood 'twould venture, far more lief,
Than underprize one drop of Sorrow's own,
Or grudge one hour of mournful idleness.
To idle time indeed, to moan our moan,
And then go shivering from a folded gate, –
Broken in heart and life, exheredate
Of all we loved! Yet some, from dire distress,
Accounting tears no loss, and grief no crime,
Have gleaned up gold, and made their walk sublime:
So he, poor wanderer in steps like theirs,
May find *his* griefs, though it must be with tears,
Gold grit and grail, washed from the sands of Time.

XXVIII

Yet sometimes, with the sad respectant mind,
We look upon lost hours of want and wail,
As on a picture, with contentment pale;
And even the present seems with voices kind
To soothe our sorrow, and the past endears:
Or like a sick man's happy trance appears,
When on the first soft waves of Slumber's calm;
And like a wreck that has outlived the gale, –
No longer lifted by the wrenching billow,
He rides at rest; while from the distant dam,   10
Dim and far off, as in a dream, he hears
The pulsing hammer play, – or the vague wind
Rising and falling in the wayside willow;
Or the faint rustling of the watch beneath his pillow.

XXIX

How oft in schoolboy-days, from the school's sway
Have I run forth to Nature as to a friend, –
With some pretext of o'erwrought sight, to spend
My school-time in green meadows far away!
Careless of summoning bell, or clocks that strike,
I marked with flowers the minutes of my day:
For still the eye that shrank from hated hours,
Dazzled with decimal and dividend,
Knew each bleached alder-root that plashed across
The bubbling brook, and every mass of moss;   10
Could tell the month, too, by the vervain-spike, –
How far the ring of purple tiny flowers
Had climbed; just starting, may-be, with the May,
Half-high, or tapering off at Summer's end.

XXX

Yet, even mid merry boyhood's tricks and scapes,
Early my heart a deeper lesson learnt;
Wandering alone by many a mile of burnt
Black woodside, that but the snow-flake decks and
        drapes.
And I have stood beneath Canadian sky,
In utter solitudes, where the cricket's cry
Appals the heart, and fear takes visible shapes;
And on Long Island's void and isolate capes
Heard the sea break like iron bars: and still,
In all, I seemed to hear the same deep dirge;
Borne in the wind, the insect's tiny trill,
And crash and jangle of the shaking surge;
And knew not what they meant, – prophetic woe?
Dim bodings, wherefore? Now, indeed, I know!

XXXI

My Anna! when for thee my head was bowed,
The circle of the world, sky, mountain, main,
Drew inward to one spot; and now again
Wide Nature narrows to the shell and shroud.
In the late dawn they will not be forgot,
And evenings early-dark, when the low rain
Begins at nightfall, though no tempests rave,
I know the rain is falling on her grave;
The morning views it, and the sunset cloud
Points with a finger to that lonely spot;
The crops, that up the valley rolling go,
Ever towards her slumber bow and blow!
I look on the sweeping corn, and the surging rye,
And with every gust of wind my heart goes by!

XXXII

Oh, for the face and footstep! woods and shores!
That looked upon us in life's happiest flush;
That saw our figures breaking from the brush;
That heard our voices calling through the bowers!
How are ye darkened! Deepest tears upgush
From the heart's heart; and, gathering more and more,
Blindness, and strangling tears, – as now before
Your shades I stand, and find ye still so fair!
And thou, sad mountain-stream! thy stretches steal
Thro' fern and flag, as when we gathered flowers   10
Along thy reeds and shallows cold; or where –
Over the red reef, with a rolling roar –
The woods, thro' glimmering gaps of green, reveal,
Sideward, the River turning like a wheel.

XXXIII

One still dark night, I sat alone and wrote:
So still it was, that distant Chanticleer
Seemed to cry out his warning at my ear, –
Save for the brooding echo in his throat.
Sullen I sat; when, like the night-wind's note,
A voice said, 'Wherefore doth he weep and fear?
Doth he not know no cry to God is dumb?'
Another spoke: 'His heart is dimmed and drowned
With grief.' I knew the shape that bended then
To kiss me; when suddenly I once again,   10
Across the watches of the starless gloom,
Heard the cock scream and pause; the morning bell,
Into the gulfs of Night, dropped One! the vision fell, –
And left me listening to the sinking sound.

XXXIV

My Anna! though thine earthly steps are done;
Nor in the garden, nor beside the door,
Shall I behold thee standing any more, –
I would not hide my face from light, nor shun
The full completion of this worldly day.
What though beside my feet no other one
May set her own, to walk the forward way?
I will not fear to take the path alone;
Loving, for thy sake, things that cheer and bless, –
Kind words, pure deeds, and gentlest charities.
Nor will I cease to hold a hope and aim;
But, prophet-like, of these will make my bread,
And feed my soul at peace; as Esdras fed
On flowers, until the Vision and the glory came!

XXXV

Nor all of solemn is my thought of her:
Though changed and glorified, must there not be
Place still for mirth, and innocent gayety,
And pure young hearts? Or do we gravely err,
And is their happiness too deep for joy?
It cannot be: the natural heart's employ
Pours praise as pure as any worshipper
Lost in his rite; too raptured to be gay!
Yes; and such service in its flight outstrips
The cries of suffering hearts that wail and bleed,
The groans of grief, wrung from some bitter need. –
This is the faith I bear; and look indeed
To hear her laugh again, – and feel her lips
Kiss from my brow the heavy thoughts away.

XXXVI

Farewell! farewell, O noble heart! I dreamed
That Time nor Death could from my side divorce
Thy fair young life, beside whose pure, bright course
My earthy nature stationary seemed;
Yet, by companionship, direction took,
And progress, as the bank runs with the brook. –
Oh! round that mould which all thy mortal hath,
Our children's, and about my own sere path,
May these dim thoughts not fall as dry and vain,
But, fruitful as March-dust, or April rain,   10
Forerun the green! foretell the perfect day
Of restoration, – when, in fields divine,
And walking as of old, thy hand in mine,
By the still waters we may softly stray!

————

As Eponina brought, to move the king,
In the old day, her children of the tomb,
Begotten and brought forth in charnel gloom, –
To plead a father's cause; so I, too, bring
Unto thy feet, my Maker, tearfully,
These offspring of my sorrow; hidden long,
And scarcely able to abide the light.
May their deep cry inaudible, come to Thee,
Clear, through the cloud of words, the sobs of song,
And, sharper than that other's, pierce thine ears!   10
That so, each thought, aim, utterance, dark or bright,
May find thy pardoning love; more blest than she
Who joyful passed with them to death and night,
With whom she had been buried nine long years!

from *Sonnets, Part III*

I

Once on a day, alone, but not elate,
I sat perusing a forgotten sage,
And turning hopelessly a dim old page
Of history, long disus'd, and out of date:
Reading 'his Method' till I lost my own;
When suddenly there fell a gold presage
Of sunset sunshine on the letters thrown.
The day had been one cloud, but now a bird
Shot into song; I left my hermitage
With happy heart: but ere I reach'd the gate
The sun was gone, – the bird! and bleak and drear
All but an icy breath the balsams stirr'd:
I turn'd again, and entering with a groan
Sat darkly down to Dagoraus Whear.

II

But Nature in her mood, pushes or pulls
At her caprice; we see what is not shown
By that which we behold: nor this alone;
To commonest matters let us fix a bound
Or purport, straight another use is found
And this annihilates and that annuls.
And every straw of grass, or dirt, or stone,
Have different function from the kind well-known:
Commerce and custom, dikes and watermills.
Not to the sea alone, from inland earth,
The stream draws down its freight of floats and hulls,
But backward far, upwinding to the north,
The River gleams, a highway for the gulls
That fly not over land, into the hills.

III

Yet not for him lifts the low weather cloud,
Not for his solace comes the clearing gale,
Who dreams but on himself: whose breath may fail
And leave no crown his due, no god his debtor;
Of his own gloom, sole builder and begetter;
But Nature for thy mirth shall laugh aloud,
O trustful child, who on her heart hast lain
In every flow of storm and fit of rain!
So let the day be wilder, windier, wetter,
It irks not thee, nor bids thy fealty end,   10
Affection wasted, and allegiance vain;
But rather seems like an embracing Friend
Who puts thee from him, but to view thee better,
And better so to fold thee close again.

from *Sonnets, Part IV*

I

Still, like a City, seated on a height
Appears my Soul, and gather'd in her place:
Whilst faintly hovering, swarm about her base
Still nearer drawing with the nearer night,
Dim cloudlike groups of men and groups of horse;
Outposts and riders of some mightier Force
That lies along the hills: while from them thrown
Rise shadowing shafts, with storms of summoning stone
And the bolt falleth where the crossbolt fell;
Till Doubt contends with Hope, and Fear conspires   10
To thwart them both: so that the Soul retires
Even to her inmost keep and citadel;
God views along the horizon darkening far,
Vague tumult, lights of wo, and moving war.

II

But Thought, like a mail'd warder helm'd and tall,
Treads ever on the outward battlement:
Striving to pierce thro' embrasure and rent
The secret of the gloom that girdleth all,
The immeasurable gulf and interval!
Nor heeds the random showers about him sent –
But whilst the cloudy squadrons tramp and wheel,
Busy with weight, and bar, and implement,
He casteth where to make his missiles fall;
Training his engine now, now lower, now higher
As a strong archer sets his bow of steel!
Yet some may pass like meteors to the mark,
Of those blind ventures loos'd into the dark
So swift the arrow flies, it taketh fire!

III

And thus the Mind by its own impulse deep,
As lightning instantly enlighteneth,
May cleave the shades of sin, the shapes of death
That pace it round all day, and never sleep,
That watch the wall all night and pace it round.
Yet not its own: in man's extremity
God lends the light we use, the strength we keep.
So let us use that light, that we may be
Oh! not perhaps with others, thron'd and crown'd,
But at the last in white arrayment found!
So daily use it, that the mystery
Of life we touch, in cloud and wind and tree;
In human faces that about us dwell,
And the deep soul that knoweth heaven and hell.

IV

Yes! pray thy God to give, whate'er thou art,
Some work to be by thee with reverence wrought:
Some trumpet note obey'd, some good fight fought,
Ere thou lay down thy weapons and depart.
Brood on thyself, until thy lamp be spent;
Bind all thy force to compass and invent;
But shun the reveries of voluptuous thought,
Day-musings, the Floralia of the heart,
And vain imaginations: else, may start
Besides the portals of thy tower or tent,   10
Rending thy trance with dissonant clang and jar,
A summons that shall drive thee wild to hear!
Loud, as when in the dreaming Conqueror's ear,
Antigenidas blew a point of war!

V

Yet some there be, believers for the nonce,
Who God's commands unwelcomely obey;
Lost in the path, they keep the heavenward way
But trip at absolute heaven, and drop at once
In the red gulf: not so, do thou essay
To snatch the splendour, and to see the thrones!
Take patience! hope! nor miserably mourn;
If ill enureth, yet abides the good.
Even now, could we look where the white ones wait
Nigh before God; and for a moment scan   10
The angelic faces: even though we stood
In audience of their voices, could we learn
More, than 'tis love that lifts us near their state,
And the dear fellow aid of man to man.

VIII

Nor strange it is, to us, who walk in bonds
Of flesh and time, if Virtue's self, awhile
Gleam dull like sunless ice: whilst graceful Guile,
Blood-fleck'd like hæmatite, or diamonds
With a red inward spark, to reconcile
Beauty and Evil seems; and corresponds
So well with Good, that the mind joys to have
Full wider jet and scope: nor swings and sleeps
Forever in one cradle wearily!
10   Like those vast weeds that off d'Acunha's isle
Wash with the surf, and flap their mighty fronds
Mournfully to the dipping of the wave:
Yet cannot be disrupted from their deeps
By the whole heave and settle of the sea.

IX

Here, where the red man swept the leaves away
To dig for cordial bark or cooling root,
The wayside apple drops its surly fruit.
Right thro' the deep heart of his midmost wood,
Thro' range and river and swampy solitude,
The common highway landward runs today,
The train booms by with long derisive hoot:
And following fast, rise factory, school, and forge.
I heed them not: but where yon alders shoot,
10   Searching strange plants to medicine my mood –
With a quick savage sense, I stop: or stray
Thro' the brush pines and up the mountain gorge:
With patient eye, and with as safe a foot,
As though I walk'd the wood with sagamore George.

X

Hast thou seen revers'd, the Prophet's miracle?
The worm, that touch'd, a twig-like semblance takes?
Or hast thou mus'd what giveth the craft that makes
The twirling spider at once invisible?
And the spermal odour to the barberry flower?
Or heard the singing sand by the cold coast foam?
Or late in inland autumn groves afar
Hast thou pluck'd the little chick-winter-green star
And tasted the sour of its leaf? then come
With me betimes, and I will show thee more   10
Than these, of Nature's secrecies the least.
In the first morning, overcast and chill,
And in the day's young sunshine, seeking still
For earliest flowers, and gathering to the east.

from *Sonnets, Part V*

I

But Nature where she gives, must give in kind;
Grant to the rich and from the poor withhold;
And much that we in manifest behold,
Is faint to some: while other some still find
Truths, that to our sense may be veil'd and furl'd,
Publish'd as light, notorious as wind.
But the old Mother moves about her fire,
Replenishes its flame and feeds the world;
And so fulfils her births and offices;
Causal or consequential, cares not she,   10
Or ortive or abortive: her desire
Is but to serve, and her necessity.
The invention and authority are His,
In the whole Past, or what remains to be.

II

Nor, though she seem to cast with backward hand
Strange measure, sunny cold or cloudy heat,
Or break with stamping rain the farmer's wheat:
Yet in such waste, no waste the soul descries,
Intent to glean by barrenest sea and land.
For whoso waiteth, long and patiently,
Will see a movement stirring at his feet:
If he but wait, nor think himself much wise.
Nay, from the mind itself, a glimpse will rest
Upon the dark: summoning from vacancy
Dim shapes about his intellectual lamp,
Calling these in, and causing him to see;
As the night-heron wading in the swamp
Lights up the pools with her phosphoric breast.

VI

Licentiate of the schools, with knowledge hot,
A stranger hither came, our dames to frighten:
Who talk'd to us of Christ, the Sibyl's Grot,
Glanc'd at Copernick, though he knew him not,
And show'd us hell; and where the blest abide
'The stars,' he said, 'that round the Northstar glide
For *there* is heaven! tell nightly, as they brighten!'
'But do they move?' I said, 'or is it so?'
He answer'd tranquilly, 'we see they do!'
It was enough! the crowd was satisfied,
And I was hush'd: yet felt my colour heighten.
Was he a knave? a coxcomb? or a clown?
Who stooping thus, our ignorance to enlighten,
Ended by so illuminating his own?

VIII

A garden lodge, shut in with quaintest growth,
A slender girl with still kine pasturing near,
And bright look half-expectant, need I fear
Thus to recall that morning when we both
Rode on to the wide City, loud and drear?
Yes, in the shock and tumult hurrying here,
Let me remind thee of that place of peace:
The maiden's smile, the look of happy doubt!
Nor in the stream of things, do thou too, fail
Still to remember me of more than these: 10
The little valley hidden in the pine, –
The low-built cottage buried in the vale,
Wooded and over-wooded, bush'd about
With holm tree, ople tree, and sycamine.

IX

For these, my friend! were but the foldings fair,
The furling leaves about the jewel-flower;
The shade that lent her beauty half its dower,
The beauty that made rich, the shadow there:
Touching all objects with transfiguring power!
The housedog at the door, the village school,
The village in the hills, the hills of Ule!
And thou, Aurania! with thy brow of pearl,
So lov'd from all the world: didst overrule
All time, all thought, in thy sweet kingdom, girl!   10
Thro' the slow weeks my fancy found but her,
And day by day, at dusk, and dawn-break cool:
All the long moonlight nights I dream'd of Ule,
And in the dark half of the month, my heart was there.

X

A poet's moonshine! Yes, for Love must lend
An ear to Reason, though 'tis bitter breath:
Better wild roses died their natural death,
Than evilly, or idly them to rend.
The girl was fair, as flower the moon beneath,
Gentle and good, and constant to her friend;
Yet out of her own place, not so complete:
Was wedded to her kind – had leave to lack,
But old associations rarely slip: –
Tight as a stem of grass within its sheath
You yet may draw and nibble: touch the sweet
With the tip-tongue, and browse the tender end,
Half-vacantly: but not to be put back,
Or swallow'd in, but sputter'd from the lip!

XI

Another! opposite as sky and lands –
As distant too, thy beauty gleams on me:
Bend downward! from thy heaven of chastity
And I will reach with earthy flickering hands!
For I am grim and stain'd. Thou, white and shrin'd!
'Tis better so! no common love our doom,
Half-nurs'd, half-forc'd, in common cold and gloom:
But quick, convulsively, our souls shall strike
And in the dance of life, tumultuous wind
Like fresh and salt indeed! O! thus may we
Join instantly, like to the cloud and sea
In whirling Pillar! nor meet in darkness like
Stalactite and stalagmite, ignorantly
Nearing each other, slow and of one kind!

XII

'Twas granted: – but the bitter god of Love
As in revenge for some disparagement,
Left us to strive, inextricably blent,
Before we knew in truth, for what we strove:
Or why we went, unwillingly who went,
Or whither driven, or who he was that drove.
The countless haps that draw vague heart to heart,
The countless hands that push true hearts apart –
Of these we nothing reck'd, and nothing knew.
The wonder of the world, the faint surmise,   10
The clouded looks of hate, the harrowing eyes;
But pierc'd and pinn'd together! 'Twas one to us
With the same arrow smitten thro' and thro',
We fell, like Phædimus and Tantalus!

XIII

A wash of rippling breath that just arrives,
Thin yellow tufts shattering and showering down:
And underfoot, and all about me blown
Thin yellow tufts and threads, bunches of fives;
Too curiously I note each lightest thing.
But where are they? my friends, whose fair young lives
Gave these dead bowers the freshness of the spring?
Gone! and save tears and memory, all is gone!
Fate robs us not of these, nor Death deprives.
But when will Nature here, new beauty bring?   10
Or thou, behold those faces gathering?
I mark the glimmering moss that yet survives,
I touch the trees, I tread the shedded shives,
But when will come the new awakening?

XIV

And me – my winter's task is drawing over,
Though night and winter shake the drifted door:
Critic or friend, dispraiser or approver,
I come not now, nor fain would offer more.
But when buds break, and round the fallen limb
The wild weeds crowd in cluster and corymb:
When twilight rings with the red robin's plaint,
Let me give something, though my heart be faint,
To thee, my more than friend! Believer! Lover!
10   The gust has fallen now, and all is mute –
Save pricking on the pane the sleety showers,
The clock that ticks like a belated foot,
Time's hurrying step, the twanging of the hours:
Wait for those days, my friend! or get thee fresher
         flowers!

XV

Let me give something! though my Spring be done,
Give to the children, ere their summer time:
Though stirr'd with grief, like rain let fall my rhyme
And tell of one whose aim was much: of one
Whose strife was this, that in his thought should be
Some power of wind, some drenching of the sea;
Some drift of stars across a darkling coast,
Imagination, Insight, Memory, Awe,
And dear New England nature, first and last!
10   Whose end was high, whose work was well-begun:
Of one, who from his window look'd and saw
His little hemlocks in the morning sun,
And while he gaz'd, into his heart, almost
The peace that passeth understanding, past.

XVI

Let me give something! as the years unfold,
Some faint fruition, though not much my most;
Perhaps a monument of labour lost.
But Thou, who givest all things, give not me
To sink in silence, sear'd with early cold!
Frost burnt and blacken'd, but quick fire for frost!
As once I saw at a houseside, a Tree
Struck scarlet by the lightning, utterly
To its last limb and twig; so strange it seem'd,
I stopp'd to think if this indeed were May,   10
And were those windflowers? or had I dream'd?
But there it stood, close by the cottage eaves,
Red-ripen'd to the heart: shedding its leaves
And autumn sadness on the dim spring day.

The Cricket

I

The humming bee purrs softly o'er his flower,
   From lawn and thicket,
The dogday locust singeth in the sun
   From hour to hour:
Each has his bard, and thou, ere day be done,
   Shalt have no wrong;
So bright that murmur mid the insect crowd,
Muffled and lost in bottom-grass, or loud
   By pale and picket:
Shall I not take to help me in my song,   10
   A little cooing cricket?

II

The afternoon is sleepy, – let us lie
Beneath these branches whilst the burden'd brook,
Muttering and moaning to himself, goes by;
And mark our minstrels carol whilst we look
Toward the faint horizon swooning blue.
    Or in a garden bower
Trellis'd and trammel'd with deep drapery
    Of hanging green,
20   Light glimmering thro' –
There let the dull hop be
Let bloom, with poppy's dark refreshing flower:
Let the dead fragrance round our temples beat,
Stunning the sense to slumber, whilst between
The falling water and fluttering wind,
    Mingle and meet,
    Murmur and mix;
No few faint pipings from the glades behind,
    Or alder-thicks:
30 But louder as the day declines,
From tingling tassel, blade, and sheath,
Rising from nets of river vines,
    Winrows and ricks;
    Above, beneath,
    At every breath,
At hand, around, illimitably
Rising and falling like the sea,
    Acres of cricks!

III

Dear to the child who hears thy rustling voice
40 Cease at his footstep, though he hears thee still,
Cease and resume with vibrance crisp and shrill,
Thou sittest in the sunshine to rejoice.
Night lover too, bringer of all things dark,
And rest and silence; yet thou bringest to me
Always that burthen of the unresting Sea,
The moaning cliffs, the low rocks blackly stark;

These upland inland fields no more I view,
But the long flat seaside beach, the wild seamew,
   And the overturning wave!
Thou bringest too, dim accents from the grave   50
To him who walketh when the day is dim,
Dreaming of those who dream no more of him,
With edg'd remembrances of joy and pain;
And heyday looks and laughter come again:
Forms that in happy sunshine lie and leap,
With faces where but now a gap must be,
Renunciations, and partitions deep
And perfect tears, and crowning vacancy!
And to thy poet at the twilight's hush,
No chirping touch of lips with laugh and blush,   60
But wringing arms, hearts wild with love and woe,
Closed eyes, and kisses that would not let go!

IV
So wert thou loved in that old graceful time
   When Greece was fair,
While god and hero hearken'd to thy chime,
   Softly astir
Where the long grasses fringed Caÿster's lip;
Long-drawn, with shimmering sails of swan and
     ship,
   And ship and swan;
   Or where   70
   Reedy Eurotas ran.
Did that low warble teach thy tender flute
   Xenophyle?
Its breathings mild? say! did the grasshopper
Sit golden in thy purple hair
   O Psammathe?
   Or wert thou mute,
Grieving for Pan amid the alders there?
And by the water and along the hill
That thirsty tinkle in the herbage still,   80
Though the lost forest wailed to horns of Arcady?

V

Like the Enchanter old –
Who sought 'mid the dead water's weeds and scum,
For evil growths beneath the moonbeam cold,
   Or mandrake or dorcynium;
And touched the leaf that open'd both his ears,
So that articulate voices now he hears
In cry of beast, or bird, or insect's hum, –
Might I but find thy knowledge in thy song!
   That twittering tongue,
Ancient as light, returning like the years.
   So might I be,
Unwise to sing, thy true interpreter
Thro' denser stillness and in sounder dark,
Than ere thy notes have pierced to harrow me.
   So might I stir
   The world to hark
To thee my lord and lawgiver,
   And cease my quest:
Content to bring thy wisdom to the world;
Content to gain at last some low applause,
   Now low, now lost
Like thine from mossy stone, amid the stems and
     straws,
Or garden gravemound tricked and drest –
   Powder'd and pearl'd
   By stealing frost –
In dusky rainbow beauty of euphorbias!
For larger would be less indeed, and like
The ceaseless simmer in the summer grass
To him who toileth in the windy field,
   Or where the sunbeams strike,
Naught in innumerable numerousness.
   So might I much possess,
   So much must yield;
But failing this, the dell and grassy dike,

90

100

110

The water and the waste shall still be dear,
And all the pleasant plots and places
Where thou hast sung, and I have hung
   To ignorantly hear.
Then Cricket, sing thy song! or answer mine!   120
Thine whispers blame, but mine has naught but
     praises.
It matters not. Behold! the Autumn goes,
   The Shadow grows,
The moments take hold of eternity;
Even while we stop to wrangle or repine
   Our lives are gone,
   Like thinnest mist,
Like yon escaping colour in the tree;
Rejoice! rejoice! whilst yet the hours exist,
Rejoice or mourn, and let the World swing on   130
Unmoved by Cricket song of thee or me.

EDWIN ARLINGTON
ROBINSON

Preface

Edwin Arlington Robinson was not yet an established poet when he wrote to Daniel Mason on 18 May 1900: 'I believe my uncomfortable abstraction called "Luke Havergal" is also to be soused in anthological pickle – along with two or three others of the forlornly joyous breed.' The anthology at issue was Edmund Clarence Stedman's *An American Anthology, 1787–1900*. What a forlorn joy indeed, for a young writer in 1900: to find a place among the American poets, yes; but also to be enclosed in the one barrel with the rest of the previous century. As Louis O. Coxe writes, in 'E. A. Robinson: the Lost Tradition', 'if any poet has been damned by the anthologists it is Robinson'.[1]

With the hope of resisting this danger, the Robinson poems in this selection have been chosen under the principle that poetry seemingly worn out by overuse can be resharpened when brought into contact with less familiar pieces. The famous poems are here, along with some that have seldom appeared outside their original volumes or the *Collected Poems*. Robinson's first, self-published book, *The Torrent and the Night Before*, is the most heavily represented, though not because of any design to favour the young Robinson. While being sure to include the 'essential' Robinson that has lodged in major anthologies and critical essays (with special attention to the most thorough criticism, found in Yvor Winters's *Edwin Arlington Robinson*), I have used my own reason and taste in seeking Robinson's best. Also, to give a sense of the maturation of Robinson's writing, I have included poems from every one of the books that contain short poetry.

To establish the text I have used the *Collected Poems* edition

of 1929, which was the last to be published during Robinson's
life. Robinson made some minor revisions of several poems,
usually altering no more than a word or a few marks of punctu-
ation, and I have maintained his changes. For poems not appear-
ing in *Collected Poems* (1929), I have used first editions of the
books in which they appeared.

I have excluded selections from the longer poems. Yvor
Winters writes, 'Robinson's long poems are mostly unsuccessful
and represent a waste of effort . . . Robinson's most successful
work is to be found among his shorter poems and poems of
medium length.'[2] Like Tennyson, whose *Idylls of the King* shine
most in their smaller scenes, Robinson is strongest when the
focus remains on one thing, whether a person, the relation of
one individual to another, or the struggle of one man with an
idea.

For many years Robinson was himself a struggling man. His
adolescence in the small Maine town of Gardiner was troubled
by the drug addiction and failed medical career of his elder
brother Dean, and by the fact that a blow on the head (by most
accounts given by a teacher) had left Edwin with a chronic,
intensely painful inner ear (an exquisitely coincidental affliction
for a poet with the initials E.A.R.). For medical treatment Robin-
son saw a specialist in Boston. While there, he began attending
Harvard as a non-degree student. In 1893 he left Harvard and
returned to Gardiner, where his father's death and his brother
Herman's mismanagement of funds had left the family in a
dismal strait. Since Robinson had no ambition other than to be
a poet, he settled into a lonely life of writing.

Gardiner is usually identified as the model for Robinson's
'Tilbury Town', where many of the early poems are set. The
poet himself referred to it as 'my mythical town, which is more
or less Gardiner'. But readers should beware the danger of
viewing Tilbury Town as a mere venue for social or political
critique of small-town attitudes, or as a wholly interconnected
world like that of Edgar Lee Masters in *Spoon River Anthology*.[3]
When John Evereldown rides the 'two long leagues to Tilbury
Town', it is not necessary to imagine that he passes the house of
Richard Cory or the 'patch-clad' form of Captain Craig. The

emotional and mental situations of the characters are of first
importance, not the locale. One must always guard against the
tendency to make connections where none are implied by the
poems.

That being said, it is certain that Robinson spent the years
1893–6 in close observation of his fellow denizens of Gardiner.
The Torrent and the Night Before, which was printed privately
in 1896 and paid for out of Robinson's own pocket, contains
many character sketches which one cannot help imagining to be
inspired by real people. There are also poems that engage the
authors Robinson was reading during this time: 'Thomas Hood',
'George Crabbe' and 'For a Book by Thomas Hardy'. These
authors have as much personal (if not physical) presence as
'Aaron Stark' or 'The Clerks' of Tilbury Town. The loneliness
of Robinson's early career was relieved by the companionship
of the poetry he admired.

No hint of the worldly success that was to follow greeted
Robinson during the next nine years of his writing. *The Children
of the Night*, which included most of the contents of *The Torrent
and the Night Before* as well as a few additional poems, was
published in 1897 through the generosity of Robinson's friend
William Butler. He was unable to find a real publisher. In late
1899, with a new century ahead, he moved to New York City.
There he continued the wide reading that had occupied him in
Gardiner and Boston while he laboured over the poems that
would eventually be published in *Captain Craig* (1902). For
sustenance, he worked as a 'time checker', keeping track of the
workers as they built the New York subway.

The break came in 1905, when President Theodore Roose-
velt's son Kermit showed some of Robinson's poems to his
father. The President offered his new favourite poet several
sinecures, and Robinson, insisting that he be able to remain in
New York City, was appointed Special Agent of the Treasury in
the US Customs office at the Port of New York. As similar
custom house positions had once done for Hawthorne and
for Melville, the job eased Robinson's financial pressure and
allowed him time to write. Until he began to sell books in large
quantities (in the late 1920s), Robinson thereafter continued to

enjoy the generosity of wealthy friends who wanted to see him devote all his energies to his art.

While Robinson's shorter poems are today generally considered his best work, it was during the writing of the longer poems that he enjoyed popular and critical acclaim. After the first ever Pulitzer prize for poetry was awarded to his *Collected Poems* of 1921, Robinson turned to blank verse in such long narrative poems as *Roman Bartholow* (1923), *The Man Who Died Twice* (1924) and *Tristram* (1927). These latter two won him more Pulitzers, and by the time of *Tristram* Robinson was a rare animal: a poet on the best-seller list. In 1933, fellow poet and critic Allen Tate referred to him as the 'most famous of living poets'.

Once he had attained the heights of fame, and during the years after his death in 1935, Robinson's reputation suffered the Modernist backlash against popular and successful poets. If he was so widely liked, he could not be any good. A 1930 review of *Cavender's House* (1929) in T. S. Eliot's magazine the *Criterion*, with a perhaps disdainful misidentification of the poet as '*Edward* Arlington Robinson', snubbed politely:

Mr Arlington Robinson's staid march in blank verse is pursued with little deference to either ancient or modern; it merely happens that his idiom was formed before this generation, and there is an end of it . . . It may be now too late for Mr Robinson to accept a hint from the junior modes; but to isolate oneself from 'the next modernity', even when one has created a style and a reputation, is as dangerous as to become its slave.[4]

Robinson's first Pulitzer prize was awarded in the year that saw the publication of *The Waste Land* (1922), and it was easy for some to make Robinson a target among the decaying old order. 'I must be very far behind the times,' he wrote to his friend Laura Richards on 2 December 1934, four months before his death. 'Once I was so modern that people wouldn't have me.' Indeed, his acute psychological character-studies and spareness of language and detail are clues that Robinson was one of the first Modernists. However, this fact became

obscured by the figure of Robinson as the amazingly success-
ful, established poet who stuck to the safe 'staid march' of the
long, blank-verse narratives. Proud of his friend for remaining
himself amid the winds of changes, Robert Frost wrote in his
introduction to Robinson's last book *King Jasper* (1935):
'Robinson stayed content with the old-fashioned way to be
new.'

The truth about Robinson's position in literary history is
better served if we resist the urge to place him on one side or the
other of some border, as that between the Romantic tradition
and the Modern, between the neo-Tennysonians and T. S. Eliot.
He requires his own space, like the lonely one he chose to occupy
through much of his life. Marianne Moore knew him as a
singular writer when she wrote:

Mr Robinson is at all times a poet – at all times circumstantially exact,
the actuality of his treatment of characters in the Bible or in history
making it difficult to think of him as restricted to one place or to an
epoch.[5]

Robinson was at the front as poetry fought its way out of the
preciosity and illusion of feeling that threatened its vitality at
the end of the nineteenth century. For that, he is owed a debt by
the Modernists and those who have come after.

To the readers of today, for whom Robinson may be but a
dim echo from the schoolroom or a dusty few pages in a fat
anthology, this selection of his poetry is offered with the wish
that they lend a fresh ear to a poet who will be forever old and
new.

NOTES

1. Louis O. Coxe, 'E. A. Robinson: The Lost Tradition', *Appreciation
of Edwin Arlington Robinson* (Waterville, Maine, 1967), p. 164.
2. Edgar Lee Masters, *Spoon River Anthology* (New York, 1915).
3. Ivor Winters, *Edwin Arlington Robinson* (New York, 1946),
p. 159.

4. Sherard Vines, review of *Cavender's House*, *Criterion*, vol. X (1930), p. 162.

5. Marianne Moore, review of *The Man Who Died Twice*, *Dial*, vol. 77 (1964), p. 168.

The Torrent

I found a torrent falling in a glen
Where the sun's light shone silvered and leaf-split;
The boom, the foam, and the mad flash of it
All made a magic symphony; but when
I thought upon the coming of hard men
To cut those patriarchal trees away,
And turn to gold the silver of that spray,
I shuddered. But a gladness now and then
Did wake me to myself till I was glad
In earnest, and was welcoming the time   10
For screaming saws to sound above the chime
Of idle waters, and for me to know
The jealous visioning that I had had
Were steps to the great place where trees and torrents go.

Aaron Stark

Withal a meagre man was Aaron Stark,
Cursed and unkempt, shrewd, shrivelled, and morose.
A miser was he, with a miser's nose,
And eyes like little dollars in the dark.
His thin, pinched mouth was nothing but a mark;
And when he spoke there came like sullen blows
Through scattered fangs a few snarled words and close,
As if a cur were chary of its bark.

Glad for the murmur of his hard renown,
Year after year he shambled through the town,   10
A loveless exile moving with a staff;
And oftentimes there crept into his ears
A sound of alien pity, touched with tears, –
And then (and only then) did Aaron laugh.

Dear Friends

Dear friends, reproach me not for what I do,
Nor counsel me, nor pity me; nor say
That I am wearing half my life away
For bubble-work that only fools pursue.
And if my bubbles be too small for you,
Blow bigger then your own: the games we play
To fill the frittered minutes of a day,
Good glasses are to read the spirit through.

And whoso reads may get him some shrewd skill;
And some unprofitable scorn resign,
To praise the very thing that he deplores;
So, friends (dear friends), remember, if you will,
The shame I win for singing is all mine,
The gold I miss for dreaming is all yours.

Sonnet

When we can all so excellently give
The measure of love's wisdom with a blow, –
Why can we not in turn receive it so,
And end this murmur for the life we live?
And when we do so frantically strive
To win strange faith, why do we shun to know
That in love's elemental over-glow
God's wholeness gleams with light superlative?

O brother men, if you have eyes at all,
Look at a branch, a bird, a child, a rose –
Or anything God ever made that grows –
Nor let the smallest vision of it slip
Till you can read, as on Belshazzar's wall,
The glory of eternal partnership!

Her Eyes

Up from the street and the crowds that went,
  Morning and midnight, to and fro,
Still was the room where his days he spent,
  And the stars were bleak, and the nights were slow.

Year after year, with his dream shut fast,
  He suffered and strove till his eyes were dim,
For the love that his brushes had earned at last,
  And the whole world rang with the praise of him.

But he cloaked his triumph, and searched, instead,
  Till his cheeks were sere and his hairs were gray.   10
'There are women enough, God knows,' he said . . .
  'There are stars enough – when the sun's away.'

Then he went back to the same still room
  That had held his dream in the long ago,
When he buried his days in a nameless tomb,
  And the stars were bleak, and the nights were slow.

And a passionate humor seized him there –
  Seized him and held him until there grew
Like life on his canvas, glowing and fair,
  A perilous face – and an angel's too.   20

Angel and maiden, and all in one, –
  All but the eyes. They were there, but yet
They seemed somehow like a soul half done.
  What was the matter? Did God forget? . . .

But he wrought them at last with a skill so sure
  That her eyes were the eyes of a deathless woman, –
With a gleam of heaven to make them pure,
  And a glimmer of hell to make them human.

God never forgets. – And he worships her
30   There in that same still room of his,
For his wife, and his constant arbiter
     Of the world that was and the world that is.

And he wonders yet what her love could be
     To punish him after that strife so grim;
But the longer he lives with her eye to see,
     The plainer it all comes back to him.

George Crabbe

Give him the darkest inch your shelf allows,
Hide him in lonely garrets, if you will, –
But his hard, human pulse is throbbing still
With the sure strength that fearless truth endows.
In spite of all fine science disavows,
Of his plain excellence and stubborn skill
There yet remains what fashion cannot kill,
Though years have thinned the laurel from his
     brows.

Whether or not we read him, we can feel
10   From time to time the vigor of his name
Against us like a finger for the shame
And emptiness of what our souls reveal
In books that are as altars where we kneel
To consecrate the flicker, not the flame.

Sonnet

Oh, for a poet – for a beacon bright
To right this changeless glimmer of dead gray:
To spirit back the Muses, long astray,
And flush Parnassus with a newer light:

To put these little sonnet-men to flight
Who fashion, in a shrewd mechanic way,
Songs without souls that flicker for a day
To vanish in irrevocable night.

What does it mean, this barren age of ours?
Here are the men, the women, and the flowers, –   10
The seasons, and the sunset, as before.
What does it mean? – Shall not one bard arise
To wrench one banner from the western skies,
And mark it with his name for evermore?

Luke Havergal

Go to the western gate, Luke Havergal,
There where the vines cling crimson on the wall,
And in the twilight wait for what will come.
The leaves will whisper there of her, and some,
Like flying words, will strike you as they fall;
But go, and if you listen she will call.
Go to the western gate, Luke Havergal –
Luke Havergal.

No, there is not a dawn in eastern skies
To rift the fiery night that's in your eyes;   10
But there, where western glooms are gathering,
The dark will end the dark, if anything:
God slays Himself with every leaf that flies,
And hell is more than half of paradise.
No, there is not a dawn in eastern skies –
In eastern skies.

Out of a grave I come to tell you this,
Out of a grave I come to quench the kiss
That flames upon your forehead with a glow
That blinds you to the way that you must go.   20

Yes, there is yet one way to where she is,
Bitter, but one that faith may never miss.
Out of a grave I come to tell you this –
To tell you this.

There is the western gate, Luke Havergal,
There are the crimson leaves upon the wall.
Go, for the winds are tearing them away, –
Nor think to riddle the dead words they say,
Nor any more to feel them as they fall;
30   But go, and if you trust her she will call.
There is the western gate, Luke Havergal –
Luke Havergal.

The Chorus of Old Men in 'Ægeus'

Ye gods that have a home beyond the world,
Ye that have eyes for all man's agony,
Ye that have seen this woe that we have seen, –
Look with a just regard,
And with an even grace,
Here on the shattered corpse of a shattered king,
Here on a suffering world where men grow old
And wander like sad shadows till, at last,
Out of the flare of life,
10   Out of the whirl of years,
Into the mist they go,
Into the mist of death.

O shades of you that loved him long before
The cruel threads of that black sail were spun,
May loyal arms and ancient welcomings
Receive him once again
Who now no longer moves
Here in this flickering dance of changing days,
Where a battle is lost and won for a withered wreath,
20   And the black master Death is over all

To chill with his approach,
To level with his touch,
The reigning strength of youth,
The fluttered heart of age.

Woe for the fateful day when Delphi's word was lost –
Woe for the loveless prince of Æthra's line!
Woe for a father's tears and the curse of a king's
      release –
Woe for the wings of pride and the shafts of doom! –
And thou, the saddest wind
That ever blew from Crete,   30
Sing the fell tidings back to that thrice unhappy
      ship! –
Sing to the western flame,
Sing to the dying foam.
A dirge for the sundered years and a dirge for the
      years to be!

Better his end had been as the end of a cloudless day,
Bright, by the word of Zeus, with a golden star,
Wrought of a golden fame, and flung to the central
      sky,
To gleam on a stormless tomb for evermore: –
Whether or not there fell
To the touch of an alien hand   40
The sheen of his purple robe and the shine of his
      diadem,
Better his end had been
To die as an old man dies, –
But the fates are ever the fates, and a crown is ever a
      crown.

Horace to Leuconoë

I pray you not, Leuconoë, to pore
With unpermitted eyes on what may be
Appointed by the gods for you and me,
Nor on Chaldean figures any more.
'T were infinitely better to implore
The present only: – whether Jove decree
More winters yet to come, or whether he
Make even this, whose hard, wave-eaten shore
Shatters the Tuscan seas to-day, the last –
Be wise withal, and rack your wine, nor fill
Your bosom with large hopes; for while I sing,
The envious close of time is narrowing; –
So seize the day, or ever it be past,
And let the morrow come for what it will.

Reuben Bright

Because he was a butcher and thereby
Did earn an honest living (and did right),
I would not have you think that Reuben Bright
Was any more a brute than you or I;
For when they told him that his wife must die,
He stared at them, and shook with grief and fright,
And cried like a great baby half the night,
And made the women cry to see him cry.

And after she was dead, and he had paid
The singers and the sexton and the rest,
He packed a lot of things that she had made
Most mournfully away in an old chest
Of hers, and put some chopped-up cedar boughs
In with them, and tore down the slaughter house.

The Ballade of Dead Friends

As we the withered ferns
By the roadway lying,
Time, the jester, spurns
All our prayers and prying, –
All our tears and sighing,
Sorrow, change, and woe, –
All our where-and-whying
For friends that come and go.

Life awakes and burns,
Age and death defying,   10
Till at last it learns
All but Love is dying; –
Love's the trade we're plying,
God has willed it so;
Shrouds are what we're buying
For friends that come and go.

Man forever yearns
For the thing that's flying:
Everywhere he turns,
Men to dust are drying –   20
Dust that wanders, eyeing
(With eyes that hardly glow)
New faces, dimly spying
For friends that come and go.

Envoy

And thus we all are nighing
The truth we fear to know:
Death will end our crying
For friends that come and go.

Thomas Hood

The man who cloaked his bitterness within
This winding-sheet of puns and pleasantries,
God never gave to look with common eyes
Upon a world of anguish and of sin: –
His brother was the branded man of Lynn;
And there are woven with his jollities
The nameless and eternal tragedies
That render hope and hopelessness akin.

We laugh, and crown him; but anon we feel
A still chord sorrow swept, – a weird unrest;
And thin dim shadows home to midnight steal,
As if the very ghost of mirth were dead –
As if the joys of time to dreams had fled,
Or sailed away with Ines to the West.

For a Book by Thomas Hardy

With searching feet, through dark circuitous ways,
I plunged and stumbled; round me, far and near,
Quaint hordes of eyeless phantoms did appear,
Twisting and turning in a bootless chase, –
When, like an exile given by God's grace
To feel once more a human atmosphere,
I caught the world's first murmur, large and clear,
Flung from a singing river's endless race.

Then, through a magic twilight from below,
I heard its grand sad song as in a dream:
Life's wild infinity of mirth and woe
It sang me; and, with many a changing gleam,
Across the music of its onward flow,
I saw the cottage lights of Wessex beam.

Supremacy

There is a drear and lonely tract of hell
From all the common gloom removed afar:
A flat, sad land it is, where shadows are
Whose lorn estate my verse may never tell.
I walked among them and I knew them well:
Men I had slandered on life's little star
For churls and sluggards; and I knew the scar
Upon their brows of woe ineffable.

But as I went majestic on my way,
Into the dark they vanished, one by one,   10
Till, with a shaft of God's eternal day,
The dream of all my glory was undone, –
And, with a fool's importunate dismay,
I heard the dead men singing in the sun.

Three Quatrains

I

As long as Fame's imperious music rings
Will poets mock it with crowned words august;
And haggard men will clamber to be kings
As long as Glory weighs itself in dust.

II

Drink to the splendor of the unfulfilled,
Nor shudder for the revels that are done: –
The wines that flushed Lucullus are all spilled,
The strings that Nero fingered are all gone.

III

We cannot crown ourselves with everything,
10   Nor can we coax the Fates for us to quarrel: –
No matter what we are, or what we sing,
Time finds a withered leaf in every laurel.

John Evereldown

'Where are you going to-night, to-night, –
     Where are you going, John Evereldown?
There's never the sign of a star in sight,
     Nor a lamp that's nearer than Tilbury Town.
Why do you stare as a dead man might?
Where are you pointing away from the light?
And where are you going to-night, to-night, –
     Where are you going, John Evereldown?'

'Right through the forest, where none can see,
10   That's where I'm going, to Tilbury Town.
The men are asleep, – or awake, may be –
     But the women are calling John Evereldown.
Ever and ever they call for me,
And while they call can a man be free?
So right through the forest, where none can see,
     There's where I'm going, to Tilbury Town.'

'But why are you going so late, so late, –
     Why are you going, John Evereldown?
Though the road be smooth and the way be straight,
20   There are two long leagues to Tilbury Town.
Come in by the fire, old man, and wait!
Why do you chatter out there by the gate?
And why are you going so late, so late, –
     Why are you going, John Evereldown?'

'I follow the women wherever they call, –
    That's why I'm going to Tilbury Town.
God knows if I pray to be done with it all,
    But God is no friend to John Evereldown.
So the clouds may come and the rain may fall,
The shadows may creep and the dead men crawl, – 30
But I follow the women wherever they call,
    And that's why I'm going to Tilbury Town.'

The Clerks

I did not think that I should find them there
When I came back again; but there they stood,
As in the days they dreamed of when young blood
Was in their cheeks and women called them fair.
Be sure, they met me with an ancient air, –
And yes, there was a shop-worn brotherhood
About them; but the men were just as good,
And just as human as they ever were.

And you that ache so much to be sublime,
And you that feed yourselves with your descent,   10
What comes of all your visions and your fears?
Poets and kings are but the clerks of Time,
Tiering the same dull webs of discontent,
Clipping the same sad alnage of the years.

Verlaine

Why do you dig like long-clawed scavengers
To touch the covered corpse of him that fled
That uplands for the fens and rioted
Like a sick satyr with doom's worshippers? –

Come! – let the grass grow there; and leave his verse
To tell the story of the life he led.
Let the man go: let the dead flesh be dead,
And let the worms be its biographers.

Song sloughs away the sin to find redress
In art's complete remembrance: nothing clings
For long but laurel to the stricken brow
That felt the Muse's finger; nothing less
Than hell's fulfilment of the end of things
Can blot the star that shines on Paris now.

Walt Whitman

The master-songs are ended, and the man
That sang them is a name. And so is God
A name; and so is love, and life, and death,
And everything. – But we, who are too blind
To read what we have written, or what faith
Has written for us, do not understand:
We only blink, and wonder.

Last night it was the song that was the man,
But now it is the man that is the song.
We do not hear him very much to-day; –
His piercing and eternal cadence rings
Too pure for us – too powerfully pure,
Too lovingly triumphant, and too large;
But there are some that hear him, and they know
That he shall sing to-morrow for all men,
And that all time shall listen.

The master-songs are ended? – Rather say
No songs are ended that are ever sung,
And that no names are dead names. When we write
Men's letters on proud marble or on sand,
We write them there forever.

Boston

My northern pines are good enough for me,
But there's a town my memory uprears –
A town that always like a friend appears,
And always in the sunrise by the sea.
And over it, somehow, there seems to be
A downward flash of something new and fierce
That ever strives to clear, but never clears
The dimness of a charmed antiquity.

I know my Boston is a counterfeit, –
A frameless imitation, all bereft   10
Of living nearness, noise, and common speech;
But I am glad for every glimpse of it, –
And there it is – plain as a name that's left
In letters by warm hands I cannot reach.

Richard Cory

Whenever Richard Cory went down town,
We people on the pavement looked at him:
He was a gentleman from sole to crown,
Clean favored, and imperially slim.

And he was always quietly arrayed,
And he was always human when he talked;
But still he fluttered pulses when he said,
'Good-morning,' and he glittered when he walked.

And he was rich – yes, richer than a king –
And admirably schooled in every grace: 10
In fine, we thought that he was everything
To make us wish that we were in his place.

So on we worked, and waited for the light,
And went without the meat, and cursed the bread;
And Richard Cory, one calm summer night,
Went home and put a bullet through his head.

Amaryllis

Once, when I wandered in the woods alone,
An old man tottered up to me and said,
'Come, friend, and see the grave that I have made
For Amaryllis.' There was in the tone
Of his complaint such quaver and such moan
That I took pity on him and obeyed,
And long stood looking where his hands had laid
An ancient woman, shrunk to skin and bone.

Far out beyond the forest I could hear
The calling of loud progress, and the bold
Incessant scream of commerce ringing clear;
But though the trumpets of the world were glad,
It made me lonely and it made me sad
To think that Amaryllis had grown old.

Cliff Klingenhagen

Cliff Klingenhagen had me in to dine
With him one day; and after soup and meat,
And all the other things there were to eat,
Cliff took two glasses and filled one with wine
And one with wormwood. Then, without a sign
For me to choose at all, he took the draught
Of bitterness himself, and lightly quaffed
It off, and said the other one was mine.

And when I asked him what the deuce he meant
By doing that, he only looked at me   10
And smiled, and said it was a way of his.
And though I know the fellow, I have spent
Long time a-wondering when I shall be
As happy as Cliff Klingenhagen is.

Octaves

I

We thrill too strangely at the master's touch;
We shrink too sadly from the larger self
Which for its own completeness agitates
And undetermines us; we do not feel –
We dare not feel it yet – the splendid shame
Of uncreated failure; we forget,
The while we groan, that God's accomplishment
Is always and unfailingly at hand.

II

Tumultuously void of a clean scheme
Whereon to build, whereof to formulate,   10
The legion life that riots in mankind
Goes ever plunging upward, up and down,
Most like some crazy regiment at arms,
Undisciplined of aught but Ignorance,
And ever led resourcelessly along
To brainless carnage by drunk trumpeters.

III

To me the groaning of world-worshippers
Rings like a lonely music played in hell
By one with art enough to cleave the walls
Of heaven with his cadence, but without   20

The wisdom or the will to comprehend
The strangeness of his own perversity,
And all without the courage to deny
The profit and the pride of his defeat.

IV

While we are drilled in error, we are lost
Alike to truth and usefulness. We think
We are great warriors now, and we can brag
Like Titans; but the world is growing young,
And we, the fools of time, are growing with it: –
We do not fight to-day, we only die;
We are too proud of death, and too ashamed
Of God, to know enough to be alive.

V

There is one battle-field whereon we fall
Triumphant and unconquered; but, alas!
We are too fleshly fearful of ourselves
To fight there till our days are whirled and blurred
By sorrow, and the ministering wheels
Of anguish take us eastward, where the clouds
Of human gloom are lost against the gleam
That shines on Thought's impenetrable mail.

VI

When we shall hear no more the cradle-songs
Of ages – when the timeless hymns of Love
Defeat them and outsound them – we shall know
The rapture of that large release which all
Right science comprehends; and we shall read,
With unoppressed and unoffended eyes,
That record of All-Soul whereon God writes
In everlasting runes the truth of Him.

VII

The guerdon of new childhood is repose: –
Once he has read the primer of right thought,   50
A man may claim between two smithy strokes
Beatitude enough to realize
God's parallel completeness in the vague
And incommensurable excellence
That equitably uncreates itself
And makes a whirlwind of the Universe.

VIII

There is a loneliness: – no matter where
We go, nor whence we come, nor what good friends
Forsake us in the seeming, we are all
At one with a complete companionship;   60
And though forlornly joyless be the ways
We travel, the compensate spirit-gleams
Of Wisdom shaft the darkness here and there,
Like scattered lamps in unfrequented streets.

IX

When one that you and I had all but sworn
To be the purest thing God ever made
Bewilders us until at last it seems
An angel has come back restigmatized, –
Faith wavers, and we wonder what there is
On earth to make us faithful any more,   70
But never are quite wise enough to know
The wisdom that is in that wonderment.

X

Where does a dead man go? – The dead man dies;
But the free life that would no longer feed
On fagots of outburned and shattered flesh
Wakes to a thrilled invisible advance,
Unchained (or fettered else) of memory;
And when the dead man goes it seems to me
'Twere better for us all to do away
80   With weeping, and be glad that he is gone.

XI

Still through the dusk of dead, blank-legended,
And unremunerative years we search
To get where life begins, and still we groan
Because we do not find the living spark
Where no spark ever was; and thus we die,
Still searching, like poor old astronomers
Who totter off to bed and go to sleep,
To dream of untriangulated stars.

XII

With conscious eyes not yet sincere enough
90   To pierce the glimmered cloud that fluctuates
Between me and the glorifying light
That screens itself with knowledge, I discern
The searching rays of wisdom that reach through
The mist of shame's infirm credulity,
And infinitely wonder if hard words
Like mine have any message for the dead.

XIII

I grant you friendship is a royal thing,
But none shall ever know that royalty
For what it is till he has realized
His best friend in himself. 'T is then, perforce,   100
That man's unfettered faith indemnifies
Of its own conscious freedom the old shame,
And love's revealed infinitude supplants
Of its own wealth and wisdom the old scorn.

XIV

Though the sick beast infect us, we are fraught
Forever with indissoluble Truth,
Wherein redress reveals itself divine,
Transitional, transcendent. Grief and loss,
Disease and desolation, are the dreams
Of wasted excellence; and every dream   110
Has in it something of an ageless fact
That flouts deformity and laughs at years.

XV

We lack the courage to be where we are: —
We love too much to travel on old roads,
To triumph on old fields; we love too much
To consecrate the magic of dead things,
And yieldingly to linger by long walls
Of ruin, where the ruinous moonlight
That sheds a lying glory on old stones
Befriends us with a wizard's enmity.   120

XVI

Something as one with eyes that look below
The battle-smoke to glimpse the foeman's charge,
We through the dust of downward years may scan
The onslaught that awaits this idiot world
Where blood pays blood for nothing, and where life
Pays life to madness, till at last the ports
Of gilded helplessness be battered through
By the still crash of salvatory steel.

XVII

To you that sit with Sorrow like chained slaves,
130   And wonder if the night will ever come,
I would say this: The night will never come,
And sorrow is not always. But my words
Are not enough; your eyes are not enough;
The soul itself must insulate the Real,
Or ever you do cherish in this life –
In this life or in any life – repose.

XVIII

Like a white wall whereon forever breaks
Unsatisfied the tumult of green seas,
Man's unconjectured godliness rebukes
140   With its imperial silence the lost waves
Of insufficient grief. This mortal surge
That beats against us now is nothing else
Than plangent ignorance. Truth neither shakes
Nor wavers; but the world shakes, and we shriek.

XIX

Nor jewelled phrase nor mere mellifluous rhyme
Reverberates aright, or ever shall,
One cadence of that infinite plain-song
Which is itself all music. Stronger notes
Than any that have ever touched the world
Must ring to tell it – ring like hammer-blows,   150
Right-echoed of a chime primordial,
On anvils, in the gleaming of God's forge.

XX

The prophet of dead words defeats himself:
Whoever would acknowledge and include
The foregleam and the glory of the real,
Must work with something else than pen and ink
And painful preparation: he must work
With unseen implements that have no names,
And he must win withal, to do that work,
Good fortitude, clean wisdom, and strong skill.   160

XXI

To curse the chilled insistence of the dawn
Because the free gleam lingers; to defraud
The constant opportunity that lives
Unchallenged in all sorrow; to forget
For this large prodigality of gold
That larger generosity of thought, –
These are the fleshly clogs of human greed,
The fundamental blunders of mankind.

XXII

Forebodings are the fiends of Recreance;
The master of the moment, the clean seer
Of ages, too securely scans what is,
Ever to be appalled at what is not;
He sees beyond the groaning borough lines
Of Hell, God's highways gleaming, and he knows
That Love's complete communion is the end
Of anguish to the liberated man.

XXIII

Here by the windy docks I stand alone,
But yet companioned. There the vessel goes,
And there my friend goes with it; but the wake
That melts and ebbs between that friend and me
Love's earnest is of Life's all-purposeful
And all-triumphant sailing, when the ships
Of Wisdom loose their fretful chains and swing
Forever from the crumbled wharves of Time.

The Growth of 'Lorraine'

I

While I stood listening, discreetly dumb,
Lorraine was having the last word with me:
'I know,' she said, 'I know it, but you see
Some creatures are born fortunate, and some
Are born to be found out and overcome, –
Born to be slaves, to let the rest go free;
And if I'm one of them (and I must be)
You may as well forget me and go home.

'You tell me not to say these things, I know,
But I should never try to be content: 10
I've gone too far; the life would be too slow.
Some could have done it – some girls have the stuff;
But I can't do it: I don't know enough.
I'm going to the devil.' – And she went.

II

I did not half believe her when she said
That I should never hear from her again;
Nor when I found a letter from Lorraine,
Was I surprised or grieved at what I read:
'Dear friend, when you find this, I shall be dead.
You are too far away to make me stop.   20
They say that one drop – think of it, one drop! –
Will be enough, – but I'll take five instead.

'You do not frown because I call you friend,
For I would have you glad that I still keep
Your memory, and even at the end –
Impenitent, sick, shattered – cannot curse
The love that flings, for better or for worse,
This worn-out, cast-out flesh of mine to sleep.'

The Corridor

It may have been the pride in me for aught
I know, or just a patronizing whim;
But call it freak or fancy, or what not,
I cannot hide that hungry face of him.

I keep a scant half-dozen words he said,
And every now and then I lose his name;
He may be living or he may be dead,
But I must have him with me all the same.

I knew it, and I knew it all along, –
10   And felt it once or twice, or thought I did;
But only as a glad man feels a song
That sounds around a stranger's coffin lid.

I knew it, and he knew it, I believe,
But silence held us alien to the end;
And I have now no magic to retrieve
That year, to stop that hunger for a friend.

Pasa Thalassa Thalassa

'The sea is everywhere the sea'

I

Gone – faded out of the story, the sea-faring friend I
     remember?
Gone for a decade, they say: never a word or a sign.
Gone with his hard red face that only his laughter could
     wrinkle,
Gone where men go to be still, by the old way of the sea.

Never again will he come, with rings in his ears like a
     pirate,
Back to be living and seen, here with his roses and vines;
Here where the tenants are shadows and echoes of years
     uneventful,
Memory meets the event, told from afar by the sea.

Smoke that floated and rolled in the twilight away from
     the chimney
10 Floats and rolls no more. Wheeling and falling, instead,
Down with a twittering flash go the smooth and
     inscrutable swallows,
Down to the place made theirs by the cold work of the sea.

Roses have had their day, and the dusk is on yarrow and
    wormwood –
Dusk that is over the grass, drenched with memorial dew;
Trellises lie like bones in a ruin that once was a garden,
Swallows have lingered and ceased, shadows and echoes are
    all.

II

Where is he lying to-night, as I turn away down to the
    valley,
Down where the lamps of men tell me the streets are alive?
Where shall I ask, and of whom, in the town or on land or
    on water,
News of a time and a place buried alike and with him?   20

Few now remain who may care, nor may they be wiser for
    caring,
Where or what manner the doom, whether by day or by
    night;
Whether in Indian deeps or on flood-laden fields of Atlantis,
Or by the roaring Horn, shrouded in silence he lies.

Few now remain who return by the weed-weary path to his
    cottage,
Drawn by the scene as it was – met by the chill and the
    change;
Few are alive who report, and few are alive who remember,
More of him now than a name carved somewhere on the
    sea.

'Where is he lying?' I ask, and the lights in the valley are
    nearer;
Down to the streets I go, down to the murmur of men.   30
Down to the roar of the sea in a ship may be well for
    another –
Down where he lies to-night, silent, and under the storms.

Momus

'Where's the need of singing now?' –
Smooth your brow,
Momus, and be reconciled,
For King Kronos is a child –
Child and father,
Or god rather,
And all gods are wild.

'Who reads Byron any more?' –
Shut the door,
10   Momus, for I feel a draught;
Shut it quick, for some one laughed. –
'What's become of
Browning? Some of
Wordsworth lumbers like a raft?

'What are poets to find here?' –
Have no fear:
When the stars are shining blue
There will yet be left a few
Themes availing –
20   And these failing,
Momus, there'll be you.

Uncle Ananias

His words were magic and his heart was true,
    And everywhere he wandered he was blessed.
Out of all ancient men my childhood knew
    I choose him and I mark him for the best.
Of all authoritative liars, too,
    I crown him loveliest.

How fondly I remember the delight
  That always glorified him in the spring;
The joyous courage and the benedight
  Profusion of his faith in everything!
He was a good old man, and it was right
  That he should have his fling.

And often, underneath the apple-trees,
  When we surprised him in the summer time,
With what superb magnificence and ease
  He sinned enough to make the day sublime!
And if he liked us there about his knees,
  Truly it was no crime.

All summer long we loved him for the same
  Perennial inspiration of his lies;
And when the russet wealth of autumn came,
  There flew but fairer visions to our eyes –
Multiple, tropical, winged with a feathery flame,
  Like birds of paradise.

So to the sheltered end of many a year
  He charmed the seasons out with pageantry
Wearing upon his forehead, with no fear,
  The laurel of approved iniquity.
And every child who knew him, far or near,
  Did love him faithfully.

How Annandale Went Out

'They called it Annandale – and I was there
To flourish, to find words, and to attend:
Liar, physician, hypocrite, and friend,
I watched him; and the sight was not so fair

As one or two that I have seen elsewhere:
An apparatus not for me to mend –
A wreck, with hell between him and the end,
Remained of Annandale; and I was there.

'I knew the ruin as I knew the man;
So put the two together, if you can,
Remembering the worst you know of me.
Now view yourself as I was, on the spot –
With a slight kind of engine. Do you see?
Like this . . . You wouldn't hang me? I thought not.'

Miniver Cheevy

Miniver Cheevy, child of scorn,
    Grew lean while he assailed the seasons;
He wept that he was ever born,
    And he had reasons.

Miniver loved the days of old
    When swords were bright and steeds were
        prancing;
The vision of a warrior bold
    Would set him dancing.

Miniver sighed for what was not,
    And dreamed, and rested from his labors;
He dreamed of Thebes and Camelot,
    And Priam's neighbors.

Miniver mourned the ripe renown
    That made so many a name so fragrant;
He mourned Romance, now on the town,
    And Art, a vagrant.

Miniver loved the Medici,
   Albeit he had never seen one;
He would have sinned incessantly
   Could he have been one.   20

Miniver cursed the commonplace
   And eyed a khaki suit with loathing;
He missed the mediæval grace
   Of iron clothing.

Miniver scorned the gold he sought,
   But sore annoyed was he without it;
Miniver thought, and thought, and thought,
   And thought about it.

Miniver Cheevy, born too late,
   Scratched his head and kept on thinking;   30
Miniver coughed, and called it fate,
   And kept on drinking.

For a Dead Lady

No more with overflowing light
Shall fill the eyes that now are faded,
Nor shall another's fringe with night
Their woman-hidden world as they did.
No more shall quiver down the days
The flowing wonder of her ways,
Whereof no language may requite
The shifting and the many-shaded.

The grace, divine, definitive,
Clings only as a faint forestalling;   10
The laugh that love could not forgive
Is hushed, and answers to no calling;

The forehead and the little ears
Have gone where Saturn keeps the years;
The breast where roses could not live
Has done with rising and with falling.

The beauty, shattered by the laws
That have creation in their keeping,
No longer trembles at applause,
Or over children that are sleeping;
And we who delve in beauty's lore
Know all that we have known before
Of what inexorable cause
Makes Time so vicious in his reaping.

Eros Turannos

She fears him, and will always ask
    What fated her to choose him;
She meets in his engaging mask
    All reasons to refuse him;
But what she meets and what she fears
Are less than are the downward years,
Drawn slowly to the foamless weirs
    Of age, were she to lose him.

Between a blurred sagacity
    That once had power to sound him,
And Love, that will not let him be
    The Judas that she found him,
Her pride assuages her almost,
As if it were alone the cost. –
He sees that he will not be lost,
    And waits and looks around him.

A sense of ocean and old trees
    Envelops and allures him;
Tradition, touching all he sees,
    Beguiles and reassures him;   20
And all her doubts of what he says
Are dimmed with what she knows of days –
Till even prejudice delays
    And fades, and she secures him.

The falling leaf inaugurates
    The reign of her confusion;
The pounding wave reverberates
    The dirge of her illusion;
And home, where passion lived and died,
Becomes a place where she can hide,   30
While all the town and harbor side
    Vibrate with her seclusion.

We tell you, tapping on our brows,
    The story as it should be, –
As if the story of a house
    Were told, or ever could be;
We'll have no kindly veil between
Her visions and those we have seen, –
As if we guessed what hers have been,
    Or what they are or would be.   40

Meanwhile we do no harm; for they
    That with a god have striven,
Not hearing much of what we say,
    Take what the god has given;
Though like waves breaking it may be
Or like a changed familiar tree,
Or like a stairway to the sea
    Where down the blind are driven.

Theophilus

By what serene malevolence of names
Had you the gift of yours, Theophilus?
Not even a smeared young Cyclops at his games
Would have you long, – and you are one of us.

Told of your deeds I shudder for your dreams
And they, no doubt, are few and innocent.
Meanwhile, I marvel; for in you, it seems,
Heredity outshines environment.

What lingering bit of Belial, unforeseen,
Survives and amplifies itself in you?
What manner of devilry has ever been
That your obliquity may never do?

Humility befits a father's eyes,
But not a friend of us would have him weep.
Admiring everything that lives and dies,
Theophilus, we like you best asleep.

Sleep – sleep; and let us find another man
To lend another name less hazardous:
Caligula, maybe, or Caliban,
Or Cain, – but surely not Theophilus.

Veteran Sirens

The ghost of Ninon would be sorry now
To laugh at them, were she to see them here,
So brave and so alert for learning how
To fence with reason for another year.

Age offers a far comelier diadem
Than theirs; but anguish has no eye for grace,
When time's malicious mercy cautions them
To think a while of number and of space.

The burning hope, the worn expectancy,
The martyred humor, and the maimed allure,   10
Cry out for time to end his levity,
And age to soften its investiture;

But they, though others fade and are still fair,
Defy their fairness and are unsubdued;
Although they suffer, they may not forswear
The patient ardor of the unpursued.

Poor flesh, to fight the calendar so long;
Poor vanity, so quaint and yet so brave;
Poor folly, so deceived and yet so strong,
So far from Ninon and so near the grave.   20

Another Dark Lady

Think not, because I wonder where you fled,
That I would lift a pin to see you there;
You may, for me, be prowling anywhere,
So long as you show not your little head:
No dark and evil story of the dead
Would leave you less pernicious or less fair –
Not even Lilith, with her famous hair;
And Lilith was the devil, I have read.

I cannot hate you, for I loved you then.
The woods were golden then. There was a road   10
Through beeches; and I said their smooth feet showed
Like yours. Truth must have heard me from afar,
For I shall never have to learn again
That yours are cloven like no beeches are.

Bewick Finzer

Time was when his half million drew
  The breath of six per cent;
But soon the worm of what-was-not
  Fed hard on his content;
And something crumbled in his brain
  When his half million went.

Time passed, and filled along with his
  The place of many more;
Time came, and hardly one of us
10   Had credence to restore,
From what appeared one day, the man
  Whom we had known before.

The broken voice, the withered neck,
  The coat worn out with care,
The cleanliness of indigence,
  The brilliance of despair,
The fond imponderable dreams
  Of affluence, – all were there.

Poor Finzer, with his dreams and schemes,
20   Fares hard now in the race,
With heart and eye that have a task
  When he looks in the face
Of one who might so easily
  Have been in Finzer's place.

He comes unfailing for the loan
  We give and then forget;
He comes, and probably for years
  Will he be coming yet, –
Familiar as an old mistake,
30   And futile as regret.

The Man Against the Sky

Between me and the sunset, like a dome
Against the glory of a world on fire,
Now burned a sudden hill,
Bleak, round, and high, by flame-lit height made
    higher,
With nothing on it for the flame to kill
Save one who moved and was alone up there
To loom before the chaos and the glare
As if he were the last god going home
Unto his last desire.

Dark, marvelous, and inscrutable he moved on   10
Till down the fiery distance he was gone,
Like one of those eternal, remote things
That range across a man's imaginings
When a sure music fills him and he knows
What he may say thereafter to few men, –
The touch of ages having wrought
An echo and a glimpse of what he thought
A phantom or a legend until then;
For whether lighted over ways that save,
Or lured from all repose,   20
If he go on too far to find a grave,
Mostly alone he goes.

Even he, who stood where I had found him,
On high with fire all round him,
Who moved along the molten west,
And over the round hill's crest
That seemed half ready with him to go down,
Flame-bitten and flame-cleft,
As if there were to be no last thing left

30   Of a nameless unimaginable town, –
Even he who climbed and vanished may have taken
Down to the perils of a depth not known,
From death defended though by men forsaken,
The bread that every man must eat alone;
He may have walked while others hardly dared
Look on to see him stand where many fell;
And upward out of that, as out of hell,
He may have sung and striven
To mount where more of him shall yet be given,
40   Bereft of all retreat,
To sevenfold heat, –
As on a day when three in Dura shared
The furnace, and were spared
For glory by that king of Babylon
Who made himself so great that God, who heard,
Covered him with long feathers, like a bird.

Again, he may have gone down easily,
By comfortable altitudes, and found,
As always, underneath him solid ground
50   Whereon to be sufficient and to stand
Possessed already of the promised land,
Far stretched and fair to see:
A good sight, verily,
And one to make the eyes of her who bore him
Shine glad with hidden tears.
Why question of his ease of who before him,
In one place or another where they left
Their names as far behind them as their bones,
And yet by dint of slaughter, toil and theft,
60   And shrewdly sharpened stones,
Carved hard the way for his ascendency
Through deserts of lost years?
Why trouble him now who sees and hears
No more than what his innocence requires,
And therefore to no other height aspires
Than one at which he neither quails nor tires?

He may do more by seeing what he sees
Than others eager for iniquities;
He may, by seeing all things for the best,
Incite futurity to do the rest.   70

Or with an even likelihood,
He may have met with atrabilious eyes
The fires of time on equal terms and passed
Indifferently down, until at last
His only kind of grandeur would have been,
Apparently, in being seen.
He may have had for evil or for good
No argument; he may have had no care
For what without himself went anywhere
To failure or to glory, and least of all   80
For such a stale, flamboyant miracle;
He may have been the prophet of an art
Immovable to old idolatries;
He may have been a player without a part,
Annoyed that even the sun should have the skies
For such a flaming way to advertise;
He may have been a painter sick at heart
With Nature's toiling for a new surprise;
He may have been a cynic, who now, for all
Of anything divine that his effete   90
Negation may have tasted,
Saw truth in his own image, rather small,
Forbore to fever the ephemeral,
Found any barren height a good retreat
From any swarming street,
And in the sun saw power superbly wasted;
And when the primitive old-fashioned stars
Came out again to shine on joys and wars
More primitive, and all arrayed for doom,
He may have proved a world a sorry thing   100
In his imagining,
And life a lighted highway to the tomb.

Or, mounting with infirm unsearching tread,
His hopes to chaos led,
He may have stumbled up there from the past,
And with an aching strangeness viewed the last
Abysmal conflagration of his dreams, –
A flame where nothing seems
To burn but flame itself, by nothing fed;
110   And while it all went out,
Not even the faint anodyne of doubt
May then have eased a painful going down
From pictured heights of power and lost renown,
Revealed at length to his outlived endeavor
Remote and unapproachable forever;
And at his heart there may have gnawed
Sick memories of a dead faith foiled and flawed
And long dishonored by the living death
Assigned alike by chance
120   To brutes and hierophants;
And anguish fallen on those he loved around him
May once have dealt the last blow to confound him,
And so have left him as death leaves a child,
Who sees it all too near;
And he who knows no young way to forget
May struggle to the tomb unreconciled.
Whatever suns may rise or set
There may be nothing kinder for him here
Than shafts and agonies;
130   And under these
He may cry out and stay on horribly;
Or, seeing in death too small a thing to fear,
He may go forward like a stoic Roman
Where pangs and terrors in his pathway lie, –
Or, seizing the swift logic of a woman,
Curse God and die.

Or maybe there, like many another one
Who might have stood aloft and looked ahead,
Black-drawn against wild red,
He may have built, unawed by fiery gules   140
That in him no commotion stirred,
A living reason out of molecules
Why molecules occurred,
And one for smiling when he might have sighed
Had he seen far enough,
And in the same inevitable stuff
Discovered an odd reason too for pride
In being what he must have been by laws
Infrangible and for no kind of cause.
Deterred by no confusion or surprise   150
He may have seen with his mechanic eyes
A world without a meaning, and had room,
Alone amid magnificence and doom,
To build himself an airy monument
That should, or fail him in his vague intent,
Outlast an accidental universe –
To call it nothing worse –
Or, by the burrowing guile
Of Time disintegrated and effaced,
Like once-remembered mighty trees go down   160
To ruin, of which by man may now be traced
No part sufficient even to be rotten,
And in the book of things that are forgotten
Is entered as a thing not quite worth while.
He may have been so great
That satraps would have shivered at his frown,
And all he prized alive may rule a state
No larger than a grave that holds a clown;
He may have been a master of his fate,
And of his atoms, – ready as another   170
In his emergence to exonerate
His father and his mother;

He may have been a captain of a host,
Self-eloquent and ripe for prodigies,
Doomed here to swell by dangerous degrees,
And then give up the ghost.
Nahum's great grasshoppers were such as these,
Sun-scattered and soon lost.

Whatever the dark road he may have taken,
This man who stood on high
And faced alone the sky,
Whatever drove or lured or guided him, –
A vision answering a faith unshaken,
An easy trust assumed of easy trials,
A sick negation born of weak denials,
A crazed abhorrence of an old condition,
A blind attendance on a brief ambition, –
Whatever stayed him or derided him,
His way was even as ours;
And we, with all our wounds and all our powers,
Must each await alone at his own height
Another darkness or another light;
And there, of our poor self dominion reft,
In inference and reason shun
Hell, Heaven, and Oblivion,
May thwarted will (perforce precarious,
But for our conservation better thus)
Have no misgiving left
Of doing yet what here we leave undone?
Or if unto the last of these we cleave,
Believing or protesting we believe
In such an idle and ephemeral
Florescence of the diabolical, –
If, robbed of two fond old enormities,
Our being had no onward auguries,
What then were this great love of ours to say
For launching other lives to voyage again
A little farther into time and pain,

A little faster in a futile chase
For a kingdom and a power and a Race   210
That would have still in sight
A manifest end of ashes and eternal night?
Is this the music of the toys we shake
So loud, – as if there might be no mistake
Somewhere in our indomitable will?
Are we no greater than the noise we make
Along one blind atomic pilgrimage
Whereon by crass chance billeted we go
Because our brains and bones and cartilage
Will have it so?   220
If this we say, then let us all be still
About our share in it, and live and die
More quietly thereby.

Where was he going, this man against the sky?
You know not, nor do I.
But this we know, if we know anything:
That we may laugh and fight and sing
And of our transience here make offering
To an orient Word that will not be erased,
Or, save in incommunicable gleams   230
Too permanent for dreams,
Be found or known.
No tonic and ambitious irritant
Of increase or of want
Has made an otherwise insensate waste
Of ages overthrown
A ruthless, veiled, implacable foretaste
Of other ages that are still to be
Depleted and rewarded variously
Because a few, by fate's economy,   240
Shall seem to move the world the way it goes;
No soft evangel of equality,
Safe-cradled in a communal repose
That huddles into death and may at last

Be covered well with equatorial snows –
And all for what, the devil only knows –
Will aggregate an inkling to confirm
The credit of a sage or of a worm,
Or tell us why one man in five
Should have a care to stay alive
While in his heart he feels no violence
Laid on his humor and intelligence
When infant Science makes a pleasant face
And waves again that hollow toy, the Race;
No planetary trap where souls are wrought
For nothing but the sake of being caught
And sent again to nothing will attune
Itself to any key of any reason
Why man should hunger through another season
To find out why 'twere better late than soon
To go away and let the sun and moon
And all the silly stars illuminate
A place for creeping things,
And those that root and trumpet and have wings,
And herd and ruminate,
Or dive and flash and poise in rivers and seas,
Or by their loyal tails in lofty trees
Hang screeching lewd victorious derision
Of man's immortal vision.
Shall we, because Eternity records
Too vast an answer for the time-born words
We spell, whereof so many are dead that once
In our capricious lexicons
Were so alive and final, hear no more
The Word itself, the living word
That none alive has ever heard
Or ever spelt,
And few have ever felt
Without the fears and old surrenderings
And terrors that began
When Death let fall a feather from his wings
And humbled the first man?

250

260

270

280

Because the weight of our humility,
Wherefrom we gain
A little wisdom and much pain,
Falls here too sore and there too tedious,
Are we in anguish or complacency,
Not looking far enough ahead
To see by what mad couriers we are led
Along the roads of the ridiculous,   290
To pity ourselves and laugh at faith
And while we curse life bear it?
And if we see the soul's dead end in death,
Are we to fear it?
What folly is here that has not yet a name
Unless we say outright that we are liars?
What have we seen beyond our sunset fires
That lights again the way by which we came?
Why pay we such a price, and one we give
So clamoringly, for each racked empty day   300
That leads one more last human hope away,
As quiet fiends would lead past our crazed eyes
Our children to an unseen sacrifice?
If after all that we have lived and thought,
All comes to Nought, –
If there be nothing after Now,
And we be nothing anyhow,
And we know that, – why live?
'Twere sure but weaklings' vain distress
To suffer dungeons where so many doors   310
Will open on the cold eternal shores
That look sheer down
To the dark tideless floods of Nothingness
Where all who know may drown.

The Flying Dutchman

Unyielding in the pride of his defiance,
　　Afloat with none to serve or to command,
Lord of himself at last, and all by Science,
　　He seeks the Vanished Land.

Alone, by the one light of his one thought,
　　He steers to find the shore from which we came,
Fearless of in what coil he may be caught
　　On seas that have no name.

Into the night he sails; and after night
10　　There is a dawning, though there be no sun;
Wherefore, with nothing but himself in sight,
　　Unsighted, he sails on.

At last there is a lifting of the cloud
　　Between the flood before him and the sky;
And then – though he may curse the Power aloud
　　That has no power to die –

He steers himself away from what is haunted
　　By the old ghost of what has been before, –
Abandoning, as always, and undaunted,
20　　One fog-walled island more.

Firelight

Ten years together without yet a cloud,
They seek each other's eyes at intervals
Of gratefulness to firelight and four walls
For love's obliteration of the crowd.

Serenely and perennially endowed
And bowered as few may be, their joy recalls
No snake, no sword; and over them there falls
The blessing of what neither says aloud.

Wiser for silence, they were not so glad
Were she to read the graven tale of lines   10
On the wan face of one somewhere alone;
Nor were they more content could he have had
Her thoughts a moment since of one who shines
Apart, and would be hers if he had known.

Mr Flood's Party

Old Eben Flood, climbing alone one night
Over the hill between the town below
And the forsaken upland hermitage
That held as much as he should ever know
On earth again of home, paused warily.
The road was his with not a native near;
And Eben, having leisure, said aloud,
For no man else in Tilbury Town to hear:

'Well, Mr Flood, we have the harvest moon
Again, and we may not have many more;   10
The bird is on the wing, the poet says,
And you and I have said it here before.
Drink to the bird.' He raised up to the light
The jug that he had gone so far to fill,
And answered huskily: 'Well, Mr Flood,
Since you propose it, I believe I will.'

Alone, as if enduring to the end
A valiant armor of scarred hopes outworn,
He stood there in the middle of the road
Like Roland's ghost winding a silent horn.   20

Below him, in the town among the trees,
Where friends of other days had honored him,
A phantom salutation of the dead
Rang thinly till old Eben's eyes were dim.

Then, as a mother lays her sleeping child
Down tenderly, fearing it may awake,
He set the jug down slowly at his feet
With trembling care, knowing that most things break;
And only when assured that on firm earth
30   It stood, as the uncertain lives of men
Assuredly did not, he paced away,
And with his hand extended paused again:

'Well, Mr Flood, we have not met like this
In a long time; and many a change has come
To both of us, I fear, since last it was
We had a drop together. Welcome home!'
Convivially returning with himself,
Again he raised the jug up to the light;
And with an acquiescent quaver said:
40   'Well, Mr Flood, if you insist, I might.

'Only a very little, Mr Flood –
For auld lang syne. No more sir; that will do.'
So, for the time, apparently it did,
And Eben evidently thought so too;
For soon amid the silver loneliness
Of night he lifted up his voice and sang,
Secure, with only two moons listening,
Until the whole harmonious landscape rang –

'For auld lang syne.' The weary throat gave out,
50   The last word wavered, and the song was done.
He raised again the jug regretfully
And shook his head, and was again alone.

There was not much that was ahead of him,
And there was nothing in the town below –
Where strangers would have shut the many doors
That many friends had opened long ago.

The Tree in Pamela's Garden

Pamela was too gentle to deceive
Her roses. 'Let the men stay where they are,'
She said, 'and if Apollo's avatar
Be one of them, I shall not have to grieve.'
And so she made all Tilbury Town believe
She sighed a little more for the North Star
Than over men, and only in so far
As she was in a garden was like Eve.

Her neighbors – doing all that neighbors can
To make romance of reticence meanwhile –   10
Seeing that she had never loved a man,
Wished Pamela had a cat, or a small bird,
And only would have wondered at her smile
Could they have seen that she had overheard.

Lost Anchors

Like a dry fish flung inland far from shore,
There lived a sailor, warped and ocean-browned,
Who told of an old vessel, harbor-drowned
And out of mind a century before,
Where divers, on descending to explore
A legend that had lived its way around
The world of ships, in the dark hulk had found
Anchors, which had been seized and seen no more.

Improving a dry leisure to invest
Their misadventure with a manifest
Analogy that he may read who runs,
The sailor made it old as ocean grass –
Telling of much that once had come to pass
With him, whose mother should have had no sons.

Monadnock Through the Trees

Before there was in Egypt any sound
Of those who reared a more prodigious means
For the self-heavy sleep of kings and queens
Than hitherto had mocked the most renowned, –
Unvisioned here and waiting to be found,
Alone, amid remote and older scenes,
You loomed above ancestral evergreens
Before there were the first of us around.

And when the last of us, if we know how,
See farther from ourselves than we do now,
Assured with other sight than heretofore
That we have done our mortal best and worst, –
Your calm will be the same as when the first
Assyrians went howling south to war.

Many Are Called

The Lord Apollo, who has never died,
Still holds alone his immemorial reign,
Supreme in an impregnable domain
That with his magic he has fortified;
And though melodious multitudes have tried
In ecstasy, in anguish, and in vain,
With invocation sacred and profane
To lure him, even the loudest are outside.

Only at unconjectured intervals,
By will of him on whom no man may gaze,   10
By word of him whose law no man has read,
A questing light may rift the sullen walls,
To cling where mostly its infrequent rays
Fall golden on the patience of the dead.

The Sheaves

Where long the shadows of the wind had rolled,
Green wheat was yielding to the change assigned;
And as by some vast magic undivined
The world was turning slowly into gold.

Silver Street

Here, if you will, your fancy may destroy
This house before you and see flaming down
To ashes and to mysteries the old town
Where Shakespeare was a lodger for Mountjoy;
Here played the mighty child who for his toy
Must have the world – king, wizard, sage and clown,
Queen, fiend and trollop – and with no more renown,
May be, than friends and envy might annoy.

And in this little grave-yard, if you will,
He stands again, as often long ago   10
He stood considering what it signified.
We may have doubted, or be doubting still –
But whether it be all so, or all not so,
One has to walk up Wood Street from Cheapside.

A Man in Our Town

We pitied him as one too much at ease
With Nemesis and impending indigence;
Also, as if by way of recompense,
We sought him always in extremities;
And while ways more like ours had more to please
Our common code than his improvidence,
There lurked alive in our experience
His homely genius for emergencies.

He was not one for men to marvel at,
And yet there was another neighborhood
When he was gone, and many a thrifty tear.
There was an increase in a man like that;
And though he be forgotten, it was good
For more than one of you that he was here.

Why He Was There

Much as he left it when he went from us
Here was the room again where he had been
So long that something of him should be seen,
Or felt – and so it was. Incredulous,
I turned about, loath to be greeted thus,
And there he was in his old chair, serene
As ever, and as laconic and as lean
As when he lived, and as cadaverous.

Calm as he was of old when we were young,
He sat there gazing at the pallid flame
Before him. 'And how far will this go on?'
I thought. He felt the failure of my tongue,
And smiled: 'I was not here until you came;
And I shall not be here when you are gone.'

Glass Houses

Learn if you must, but do not come to me
For truth of what your pleasant neighbor says
Behind you of your looks or of your ways,
Or of your worth and virtue generally;
If he's a pleasure to you, let him be –
Being the same to him; and let your days
Be tranquil, having each the other's praise,
And each his own opinion peaceably.

Two others once did love each other well,
Yet not so well but that a pungent word   10
From each came stinging home to the wrong ears.
The rest would be an overflow to tell,
Surely; and you may slowly have inferred
That you may not be here a thousand years.

New England

Here where the wind is always north-north-east
And children learn to walk on frozen toes,
Wonder begets an envy of all those
Who boil elsewhere with such a lyric yeast
Of love that you will hear them at a feast
Where demons would appeal for some repose,
Still clamoring where the chalice overflows
And crying wildest who have drunk the least.

Passion is here a soilure of the wits,
We're told, and Love a cross for them to bear;   10
Joy shivers in the corner where she knits
And Conscience always has the rocking-chair,
Cheerful as when she tortured into fits
The first cat that was ever killed by Care.

Reunion

By some derision of wild circumstance
Not then our pleasure somehow to perceive,
Last night we fell together to achieve
A light eclipse of years. But the pale chance
Of youth resumed was lost. Time gave a glance
At each of us, and there was no reprieve;
And when there was at last a way to leave,
Farewell was a foreseen extravagance.

Tonight the west has yet a failing red,
While silence whispers of all things not here;
And round there where the fire was that is dead,
Dusk-hidden tenants that are chairs appear.
The same old stars will soon be overhead,
But not so friendly and not quite so near.

Young Gideon
(Judges 6)

Young Gideon would have threshed his father's
        wheat
With no more words, and as obediently
As other sons were toiling in Manasseh,
Where toil was tribute and a vanity.

Another day would be another day
For Gideon now; and round him everywhere,
Whether he toiled or slept, there would be always
Eyes watching, and a presence of despair.

There were too many presences with eyes,
Invisible and alert; they were like fire,
Piercing his heart and brain, till anger made him
A slave without ambition or desire.

Why toil so long to feed a Midian mouth,
With shame his only wages? Why not make
Jehovah's wrath aware of one who feared him
Less than he feared dishonor for his sake?

If this was life, why not be done with life?
The means at hand was his, and his the choice.
So Gideon waited for the word within him,
Hearing it not. He heard instead the Voice.   20

The least of a small house in a poor land
Until today, he shook, and feared to raise
His eyes to see the common things around him
That looked as far off as old yesterdays.

He knew, and still he feared – as prisoners fear
The weariness of waking. Yet he knew;
He knew that his one doubt was a thing dying
Before it should be born. It was all true.

God found him young, and in his youth had found
Faith to mock knowledge, knowledge to mock fear.   30
Why then was he afraid if he feared nothing?
God knew his Gideons, and the way was clear.

He would have danced and sang there where he was,
With Israel pitying him, for all he cared.
Meanwhile he pitied Israel for not knowing
How many were soon to perish, or be spared.

Now that he knew the man that in himself
Had been a stranger, freedom, like a bell,
Sang through him; and he knew that while he
    trembled
His fear was only joy for Israel.   40

He trembled while he felt the Midian yoke
Releasing him; and there was in release
No fear, until a second morning found him
Fearing to find the dew upon the fleece.

Notes

HERMAN MELVILLE

The following abbreviations are used in this section of the Notes:

Battle Pieces *Battle Pieces and Aspects of the War*, August 1866
Cohen (1963) *The Battle-Pieces of Herman Melville*, ed. Hennig Cohen (New York)
Cohen (1991) *Selected Poems of Herman Melville*, ed. Hennig Cohen (New York)
Weeds and Wildings *Weeds and Wildings, with a Rose or Two*, unfinished collection
Works *The Works of Herman Melville* (London, 1924), vol. 16

The Portent

Probably written between 3 April 1865 and July 1866; published August 1866 in *Battle Pieces*. In the first edition, the title of 'The Portent' does not appear in the table of contents. The poem appears on the page immediately following the table, set in italics, positioned as a preface to the other poems. John Brown was hanged on 2 December 1859, after his conviction on charges of treason and conspiring with slaves to commit treason and murder. On 16 October 1859, Brown and about twenty men had attacked the US arsenal at Harpers Ferry, Virginia, in an attempt to get weapons and to arm slaves for insurrection. Brown's attempt was viewed in the South as evidence of a northern conspiracy, and his hanging enraged the northern abolitionists. 'Weird' (line 13) suggests the involvement of fate in the Brown affair; the three Fates of Greek mythology (as well as Shakespeare's oracular witches in *Macbeth*, I.iii.32) are called the 'weird sisters'. Brown's 'streaming beard' (line 12) is 'the meteor of the war' (line 14) because the hanging

of Brown was a precursor to further hostility, as meteors are super-
stitiously believed to portend great events. William Spengemann (in a
forthcoming article) notes the poem's allusion to Thomas Gray's ode
'The Bard' (1757), lines 17–19, in which the Welsh bards are executed
by Edward the First after his conquest of Wales:

> With haggard eyes the poet stood;
> (Loose his beard, and hoary hair
> Streamed, like a meteor, to the troubled air).

Gray's note reveals that this echoes Milton's *Paradise Lost* (1667),
I.537, 'Shone, like a meteor, streaming to the wind'.

Misgivings

Probably written between 3 April 1865 and July 1866; possibly during
the winter of 1860–61 (see *The Melville Log: A Documentary Life of
Herman Melville*, ed. Jay Leyda, New York, 1969, vol. 2, p. 631);
published August 1866 in *Battle Pieces*. Melville's note to 'The Conflict
of Convictions' refers to 'doubts and misgivings universal' in the winter
preceding the outbreak of the Civil War.

The Conflict of Convictions

Probably written between 3 April 1865 and July 1866; published
August 1866 in *Battle Pieces*. Melville added this note in the first
edition:

The gloomy lull of the early part of the winter of 1860–1, seeming big with
final disaster to our institutions, affected some minds that believed them to
constitute one of the great hopes of mankind, much as the eclipse which came
over the promise of the first French Revolution affected kindred natures,
throwing them for the time into doubts and misgivings universal.

The poem describes a Miltonic struggle between forces of good and
evil, with the onset of the Civil War representing 'man's latter Fall'
from the innocence of the young American republic. The alternation
between the irregular stanzas and the italicized choruses is an interplay
of different 'convictions' about man's destiny. The final chorus, differ-
entiated by its capital letters, does not resolve the dispute but maintains
the mystery of God's will. 'Raphael' (line 10) is described in *Paradise
Lost*, VII.41, as 'the affable archangel'. According to ancient Hebrew

writing (Enoch: 20), it is the task of Raphael to 'heal the earth which the angels [i.e. the fallen angels] have defiled'. 'Apoplex' (line 35) refers to apoplexy, meaning cerebral haemorrhage or stroke. The 'Iron Dome' of line 44 refers to the new dome added to the US Capitol building in 1861 to replace the original wooden one. 'Michael the warrior one' (line 48) is the archangel who leads the heavenly armies in battle against Satan and the fallen angels. Compare the description (in lines 46–8), of Michael's tent as a cloud with lightning glimmering from his sword as he puts it on, with a similar image in *Paradise Lost*, II.293–5:

> so much the fear
> Of thunder and the sword of Michael
> Wrought still within them.

'The light is on the youthful brow' (line 50) refers to the usual artistic depiction of Michael as a beautiful young man. 'Athwart' (line 78) means across and 'the main' means the open sea.

In his copy of *Battle Pieces*, Melville revised line 11 from 'at which' to 'whereat', line 52 from 'blinking light' to 'taper dim', and line 54 from 'A meagre wight!' to 'Which foldeth him.'

The March into Virginia, Ending in the First Manassas

Probably written between 3 April 1865 and July 1866; published August 1866 in *Battle Pieces*. On 21 July 1861 the first major battle of the Civil War took place at Bull Run, near Manassas Junction, Virginia. The confident Union Army under General Irvin McDowell was followed from Washington by groups of picnicking sightseers who expected to see an easy Union victory. When Confederate Brigadier Thomas Jackson's forces earned their commander his nickname by standing as firmly as a 'stone wall', the Union Army was routed. In line 1 'lets' means impediments. 'Moloch' (line 23) refers to the Ammonite deity whose sacrifices required children 'to pass through the fire' (2 Kings 23:10). The 'Second Manassas' of line 36 occurred on 30 August 1862 when a Union Army suffered another defeat on the same battlefield.

In his copy of *Battle Pieces*, Melville tried various revisions of this final line: 'Thy after shock, Manassas, share', 'Manassas's second throe and deadlier share' and 'Thy second shock, Manassas, share'. Since none of these revisions appears final, I give the line as it was originally printed.

Ball's Bluff, A Reverie

Probably written between 3 April 1865 and July 1866; published August 1866 in *Battle Pieces*. On 21 October 1861, a Union force under Colonel Edward Baker moved against Confederate positions near Ball's Bluff, Virginia. The Union troops were trapped between the cliffs and the Potomac River as they attempted to retreat, losing about a thousand men. The phrase 'Juny morning' (line 8), meaning June morning, is Melville's invention, along the lines of the southern American dialect's alteration of 'June bug' to 'Juny bug'. There are echoes of Keats in the last stanza, particularly in line 16 with the phrase 'easeful sleep bereft' recalling the 'Ode to a Nightingale' (1819), line 52, 'easeful death', as well as 'Isabella, or the Pot of Basil' (1820), line 323, 'of healthful midnight sleep bereft'. For a discussion of the Keatsian elements, see *Selected Poems of Herman Melville*, ed. Robert Penn Warren (New York, 1970), p. 356.

A Utilitarian View of the Monitor's Fight

Probably written between 3 April 1865 and July 1866; published August 1866 in *Battle Pieces*. On 9 March 1862, the world's first battle between ironclad warships occurred when the Confederate ship known as the 'Merrimac' was met at Hampton Roads, Virginia, by the Union vessel 'Monitor'. The battle was a draw, with neither ship seriously damaging the other, but their encounter foreshadowed the future of naval warfare and the end of wooden fighting ships. 'Fans' (line 8) are fan-shaped flags, also called fan-banners. 'Caloric' (line 18) refers to calories, a measure of heat or energy. The 'Utilitarian' philosophy holds that usefulness is the standard of whatever is good for man. Cf. the poem's title with W. S. Coleman's *Our Woodlands, Heaths, and Hedges* (1859). 'Turning from the picturesque or cymbal', recalls Milton's disparagement of 'barbarous' rhyme in the headnote to *Paradise Lost*. Lines 20–21, describing how the sound of the ironclad battle 'Still ringeth round the world', echo Emerson's 'Hymn Sung at the Completion of the Concord Monument' (1837), line 4, 'the shot heard round the world'.

In his copy of *Battle Pieces*, Melville revised line 4 from 'Orient' to 'painted' and line 27 from 'yet shall' to 'shall yet'.

Shiloh, A Requiem

Probably written between 3 April 1865 and July 1866; published August 1866 in *Battle Pieces*. The battle at Shiloh, Tennessee, took place on 6–7 April 1862 when Confederate General Albert Johnston's outnumbered troops surprised the forces of General Ulysses S. Grant. Both sides suffered very heavy casualties, totalling about 23,000 men. Cohen (1963) notes that Melville used details of the battle scene given in a *Cincinatti Gazette* story of 9 April 1862, which he probably saw in the *Rebellion Record*, a compendium of documents relating to the Civil War (vol. IV, pp. 356–417; edited by Frank Moore, published 1862–5). Compare 'dying foemen' (line 13) with Tennyson's 'The Two Voices' (1844), lines 154–5, 'Then dying of a mortal stroke / What time the foeman's line is broke'.

Malvern Hill

Probably written between 3 April 1865 and July 1866 or possibly in April 1864 when Melville visited various battlefields in Virginia, including Malvern Hill; published August 1866 in *Battle Pieces*. The 'Seven Nights and Days' (line 16) were the 'Seven Days' Battles' that ended Union General George McClellan's Peninsular Campaign to capture the Confederate capitol at Richmond. The battle with General Robert E. Lee's forces at Malvern Hill on 1 July 1862 was the last effort in the campaign, which was not successful. Cohen (1991: p. 231) cites as a possible source for Melville an article in the *Rebellion Record* (vol. V, p. 266) containing details of the battle scene, including a description of the 'ancient elms' at Malvern Hill, 'it seemed a bitter satire on the wickedness of man, this peaceful, serene, harmonious aspect of nature'. The source of 'Wag the world how it will' (line 34) is *As You Like It*, II.vii.23: 'Thus we may see, quoth he, how the world wags'.

Stonewall Jackson, Mortally Wounded at Chancellorsville

Probably written between 3 April 1865 and July 1866; published August 1866 in *Battle Pieces*. On 2 May 1862 the Confederate General Thomas 'Stonewall' Jackson was accidentally shot by his own men as he returned on horseback from a successful fight. In the prose 'Supplement' to *Battle Pieces*, Melville writes, concerning the Reconstruction and the attitudes of the North towards the heroes of the South:

If George the IV could . . . raise an honorable monument in the great fane of
Christendom over the remains of the enemy of his dynasty, Charles Edward . . .
is it probable that the grandchildren of General Grant will pursue with rancor,
or slur by sour neglect, the memory of Stonewall Jackson?

The poem is a muted memorial to Jackson, holding forth the possibility
that although his 'Cause' (Secession) is dead his deserved personal
repute will live on.

Gettysburg

Written between 4 July 1865 and July 1866; first published in *Harper's
New Monthly Magazine*, July 1866; published August 1866 in *Battle
Pieces*. The battle of Gettysburg, Pennsylvania (1–3 July 1863), was
the turning point of the Civil War. Confederate General Lee had
advanced northwards through Maryland into Pennsylvania, threaten-
ing Washington and Philadelphia. In their charge on the centre of the
Union line at Cemetery Ridge (line 28), the Confederate forces came
under withering fire. After fierce hand-to-hand fighting among the
graves on the ridge, the remaining Confederates withdrew. The 'war-
rior-monument' of line 31, as Melville explains in the notes to *Battle
Pieces*, was that of a Federal officer killed in 1862. It was one 'among
numerous head-stones or monuments on Cemetery Hill, marred or
destroyed by the enemy's concentrated fire' (Melville's note). Lines 3–
6 refer to an episode in 1 Samuel 5 of the war between the Israelites
and the Philistines. During an invasion of Israel, the Philistines captured
the Ark of God and left it as an offering before the statue of their god
Dagon. On the following day, they found Dagon 'fallen upon his face
to the earth before the ark of the Lord' (verse 3). After righting the
statue, they returned on the third day to find Dagon's head and hands
cut off. Melville draws a parallel with the events at Gettysburg, where
the Confederates were victorious on the first day of battle, beaten back
on the second and finally defeated on the third. The 'last invader' (line
8) will charge no more; both the Philistines and the Confederates were
thereafter on the defensive until their eventual defeats. The final lines
of the poem allude to the consecration (4 July 1865) of the battlefield
at Gettysburg as a National Cemetery. 'Targed' (line 5) means shielded,
and 'marge' (line 25) means margin.

In the first edition of *Battle Pieces*, the poem bore a subtitle, 'The
Check', but in his personal copy Melville removed it.

The House-Top, A Night Piece

Probably written between 3 April 1865 and July 1866; published August 1866 in *Battle Pieces*. On 11 July 1863, several days of rioting began in New York City in response to the imposition of the Enrollment Act, which allowed immunity from the draft upon payment of $300. Gangs of working-class protesters set fires and looted throughout the city. Federal units restored order by the use of military force. The ancient Romans believed that 'Sirius' (line 9), when rising with the sun during July and August, added to the Sun's heat and produced the 'dog-days' that precipitated madness. Melville adds an invented personification, 'red Arson', at line 10. In contrast to these destructive pagan elements, which stand with the 'Atheist roar of riot' (line 8), are the forces of order: 'Calvin's creed' (line 21) of humanity's predestination into classes of Elect and Reprobate, and 'Wise Draco' (line 19), the Athenian statesman whose code of Athenian laws brought order through their severity. Yet 'Draco' is also the name of a pagan (Greek) constellation representing the figure of an evil Dragon who is crushed in the heavens by Hercules. During July, Draco is high in the northern sky, after Sirius has set. The 'Roman, never to be scourged' (line 27) was the apostle Paul who in Acts 22:25 protested that he should not be scourged (i.e. whipped) until he had been condemned, because he was a Roman citizen.

In his copy of *Battle Pieces*, Melville revised line 18 from 'shakes' to 'jars'.

On the Photograph of a Corps Commander

Probably written between 3 April 1865 and July 1866; published August 1866 in *Battle Pieces*. The cover of *Harper's Weekly Magazine* for 28 May 1864 bore a picture of Union General Winfield Scott Hancock, who led a successful and heroic charge at the Battle of Spotsylvania, Virginia. The poem celebrates the manliness of this Union hero, linking him by lineage to the heroic English warriors of the past. King Henry V was called 'Harry' (line 16) as a token of his egalitarian brotherhood with his men. A 'Norman' (line 17) was a warrior of the Norman Conquest under William the Conqueror in 1066. The 'Templars' (line 18) were the Knights Templars, a military and religious order founded for the protection of Christian pilgrims visiting the Holy Land. A 'front' (line 18) is a face; the poem suggests that the modern descendants of the Templars still resemble them in their faces.

'Spottsylvania' in line 5 is Melville's spelling. 'Endued' (line 11) means endowed. 'Span' (line 23) means measure by hand.

The Swamp Angel

Probably written between 3 April 1865 and July 1866; published August 1866 in *Battle Pieces*. As Melville's note to the poem relates, 'The great Parrott gun, planted in the marshes of James Island . . . was known among our soldiers as the Swamp Angel.' This eight-inch gun was used by the Union forces to bombard the city of Charlestown, South Carolina, in August 1863. An earlier poem about the same gun, entitled 'The Swamp Angel' by 'T.N.J.', appeared in the *Rebellion Record*. Melville's poem opens with a description likening the gun to a black slave hiding in a swamp, a common refuge for escaped slaves. At line 40, the City (Charleston) calls upon the archangel Michael (St Michael's Church stood in Charleston), but he has 'fled from his tower' (line 42) to join the Swamp Angel on James Island 'over the sea' (line 43) as a sign that God sides with the Union cause. 'Blastment' (line 7) is a withering or shrivelling up caused by atmospheric, electric or unseen agency. 'It comes like a thief in the gloaming' (line 17) alludes to 1 Thessalonians 5:2, 'the day of the Lord so cometh as a thief in the night'.

The College Colonel

Probably written between 3 April 1865 and July 1866; published August 1866 in *Battle Pieces*. On 22 August 1863, Melville was among those who welcomed the return to Pittsfield of the 49th Massachusetts Regiment under the command of Colonel William Francis Bartlett. The 'College Colonel' had left Harvard University to take commission as a captain in the Union Army. His wounds occurred during the 'Seven Days' Battles' of the Peninsular Campaign (see note to 'Malvern Hill') and at Port Hudson, Louisiana. 'Lones' (line 14) is used here poetically as a verb meaning 'to give the appearance of loneliness'. 'Alloy' (line 21) means a mixture of two or more metals; here it refers to the mixture of sadness with happiness, and perhaps to the metal used to make a prosthesis for the 'leg' that 'is lost' (line 22). The 'Petersburg crater' (line 29) was caused by the implosion of a tunnel dug under Confederate lines during the siege of Petersburg, Virginia, where Colonel Bartlett was captured. 'Libby' (line 30) refers to a warehouse in Richmond used by the Confederates as a prison camp for Union officers.

At the Cannon's Mouth, Destruction of the Ram Albemarle by the Torpedo-launch

Probably written between 3 April 1865 and July 1866; published August 1866 in *Battle Pieces*. On 27 October 1864, the young Lieutenant William Cushing and a crew of volunteers in a small launch assaulted the Confederate ironclad ram *Albemarle*, sinking it with a single torpedo. The ironclad destroyed the attackers' boat and killed its crew, but Cushing managed to swim to safety. The poem admires Cushing's fame but expresses dismay at the brashness that led him to risk his young life. The source of the title is *As You Like It*, II.vii.152–3, Jaques's description of a soldier, 'Seeking the bubble reputation / Even in the cannon's mouth'. 'Die or do' (line 5) echoes Tennyson's 'Theirs but to do and die' in 'The Charge of the Light Brigade' (1854), another account of boldness in the face of certain death. Cushing's bold disregard for the beauty of living is compared to that of the youthful Adonis (line 20), who ignored his lover Aphrodite's pleas that he hunt only small game, until he was eventually killed by a boar. 'Draw' in line 20 refers to the drawing of the hunting bow. To 'imp' (line 23) is a term from falconry, meaning to engraft feathers in the wing of a bird so as to repair damage. In the final stanza, the poem's admiring tone changes to suggest that fate had a hand in winning Cushing his fame: 'The star ascended in his nativity' (line 31) means that Cushing was born under lucky astrological conditions. It also refers to the star that guided the wise men to the birth of Jesus (Matthew 2:9 ff.).

In his copy of *Battle Pieces*, Melville revised lines 11–12 from 'Had Earth no charm to stay the Boy / From the martyr-passion?' to 'Had Earth no charm to stay in the Boy / The martyr-passion?'.

'The Coming Storm', A Picture by S. R. Gifford, and owned by E. B. Included in the N. A. Exhibition, April, 1865

Written between 14 April 1865 and July 1866; published August 1866 in *Battle Pieces*. The landscape portrait 'The Coming Storm' by Sanford R. Gifford was shown at the National Academy of Design exhibition in Washington in April 1865 and is now in a private collection. It was owned by the famous Shakespearean actor Edwin Booth, brother of John Wilkes Booth, the assassin of President Lincoln. Henry T. Tuckerman (the cousin of the poet Frederick) described it as 'delineating the brooding shadow of an impending thunder storm – so grand in its shadowy gloom that it won the heart of the best living representative of Shakespeare's Hamlet' (*Book of the Artists*, 1867). The poem suggests that Edwin's close study of Shakespeare (particularly *Hamlet*, which role Edwin was himself playing in Boston at the time of Lincoln's assassination) must have given him 'Presage dim' (line 2) of the crime his brother was to commit. In line 12, 'antedate' means anticipate.

The Released Rebel Prisoner

Probably written between June 1865 and July 1866; published August 1866 in *Battle Pieces*. Melville's note to this poem in the original edition of *Battle Pieces* describes how 'for a month or two after the completion of peace, some thousands of released captives from the military prisons of the North, natives of all parts of the South, passed through the city of New York', where Melville resided in June 1865. 'Nineveh of the North' in line 3 is New York. Nineveh was an ancient city situated to the north of Babylon in the Babylonian empire, ancient enemy of the Israelites. In the eyes of the Rebels, New York would stand as Nineveh to the Babylon of Washington. 'Hill' and 'Ashby' (lines 17–18) were Confederate Generals killed in combat. 'Stuart with the Rupert-plume' (line 19) makes a connection with the English Civil War, where Prince Rupert (1619–82) was a brilliant cavalry commander under his uncle, the Stuart King Charles I. General Jeb Stuart (1833–64) was a commander of the Confederate cavalry. The 'Rupert-plume' refers to a feather worn by the Prince; it is perhaps related to the 'Prince-Rupert-drop', a small glass ball used as a decoration.

In his copy of *Battle Pieces*, Melville revised line 35 from 'drear' to 'weird'.

A Grave Near Petersburg, Virginia

Written between April 1865 and July 1866; published August 1866 in *Battle Pieces*. Petersburg was abandoned by Confederate General Robert E. Lee early in 1865 as Union General Ulysses S. Grant pushed his Army of the Potomac towards the Confederate capitol at Richmond. The Confederates buried some of their weapons during the retreat 'with a view to ultimate repossession', as Melville writes in his note to the original edition. The buried gun's name (perhaps its model name), 'Daniel Drouth', would have been pronounced to rhyme with 'mouth' in some dialects of the time.

On the Slain Collegians

Written between April 1865 and July 1866; published August 1866 in
Battle Pieces. Melville's note to the original edition read:

The records of Northern colleges attest what numbers of our noblest youth
went from them to the battle-field. Southern members of the same classes
arrayed themselves on the side of the Secession; while Southern seminaries
contributed large quotas. Of all these, what numbers marched who never
returned except on the shield.

'On the shield' refers to the ancient custom of bearing the dead and
wounded from the battlefield on shields. 'Meet' (line 14) means 'fitting,
proper'. 'Saturnians' (line 21) lived during the Golden Age in ancient
Greece when the god Saturn ruled, and 'Tempe' (line 21) was a valley
in Thessaly considered the most beautiful on earth. 'Each would slay
his Python' (line 34) refers to the giant snake of that name who lived
at Delphi and was slain by the youthful Apollo when he established his
oracle there.

In his copy of *Battle Pieces*, Melville revised line 44 from 'in both
was' to 'in all was' and line 46 from 'So be it' to 'So put it'.

The Fortitude of the North, under the Disaster of the Second Manassas

Probably written between April 1865 and July 1866; published August
1866 in *Battle Pieces* in the section subtitled 'Verses Inscriptive and
Memorial'. 'The disaster of the Second Manassas' mentioned in this
poem's subtitle was the defeat of the Union Army under General John
Pope by the Confederate forces under General Robert E. Lee on 29–
30 August 1862 at Manassas Junction, Virginia. This is the 'throe of
Second Manassas' foreseen in the final line of 'The March into Vir-
ginia'. 'The Cape-of-Storms' at line 5 is Cape Horn, at the southern
extremity of South America.

In his copy of *Battle Pieces*, Melville revised line 1 from 'They take
no shame' to 'No shame they take'.

On the Men of Maine, Killed in the Victory of Baton Rouge, Louisiana

Probably written between April 1865 and July 1866; published August 1866 in *Battle Pieces* in the section subtitled 'Verses Inscriptive and Memorial'. In August 1862, the Fourteenth Maine Regiment was among the forces who successfully defended the Union position at Baton Rouge, Louisiana, against a Confederate attack.

Inscription: For Marye's Heights, Fredericksburg

Probably written between April 1865 and July 1866; published August 1866 in *Battle Pieces* in the section subtitled 'Verses Inscriptive and Memorial'. In December 1862, Union General Ambrose Burnside crossed the Rappahannock River near Fredericksburg, Virginia, and attacked General Lee, who had taken up a defensive position on Marye's Heights. The Union forces were beaten back, with heavy losses. In May 1863 the Union succeeded in capturing the heights, only to be pushed down by Lee soon after.

On the Slain at Chickamauga

Probably written between April 1865 and July 1866; published August 1866 in *Battle Pieces* in the section subtitled 'Verses Inscriptive and Memorial'. The Battle of Chickamauga Creek occurred after the capture of Chattanooga, Tennessee, by Union forces in September 1863. Union General William S. Rosecrans mistakenly presumed that the Confederates had abandoned Chattanooga as part of a widespread retreat. Pursuing them, he met defeat when they counter-attacked.

On Sherman's Men, Who Fell in the Assault of Kenesaw Mountain, Georgia

Written between 27 June 1865 and July 1866; published August 1866 in *Battle Pieces* in the section subtitled 'Verses Inscriptive and Memorial'. Union General William Tecumseh Sherman's men assaulted the Confederate position at Kenesaw Mountain, Georgia, on 27 June 1865 during Sherman's march to the sea. 'Mailed' (line 7) means armoured; the 'mailed ones' were the knights of medieval warfare.

Commemorative of a Naval Victory

Probably written between April 1865 and July 1866; published August 1866 in *Battle Pieces* in the section subtitled 'Verses Inscriptive and Memorial'. A 'damasked blade' (line 5) is a sword made of Damascus steel, also known as watered steel. The metal is finished with a wavy pattern. 'Tempering' (line 4) means both the refinement of character through hardship and the hardening of a steel blade in water. 'Titian's picture' (line 8) is probably 'The Man with a Falcon'. The image links the accoutrements of hunting and warfare with the aspect of nobility. Compare 'The hawk, the hound, and sworded nobleman' (line 7) with Keats's 'The Eve of St Agnes' (1820), line 358, 'the arras, rich with horseman, hawk, and hound'. As Cohen (1963: p. 284) notes, 'pensive pansies' (line 20) plays with the etymology of the flower's name, which comes from the Middle French *pensée*, meaning 'thought'.

The Maldive Shark

Published September 1888 in *John Marr and Other Sailors*. The Maldives are an island chain in the Indian Ocean. 'Pilot-fish' (line 3), *Naucrates ductor*, swim very close to sharks and other predators, catching bits of food that drift from the kill. Their name comes from the (mistaken) notion that they 'guide' (line 13) the shark. 'Gorgonian' (line 8) refers to the snake-haired Gorgons of Greek mythology, one of whom was Medusa, whose glance could turn men to stone.

The Berg (A Dream)

Published September 1888 in *John Marr and Other Sailors*. 'Standards' (line 2) are naval flags. A 'lubbard' (line 33) is a large, clumsy person.

In his copy of *John Marr*, Melville revised the last line from 'dead indifference' to 'dense stolidity'.

The Enviable Isles (From 'Rammon')

Published September 1888 in *John Marr and Other Sailors*. Melville originally intended the poem as part of a larger piece of prose and verse entitled *Rammon*, which was only partially completed and of which only 'The Enviable Isles' was published during the poet's lifetime. Rammon, a son of King Solomon, is a young prince who has lost interest in the practical affairs of the kingdom. Turning away from the ebb and flow of fortune after the coronation of his half-brother

Rehoboam, seeking something beyond the ordinary world, Rammon asks an older, well-travelled merchant to tell him about the far-away, half-mythical 'Enviable Isles / Whereof King Hiram's tars used to tell'. Cohen (1991: p. 221) points out the influence of Spenser's *The Faerie Queene*, I.i.36–42. See also the description of Morpheus' house (*The Faerie Queene*, I.i.41.1–5):

> And more, to lulle him in his slumber soft,
> A trickling streame from high rocke tumbling downe
> And ever-drizling raine upon the loft,
> Mixt with a murmuring winde, much like the sowne
> Of swarming Bees, did cast him in a swowne.

Other influences include Tennyson's 'The Islet' (1864) and 'The Lotos-Eaters' (1833).

Billy in the Darbies

Early version written before 1888; published 1924 as the conclusion of the unfinished novel *Billy Budd, Foretopman*. *Billy Budd* grew from what was originally a headnote to 'Billy in the Darbies'. 'Darbies' are shackles. 'Lone Bay' (line 1) is a sailor's euphemism for the ship's brig, where prisoners are held. A 'jewel-block' (line 7) is a pulley that hangs from the end of the yard-arm in the rigging of a ship. 'Taff' (line 25) is a nickname for a Welshman, from the common name David as pronounced in Welsh: 'Taffid'. Compare line 32, 'and the oozy weeds about me twist', with Milton's 'Lycidas', line 175, 'With Nectar pure his oozy Locks he laves'. Another source is Jonah 2:5, 'The waters compassed me about, even to the soul: the depth closed me round about, the weeds were wrapped about my head.'

Timoleon (394 BC)

Published May 1891 in *Timoleon, Etc.* Melville found the historical background of the Corinthian statesman Timoleon (*c.* 411–*c.* 337 BC) in Plutarch's *Lives*. A major influence was Balzac's novel *The Two Brothers*, of which Melville owned the 1887 translation by Katherine Wormley. 'Arch rule' (line 3) means absolute power. 'Ban' at line 10 means a public notice of a prohibition, while at line 115 it means a curse or personal denunciation. 'Crowned with laurel twined with thorn' (line 21) is a combination of the traditional prize of a laurel wreath and the mock crown of thorns placed upon the head of Jesus by the Roman soldiers at the Crucifixion. Line 24 alludes to Matthew 9:20, where a woman seeks to relieve herself of disease by touching the hem of Jesus' garment. A 'bayard' (line 32) is a bay-coloured horse. The term also carries a connotation of foolish boldness, found in proverbs going back to Chaucer's *Yeoman's Tale*, 'Ye been as boold as is Bayard the blind', and Thomas Jackson's 'Commentaries Upon the Apostle's Creed' (1615), 'As boldly as blind bayard rusheth into the battle'. 'Timophanes' (line 33) was Timoleon's brother and for a time was the tyrant of Corinth. Timoleon, a champion who fought against tyranny, was brought to involvement in his brother's overthrow and murder. 'Phidian' (line 42) refers to Phidias, the most famous sculptor of ancient Greece. 'Bent' (line 57) means natural inclination. 'Lictors' (line 90) were Roman officers whose functions were to attend upon the magistrate, bearing the fasces before him, and to execute sentence of judgement upon offenders. '*Fasces*' (line 92) were bundles of rods bound up with an axe in the middle, carried as an emblem of power. The 'Furies' (line 92) were the Roman goddesses of vengeance, and 'Ate' (line 94) was the goddess of rash destructive deeds. 'Phocion' (line 136) was an Athenian general, a pupil of Plato, and for a short time ruler of Athens until he was deposed in 318 BC. A 'wilding' (line 138) is a wild plant or animal; a 'wilding place' is a wilderness. Melville titled a late, unfinished collection of poetry *Weeds and Wildings*. 'Sightless orbs' (line 147) are blind eyes; compare *Paradise Lost*, III.23-5:

> these eyes, that roll in vain
> To find thy piercing ray, and find no dawn;
> So think a drop serene hath quenched their orbs.

The Ravaged Villa

Possibly written in February or March 1857; published May 1891 in *Timoleon, Etc.* In February and March 1857, Melville toured Italy, noting in his journal on 20 February the 'ruins of villas' that he had seen near Naples. On 27 February, while he was in Rome, Melville visited the grave of John Keats, whose memory is woven into this poem.

Monody

Written after the death of Nathaniel Hawthorne (19 May 1864) and inscribed in Melville's copy of Hawthorne's last book, *Our Old Home*; published May 1891 in *Timoleon, Etc.* In August 1850 Melville published an enthusiastic review of Hawthorne's *Mosses from an Old Manse*, and the two men began a close friendship. The letters of Sophia Hawthorne show that Melville greatly admired the older writer's 'high calm intellect' and 'glowing, deep heart'. A monody is a lament, as in the headnote of Milton's 'Lycidas': 'In this monody the author bewails a learned friend, unfortunately drowned . . .' The metaphor at the end of 'Monody' perhaps alludes to Melville's long poem *Clarel* (1876) where the character 'Vine' is based on Hawthorne. 'The shyest grape' (line 12) refers to Hawthorne and his characteristic reserve.

Lone Founts

Possibly written in the spring of 1857; published May 1891 in *Timoleon, Etc.*

Art

Published May 1891 in *Timoleon, Etc.* 'Jacob's mystic heart' (line 10) refers to the patriarch Jacob's vision (Genesis 28:12–15) of God commanding that he create a new nation. In Genesis (32:24–32), Jacob wrestles all night with an angel. Held to a draw, the angel wounds Jacob on the thigh but repays him with a blessing and gives him a new name: Israel.

Fragments of a Lost Gnostic Poem of the 12th Century

Published May 1891 in *Timoleon, Etc.* The Gnostics (from the Greek *gnosis*, 'knowledge') were a 2nd–4th-century religious sect who believed that the world was made from evil matter and was not the creation of God, who is the source of all that is good and permanent. Since the world is essentially an illusion, worldly pursuits are entirely vain, and salvation and enlightenment must come from without: 'Indolence is heaven's ally here' (line 5). As an organized religion the Gnostics had been dissolved by the 4th century AD; their ideas were almost entirely unknown until the Enlightenment of the 17th century.

In a Church of Padua

Possibly written April 1857; published May 1891 in *Timoleon, Etc.* in a section subtitled 'Fruit of Travel Long Ago'. On 1 April 1857, Melville was in Padua, where he wrote in his journal, 'got a grave dark guide & started with great-coat & umbrella to see the sights'. Among the sights seen were the Church of St Anthony and the Giotto Chapel. The 'upright sombre box' (line 2) and the 'Dread diving-bell' (line 14) describe the confessional box.

The Attic Landscape

Possibly written February 1857, when Melville was touring Greece. Published May 1891 in *Timoleon, Etc.* in a section subtitled 'Fruit of Travel Long Ago'. 'Attic' means characteristic of the ancient Greek art and architecture of Attica (the region surrounding Athens), with its style of simple, intelligent elegance. 'Old Romance' (line 3) perhaps alludes to Wordsworth's 'A narrow girdle of rough stones and crags' (1800), line 38: 'Sole-sitting by the shores of old romance'. 'Tivoli' (line 4) is a town near Rome whose temples, ruins and gardens made it a favourite tourist attraction after excavation began in the 16th century.

Greek Masonry

Possibly written February 1857; published May 1891 in *Timoleon, Etc.* in a section subtitled 'Fruit of Travel Long Ago'. Melville visited the Parthenon on 10 February 1857, noting the naturalness of its artifice in his journal: 'Pavement of Parthenon – square – blocks of ice frozen together. – No mortar: – Delicacy of frostwork'.

Greek Architecture

Possibly written February 1857; published May 1891 in *Timoleon, Etc.* in the section subtitled 'Fruit of Travel Long Ago'.

Immolated

Written after summer 1862; published 1924 in *Works*. In preparing to sell Arrowhead Farm in Pittsfield, Massachusetts, and move to New York City, Melville copied out the poetry manuscripts he wanted to keep, burning the rest. The influence of Greek mythology can be seen in the personification of 'Hope' (line 4) and 'Mediocrity' (line 15), and in the fact that the first line was originally written 'Children of my Tempe prime'. 'Snugged' (line 17) means made snug.

When Forth the Shepherd Leads the Flock

Published 1924 in *Works*. This poem was part of an unfinished collection tentatively titled *Weeds and Wildings, with a Rose or Two*. 'Dibbling' (line 3) means making holes in the soil to prepare it for planting. Compare line 4, 'the world begins anew', and line 7, 'The Golden Age returns to fields', with Shelley's 'The World's Great Age' from *Hellas* (1822), lines 1–2, 'The world's great age begins anew, / The Golden years return'. 'Heart-Free' (line 12) is apparently a kind of wild flower, perhaps a colloquial name for the heart's-ease or pansy. A 'Wilding' (line 13) is any cultivated plant that grows in the wild. 'Since hearsed was Pan' (line 16) refers to the Greek god of pastures and forests, and to the tradition that at the time of the crucifixion of Jesus, a mysterious voice was heard from across the ocean crying 'Pan is Dead!'. 'Tares' (line 26) are weeds mentioned in Jesus' parable in Matthew 13:25–30, where the kingdom of heaven is likened to a man whose enemy has mingled tare seeds with the wheat the man has planted. Rather than dig up the tare seeds and risk disturbing the good wheat, the man plans to wait until the wheat and the tares grow so they can be distinguished and the tares destroyed.

Trophies of Peace, Illinois in 1840

Possibly written after March 1858; published 1924 in *Works*. This poem was part of *Weeds and Wildings*. In July 1840, Melville visited his Uncle Thomas Melville in Galena, Illinois. The poem is a memory of the prairie landscape and the days of relative national peace during which Melville first viewed it. Melville returned to Illinois on a lecture tour in March 1858. 'The floss' (line 4) is the corn silk at the top of the maize plant. Lines 5 ff. refer to the battle of Marathon (490 BC) between the Persians and the Greeks. A 'pennon' (line 7) is a pennant. 'Ceres' (line 13) is the Roman goddess of the harvest. 'Mars' (line 16) is the Roman god of war.

Field Asters

Published 1924 in *Works*. This poem was part of *Weeds and Wildings*. The flower described in the poem has a shape like a star; hence its name, 'Aster', which derives from the Greek word for 'star'.

The Avatar

Published 1924 in *Works*. This poem was part of *Weeds and Wildings*. In Hindu mythology, an 'avatar' is the earthly incarnation of a god. 'Sweet-Briar' (line 6) is a wild member of the rose family, much simpler in form than cultivated roses.

The American Aloe on Exhibition

Published 1924 in *Works*. This poem was part of *Weeds and Wildings*. The American Aloe, also known as the Century Plant, is erroneously believed to flower only once in a century. The 'bon-bons of the hour' (line 4) refer to the flower itself, which blooms for a very short time relative to the lifespan of the plant. The 'garland' (line 9) and the 'wreath' (line 14) also refer to the flower, sitting atop the stem as though placed there for decoration.

Inscription: For a Boulder near the spot . . .

Possibly written 1850–63; published 1924 in *Works*. This poem was part of *Weeds and Wildings*. The 'Hardhack' mentioned in the subtitle is a wild shrub of the rose family.

Rose Window

Published 1924 in *Works*. This poem was part of *Weeds and Wildings*, in a section subtitled 'As They Fell'. '*The Rose of Sharon*' (line 3) appears in Song of Solomon 2:1. 'Metheglin' (line 9) is spiced mead or honey wine: 'How honied a homily he drew' (line 6). 'Iris and Aurora' (line 23) are the Greek goddesses of the rainbow and of the dawn, respectively.

Thy Aim, Thy Aim?

Published 1924 in *Works*. 'Guerdon' (line 11) means reward. 'Dis' (line 20) is a Roman name for the Underworld, which is ruled by Pluto (also himself called Dis). According to mythology, Pluto captured the maiden Proserpine (who became his wife) while she was picking flowers. Proserpine's yearly return to the Earth brings the beginning of spring.

Camoëns, 1 (Before) and Camoëns in the Hospital, 2 (After)

Published 1924 in *Works*. Luís Vaz de Camoës (in English, Camoëns; 1524–80) was a Portuguese poet who wrote Portugal's epic *Os Lusíadas* (1572) and died in poverty. In 1867, after the beginning of his self-imposed retirement from the public eye, Melville acquired a copy of *Poems from the Portuguese of Luís de Camoëns, with Remarks on His Life and Writings* by Lord Strangford (London, 1824), and he underlined a passage in Sonnet VI:

> My senses lost, misjudging men declare,
> And Reason banish'd from her mental throne,
> Because I shun the crowd, and dwell alone.

Line 1 of 'Camoëns in the Hospital' ('What now avails the pageant verse') alludes to W. S. Landor's 'Rose Aylmer' (1806), line 1: 'Ah, what avails the sceptred race!'

The opening lines of 'Camoëns' in manuscript are a confused array of cross-outs and optional words. My reading differs from that in Howard Vincent's *Collected Poems of Herman Melville* (1947) in retaining Melville's original order of the lines. Another reading is seen in Cohen (1991), where he leaves out the line (retained by Vincent and by myself), 'For ever must I fan this fire'. To me, it is clear in the manuscript that 'Forever must I fan this fire?' (with question mark, which Vincent replaces with a comma) is the first line of the poem. Also, though Vincent disagrees, it does not seem to me (nor to Cohen) that Melville intended to remove the line 'The Imperfect toward Perfection pressed!'. I concur with Cohen in choosing the word 'epic' in line 13 of 'Camoëns'. The optional word, 'ancient', is given by Vincent. It is not apparent which (if either) was Melville's final choice in the manuscript.

A Spirit Appeared to Me

Published 1924 in *Works*. 'Solomon's hell' (line 4) refers to the wise king of Israel who, having died before the birth of Christ, and having never been baptized, would not be allowed into Heaven. A 'fool's Paradise' (line 6) is a proverbial saying, meaning an illusion of happiness.

Pontoosuc

Published 1924 in *Works*. The 'Chaldæans' (line 55) were an ancient people of Babylonia famous for their skills in astrology. 'Appalachee' (line 56) refers to the Appalachian Mountains of the eastern US. 'Adown' (line 61) is a poeticism for down. Keatsian influences are strong in the poem, especially from 'La Belle Dame sans Merci' (1819). Compare lines 15–22 with Keats's 'To Autumn' (1820). Also compare lines 86–7, 'Since light and shade are equal set / And all revolves, nor more ye know', with Keats's 'Ode on a Grecian Urn' (1820), lines 49–50, ' "Beauty is truth, truth beauty," – that is all / Ye know on earth, and all ye need to know.'

There is some disagreement about the title of 'Pontoosuc'. Vincent (*Collected Poems*) and Cohen (1991) read it as 'Pontoosuce'. I concur with Douglas Robillard (*Poems of Herman Melville*, 1976), who writes, 'I am all for "Pontoosuc"; that is the name of the lake near his home in Pittsfield, and it is difficult to tell whether the manuscript is blessed with a final letter or a careless doodle.' 'The Lake' appears in the manuscript as an alternative title. I agree with Vincent and Robillard that 'deep' is the authoritative reading at line 38; Cohen chooses 'brown'. Lines 47–9 appear on the verso of the manuscript page; Cohen leaves these lines out. At line 55, the phrase 'have left their place' is crossed out in the manuscript; I agree with Vincent and Robillard in restoring it.

FREDERICK GODDARD TUCKERMAN

The following abbreviations are used in this section of the Notes:

Bynner *The Sonnets of Frederick Goddard Tuckerman*, ed. Witter Bynner (New York, 1931)

Golden Golden, Samuel A., *Frederick Goddard Tuckerman* (New York, 1966)

Momaday *The Complete Poems of Frederick Goddard Tuckerman*, ed. N. Scott Momaday (New York, 1965)

November

Published November 1849 in the *Literary World* (New York); privately printed late 1860 in *Poems*, published 1863 in London and 1864 in Boston. This poem was Tuckerman's first foray into print. The stress on the second syllable of 'decadence' (line 2), which emphasizes the root word 'decay', was the standard (*Webster's Dictionary*, 1828) pronunciation in Tuckerman's time.

April

Privately printed late 1860 in *Poems*; published 1863 in London and 1864 in Boston.

Inspiration

Published 22 May 1852 in the magazine *Littell's Living Age*; reprinted late 1860 in *Poems*. This poem, with its particular references to 'names constellate' (line 41) such as Milton and Shakespeare, may have been inspired by Tuckerman's first trip to England in the summer of 1851. He made literary pilgrimages to the homes of many great poets, picking and preserving flowers that he found there. For example, on July 9 he picked pansies at Wordsworth's Grasmere cottage. The flowers are still preserved in Tuckerman's herbarium, among his papers at Harvard. 'Clotbur' (line 3) is burdock and the 'leaves' (line 4) are laurel, the traditional prize of outstanding poets.

Sonnet ('Again, again, ye part in stormy grief')

Published 22 May 1852 in *Littell's Living Age*; reprinted late 1860 in *Poems*. The 'she' who sleeps is perhaps Tuckerman's first (unsurviving) daughter, who died 29 June 1848. 'Writhled' (line 4) is an archaism meaning wrinkled, withered.

Sic Itur Ad Astra

Published late 1860 in *Poems*; reprinted June 1862 in the *Atlantic Monthly*. Hitherto in publication the title has been 'Sonnets'; Tuckerman's earlier title, which appears in two different manuscript drafts, is here adopted. Its source is Virgil's *Aeneid*, IX.641 (*Macte nova virtute, puer, sic itur ad astra*, 'Blessings on your new virtue, child, that's the way to the stars'). The first sonnet's references to nature and Greek mythology lead to the second sonnet's unification of the world under God. The 'bluet' (line 3) is known in one variety as the star violet. 'Orion' (line 14) in Greek mythology was a legendary hunter whose sight was once restored by staring at the sun. After his death he was brought 'ad astra' (literally, to the stars) to become a constellation. Tuckerman shows the range of 'His hand' (line 13) by describing two images from opposite ends of the year: the 'showers of gold' (line 13) are the flowers of spring, and Orion is a winter constellation. Compare lines 18–19 with Tennyson's 'In Memoriam' (1850), cxxiii.5–8:

> The hills are shadows, and they flow
> > From form to form, and nothing stands;
> > They melt like mist, the solid lands,
> Like clouds they shape themselves, and go.

The alexandrine (iambic hexameter) in the poem's final line recalls the stanzaic form of Spenser's *The Faerie Queene*, and it is also seen in Keats's 'The Eve of St Agnes' (1820).

Twilight

Privately printed late 1860 in *Poems*, which was published 1863 in London and 1864 in Boston. The phrase 'dusk and fail' (line 2) is perhaps influenced by Tennyson's 'The Lady of Shalott' (1833), line 11, 'Little breezes dusk and shiver'. A 'runside' (line 9) is the bank of a run, a small stream. Compare lines 42–5 with Matthew Arnold's 'Dover Beach', lines 24–8:

> But now I only hear
> Its melancholy, long, withdrawing roar,
> Retreating, to the breath
> Of the night-wind, down the vast edges drear
> And naked shingles of the world.

'Dover Beach' was not published until 1867, though it was probably written in 1851. Tuckerman read Arnold's work (see note to 'The Stranger' below), and it is possible that the two poets met during Tuckerman's autumn 1854 trip to England. Lines 82–5 allude to

Matthew 12:43, 'When the unclean spirit is gone out of a man, he walketh through dry places, seeking rest, and findeth none.'

The Stranger

Privately printed late 1860 in *Poems*, published 1863 in London and 1864 in Boston. A major influence is Arnold's 'The Scholar-Gipsy' (1853). Similarities include the title characters (both poems refer to him as an alienated 'Wanderer', Tuckerman's at line 123, Arnold's at line 63), and the inclusion of the names of rural places (Tuckerman's 'Shaking-Acres' and 'Wells's Woods'; Arnold's 'Godstow Bridge' and 'Bagley Wood'). For examples of direct allusion, cf. 'The Stranger', line 25, 'all the Tyrian hills', with 'The Scholar-Gipsy', line 232, 'some grave Tyrian trader'; 'The Stranger', lines 28, 'the folded vale', and 35, 'upland farm-field lovely and apart', with 'The Scholar-Gipsy', lines 17–18, 'While to my ear from uplands far away / The bleating of the folded flocks is borne'; 'The Stranger', line 45, 'Yet sought no succour save of sun and shade', with 'The Scholar-Gipsy', line 29, 'And bower me from the August sun with shade'; 'The Stranger', line 95, 'And in his hand a bunch of blazing leaves', with 'The Scholar-Gipsy', line 119, 'twirling in thy hand a wither'd spray'. 'Pyrola' (line 56) refers to plants of the wintergreen (*Pyrolaceae*) family, and 'Partridge-flower' (line 57) perhaps refers to the partridge-berry plant (*Mitchella repens*), a creeping evergreen herb with white, fragrant flowers. 'Thrid' (line 55) means to make one's way through a narrow place, as in Coleridge's *Aids to Reflection* (1848), i.323: 'He ... thrids his way through the odorous and flowering thickets into open spots of greenery'. The 'Poet's rock' (line 140) is an outcropping that overlooks Tuckerman's hometown of Greenfield, Mass. Next to the title of this poem in his own copy of *Poems* (1860), Tuckerman inscribed the initials RWE and NH, indicating Ralph Waldo Emerson and Nathaniel Hawthorne. Both had been sent the book and written back with praise of it.

The School-Girl, An Idyll

Privately printed late 1860 in *Poems*, published 1863 in London and 1864 in Boston. An idyll is a short poem describing a simple incident in country life. Cf. with Tennyson's idyll 'The Brook' (1855), which also incorporates ballads into blank verse. 'Bitter Mayweed' (line 11) is probably stinking camomile (*Anthemis cotula*), and 'sweet-flag' (line 22) is galingale (*Acorus calamus*), the aromatic root of which, when bruised, was used for strewing church floors and is still used to flavour beer and sweets. 'Alnage' (line 24) is an archaism meaning measurement by the ell, a unit about 45 inches in length. 'Spoonwood' (line 36) is another name for the evergreen shrub mountain-laurel (*Kalmia latifolia*), which bears pinkish-white flowers in early summer. Compare line 38 with Tuckerman's own 'The Cricket', line 109, 'the ceaseless simmer in the summer grass'. The trees in a 'sugar-orchard' (line 56) produce maple-sugar. The spelling of 'moccason' (line 124) was one of many variants in the 19th century. 'Phœbe Bellflower' (line 129) is 'the fair Quaker maid' of line 70: Tuckerman pencilled lines 70–71 and 124–31 into his copy of the 1860 *Poems*. Line 70 was partially cancelled out: 'Of Wassahoale and ~~Phœbe Bellflower~~ the fair Quaker maid'. Their story itself is obscure.

Rhotruda

Privately printed late 1860 in *Poems*; reprinted July 1861 in *The Atlantic Monthly*. Tradition holds various accounts of immorality concerning Charlemagne's daughters. Tuckerman's poem recalls the love story of Eginhard (called Eginardus in the poem), who was Charlemagne's biographer (author of the *Vita Caroli*), and Charlemagne's daughter Emma, here called Rhotruda. Tuckerman considered using the 'Eginhard' spelling, noting on the back of one draft of 'Rhotruda' that 'the etymol. requires the h'. However, he did not use this more historically correct spelling in *Poems*. 'Spray bows' (line 36) is a poeticism meaning rainbows seen in a spray of water. 'Emprise' (line 52) is an archaism meaning chivalric enterprise, as in 'Lancelot of the Laik' (*c.* 1500), line 3455: 'The worschip of knychthed and empryse.' Compare line 92, 'The strangeness and the vagary of the feat', with *Paradise Lost*, VI.613–15, 'Strait they chang'd their minds, / Flew off, and into strange vagaries fell, / As they would dance'. Vagary means departure from the usual decorum. 'Cancellate' (line 107) is a botanical term meaning marked with cross lines like lattice-work. An 'anadema' (line 117) is a headband or here a garland of flowers. Line 159 refers to the fairy tale of Rapunzel. In March 1861, Ralph Waldo Emerson wrote to Tuckerman with his praise of *Poems* (1860), saying that Rhotruda 'should be bound up as a fifth in your friend Tennyson's Idyls', referring to *Idylls of the King* (1859). Emerson later included the poem in his anthology *Parnassus* (1874).

—— ('I took from its glass a flower')

Probably composed after May 1857; privately printed late 1860 in *Poems*, published 1863 in London and 1864 in Boston. This poem is usually presented as part of the poem entitled 'Coralie', but evidence from the manuscripts and from the first published edition suggests that Tuckerman thought of it as a separate poem. On the title-pages of the 1854 manuscript notebook and the (first) edition of the *Poems* in 1860, it is listed after 'Coralie' with its title given as a long dash: '——'. In the notebook and in the printed volume, it starts on a separate page; there is space at the bottom of the last page of 'Coralie' for the beginning of 'I took from its glass a flower', but it is left blank. Also the '——' title appears at the top of the page in both the manuscript and the 1860 *Poems*. Tuckerman's 'little girl' (line 16) was his second and only surviving daughter Anna (1853-1924) who was four years old at the time of Mrs Tuckerman's death. Golden (p. 162) points out an echo in line 10, 'And the little wheels go over my heart', of Tennyson's *Maud* (1855), Part II.V.i.242, 'And the wheels go over my head'.

Sidney

Privately printed late 1860 in *Poems*, published 1863 in London and 1864 in Boston. Sidney is a woman's given name as well as a reference to Sir Philip Sidney, whose pastoral *Arcadia* is evoked. The poem's desire to 'recover from the past one Golden look' (line 73) looks back to a Golden age of pastoral literature, while the setting remains grounded in western Massachusetts: the 'dark-channelled Deerfield' (line 51) joins the Connecticut River in Tuckerman's hometown of Greenfield. 'Lozenge' (line 46) perhaps refers to a diamond-shaped mole or beauty-spot. The 'red dark bud Damascus yields' (line 92) refers to a particular variety of rose (*Rosa damascena*, the damask rose) and probably echoes Shakespeare's Sonnet 130, line 5, 'I have seen roses damasked, red and white'. 'York-and-Lancaster' (line 93) were the two English houses of nobility, emblemized by white and red roses respectively, who fought a series of civil wars in the 15th century known as the Wars of the Roses. 'Poising' (line 16) means hovering.

Paulo to Francesca

Privately printed late 1860 in *Poems*, published 1863 in London and 1864 in Boston. In the 13th-century Italian town of Rimini, Paolo the

Fair and his lover Francesca da Polenta were killed when Francesca's husband discovered their secret affair, and their doom grew into romantic legend. The episode was taken up by Dante (*Inferno*, V.73–142) and by Leigh Hunt, whose 'Story of Rimini' (1816) strongly influenced the young John Keats (see Keats's sonnet 'On *The Story of Rimini*' [1848]). It was to Hunt's poem that Tuckerman himself referred his readers, with a footnote in the 1860 edition: 'See the "Story of Rimini"'. The 'Gemelli' (line 10) and the 'Scorpion' (line 12) are constellations. 'Gemelli' means 'little twins' (i.e. the constellation Gemini) and the 'red beating of the Scorpion's heart' refers to the flickering of the bright star Antares, which forms the centre of that constellation. The constellations would not be in the positions described at that time of year: the Gemelli would be 'Low in the westward' (line 9) in May and June. Tuckerman was perhaps making a point of this to highlight the exotic and bygone setting, since the procession of the equinoxes has markedly changed the seasonal positions of the constellations since the 13th century. 'Paul' (line 37) was an apostle of Christ, and the author of several letters in the New Testament. The reference to the Greek myth of Apollo and Cassandra (line 48) was footnoted by Tuckerman in the 1854 manuscript: 'This young lady Cassandra Young was you know kissed by Apollo in the manner described, who thereby falsified (to the ears of all hearers) and rendered null his gift of prophecy'. 'Cupreous' (line 24) means copper-coloured.

Margites

Privately printed late 1860 in *Poems*, published 1863 in London and 1864 in Boston. The *Margites* was a Greek comic poem attributed to Homer and now lost. The eponymous hero was a supreme idiot, who had many ideas but little knowledge and less wisdom. In one of the prefatory notes to his *Dunciad*, Alexander Pope (as Martinus Scriblerus) writes, 'Margites was the name of this personage, whom Antiquity recordeth to have been Dunce the first.' In his *Ars Poetica*, Aristotle considered the *Margites* to bear the same relation to comedy as the *Iliad* and the *Odyssey* bore to tragedy; that is, a founding example. 'Disrelishing' (line 12) means tasting badly. Compare line 33, 'all things seem the same', with Tennyson's 'The Lotos-Eaters' (1833), line 24, 'A land where all things always seem'd the same'. 'Honey-month' (line 16) is an archaic term for honeymoon. 'Nero' (line 43) was the Roman emperor who built great palaces only to stand by and watch them burn. 'Cham' (line 44) is an archaic spelling of

'Khan'; thereby 'Cham Cublai' is Kubla Khan, whose 'stately pleasure dome' inspired Coleridge.

The Sonnets

Tuckerman wrote five sequences of sonnets. The first two sequences are contained in the notebook dated '1854' upon which *Poems* (1860) was based. The third, fourth and fifth sequences were found in a notebook among Tuckerman's papers and were not published until Witter Bynner's *Sonnets of Frederick Goddard Tuckerman* (1931). In the 1854 manuscript, the first two sequences were prefaced with the heading 'Personal Sonnets' and were positioned at the end of the book, as they were in the 1860 *Poems*. The sequences were divided by the subheadings 'Part I' and 'Part II'. The latter three sequences were not divided this way in the notebook, being separated only by blank spaces.

Sonnets, Part I

I

A strong influence is Tennyson's 'A spirit haunts the year's last hours' (1830). The 'swan's voice' (line 11) is a reference to the ancient idea that the swan, though normally mute, sings beautifully just before its death. According to legend, the souls of poets pass into swans, which were sacred to Apollo, and they sing when their souls are again released. Hence, the last work of a poet or composer is known as a swan song.

III

Compare the description of the 'voice' (line 10) with Keats's 'Ode to a Nightingale' (1819), line 63: 'The voice I hear this passing night . . .'

IV

'Stramony' (line 13) refers to the Jimson weed (*Datura stramonium*), a rank-smelling, poisonous plant with purplish flowers. *Paradise Lost*, III.1–55, is an influence on this and the following three sonnets.

VI

'Dim' (line 7) was originally 'dark' in the manuscript and in the 1860 edition of *Poems*. Many occurrences of the word 'dark' were replaced with other words in the 1863 and subsequent editions. This was apparently performed at Tuckerman's request, though only a few instances exist where we can see his pencilled changes in the 'author's copy' of the 1860 *Poems* in the Houghton Library. Since it is unlikely that an editor would have silently undertaken such a sweeping and particular revision, we must assume that Tuckerman communicated changes to the editors at Smith, Elder and Company in London when they were preparing the publication of the *Poems* in 1863. The use of 'Ample' (line 2) as a noun is a poeticism. Compare lines 1–2 with Gray's 'Elegy Written in a Country Churchyard' (1751), lines 49–50: 'But Knowledge to their eyes her ample page / Rich with the spoils of time did ne'er unroll'.

VII

'Dank' (line 1) was originally 'dark' in the manuscript and in the 1860 edition of *Poems*. (See note to *Sonnets, Part I*, VI regarding widespread changes of the word 'dark' in Tuckerman's poetry.) In this instance, Tuckerman crossed out the word 'dark' in his copy of the 1860 *Poems* and pencilled 'dank' in above it. 'Blindness' (line 9) was 'darkness' in the 1860 *Poems*; however, no pencilled change by Tuckerman is evident.

VIII

The poeticism 'plashed' (line 12) was mistakenly changed to 'splashed' (the words are synonymous) in the 1863 edition of *Poems*, creating a difficult sibilance in the line and spoiling the alliteration of 'plashed and purled'. The word 'splashed' was retained in the 1864 Ticknor and Fields edition, but an errata slip was included listing the correct word 'plashed'. The 1869 edition ignored the changes demanded by the errata slip, and 'splashed' remained. 'Purled' (line 12) means flowed with a whirling motion.

IX

Saul (line 13) was the first king of Israel. With the aid of a witch he summoned the spirit of the prophet Samuel, whose voice, foretelling doom, caused Saul to sink to his knees (1 Samuel 28:7).

X

Eugene England (*Southern Review* 12 [Spring 1976]) called this 'the first Post-Symbolist Poem'. Yvor Winters (Momaday, p. xii ff.) sees a connection with such French Symbolists as Verlaine and Rimbaud in this sonnet's 'progression into pure obscurity' in the last six lines. Admitting the difficulty in understanding the grammar and syntax of the passage, Winters suggests that 'the sensory details express the sickness of the man; the tiny details are the items on which he can concentrate; but that is all we know' (quoted in Momaday, p. xiii). One possible reading of the lines places 'where the black shingles slope' as an adverbial phrase modifying 'think', and 'boughs' and 'petals' as the direct objects of 'meet'.

XI

'Strange' (line 10) was originally 'dark' in the manuscript and in the 1860 *Poems*. Tuckerman pencilled the change into his copy of the book.

XIV

Tuckerman gave a copy of the 1860 edition of his *Poems* to Bronson Alcott, the Concord teacher, philosopher and father of Louisa May Alcott. In Alcott's copy of *Poems*, this sonnet has the words 'F. Tuckerman' pencilled vertically down the left margin. Evidently, Alcott found the poem to be an apt description of its author.

XVII

'The Preacher' (line 1) is the author of the biblical Book of Ecclesiastes, which questions, 'What profit hath a man of all his labour which he taketh under the sun?' Since both the rich man and the poor man meet the same end in death, it seems that 'all is vanity' (Ecclesiastes 1:2 ff.). The influence of Ecclesiastes is strong in Sonnets 17–28 of the first series.

XXVI

'Into mine' (line 8), i.e. into my ear. The 'sense divine' (line 4) enables the observation of an underlying unity in nature such that seeming opposites may be seen to coexist. The birds mentioned in lines 10–14 would indeed not normally be seen at the times of day indicated. Compare lines 13–14, 'the wakeful bird / That to the lighted window sings for dawn', with *Paradise Lost*, III.38–9, 'the wakeful Bird / Sings darkling', and also Tennyson's 'Morte d'Arthur' (1842), line 334, 'The lusty bird takes every hour for dawn'.

XXVII

This sonnet continues the previous sonnet's fusion of opposites, expanding it from natural phenomena to include human emotions. A consonant theme may be heard in Keats's 'Ode on Melancholy' (1820), lines 25–6, where 'in the very temple of Delight / Veiled Melancholy has her sovran shrine'. The similarity with Keats's Grecism is reinforced by Tuckerman's personification of 'Sorrow' (line 5). The final image returns the sonnet to nature, with the paradox of a 'fount' (line 13) or spring, beginning as salt water and gradually becoming fresh water as it approaches the salty sea, rather than the reverse (as would normally happen). Compare this image with Tennyson's sonnet, 'If I were loved, as I desire to be' (1833), lines 7–8: 'As I have heard that, somewhere in the main, / Fresh-water springs come up through bitter brine.'

XXVIII

The 'reconcilement' (line 2) is the deep harmony of the discordant things in the preceding two sonnets, as well as the spiritual reconciliation between the belief that 'all is vanity' (Ecclesiastes 1:2 ff.) and God, who must be approached swiftly, without 'straining thought, and stammering word' (line 11), and 'in silence, like a bird' (line 13). The poet Jones Very praised this sonnet in a letter to Tuckerman on 24 April 1861.

Sonnets, Part II

The second sequence of sonnets (totalling thirty-seven, of which all are here printed) is entitled 'Sonnets, Part II' in the 1860 and subsequent editions of *Poems*.

I

'Cradle' (line 4) means to mow (corn, etc.) with a cradle-scythe. 'Poke-berry' (line 14) is the glossy black fruit of the pokeweed plant. The juice of the berry is non-poisonous, but the seed is toxic.

II

'A still strong sleep, till but the east is red' (line 14): that is, the farm-boy's sleep will end at dawn, unlike 'her rest' (line 10), which will last until the end of time: Judgement Day, when all the dead awaken and (according to Revelation 6:12) the moon becomes red 'as blood', and (in Revelation 16:3–4) the seas and rivers of the world are turned into blood.

IV

Lines 10–14 build on the apocalypticism of *Sonnets, Part II*, II. 'The world' was 'water-drowned' (line 10) in the time of Noah (Revelation 16:8), when an angel poured a vial upon the sun, causing it to grow in heat and scorch the people on earth. The biblical element is mingled with Greek mythology: 'Hephæstian hills' (line 14) would be volcanoes, wherein Hephaestus, the Greek god of fire and metalworking, had his workshops. 'Brook-flags' (line 8) might refer to several kinds of riverside plants, such as the blue flag or the sweet flag. Compare the opening lines with Shelley's 'The Triumph of Life' (1824), lines 58–9: 'And others mournfully within the gloom / Of their own shadow walked'.

V

'Planet-struck' (line 11) probably comes from *Paradise Lost*, X.413–14, 'And Planets, Planet-strook, real Eclips / Then sufferd'.

VI

Line 5 alludes to 1 John 4:18, 'perfect love casteth out fear'.

VII

Line 3 refers to Hamilcar Barca (d. 229 BC), a successful Carthaginian general and the father of Hannibal. Barca means lightning, in reference to his swiftness of attack. 'Tan and bone-dust' (line 8) are materials for increasing the acidity or alkalinity of garden soil, respectively. A 'garden-engine' (line 12) is a portable force-pump used for watering gardens.

VIII

In the manuscript notebook from which the 1860 edition of *Poems* was printed, the end of line 7 and all of line 8 are contained by quotation marks, as in lines 9–14.

> asserting, 'thought is free;
> And wisest souls by their own action shine,'
> 'For beauty,' he said, 'is seen where'er we look . . .

However, the quotation marks did not appear in any of the editions published during Tuckerman's lifetime, and no pencilled notation was added to the lines in Tuckerman's own copy of the 1860 *Poems*. The source of 'thought is free' is perhaps *The Tempest*, III.ii.134.

IX

'The new blossom on my household-tree' (line 4) was Tuckerman's son Frederick, who was born 7 May 1857. Tuckerman's wife, Anna, died five days later as a result of complications from the birth.

X

This sonnet addresses Anna directly, the 'baby' (line 1) being the son Frederick whose birth led to Anna's death. 'Cold, cold she lies where houseless tempests blow' (line 8) perhaps arises from *King Lear*, III.iv.28–32: 'Poor naked wretches, wheresoe'er you are, / That bide the pelting of this pitiless storm, / How shall your houseless heads . . . defend you / From seasons such as these?'

XI

'Whately' (line 7) is a town in western Massachusetts. 'The witchlight of the reedy river-shore' (line 12) is the will-o'-the-wisp or *ignis fatuus* (foolish fire), a phosphorescent light caused by the spontaneous combustion of marsh gases. It is known for leading unwary travellers astray.

XIII

Line 7 refers to kinds of flowers; line 14 refers to gems, although 'girasol' is at once a kind of gem (an opal), an adjective describing other gems (meaning opalescent), and a kind of flower (the Italian *girasole articiocco*) from which the Jerusalem artichoke (a yellow flower) takes its name.

XIV

'Dim' (line 9) was originally 'dark' in the manuscript and in the 1860 edition of *Poems*. 'Loft' (line 12) is an archaic term meaning sky, as in Spenser's *Faerie Queene*, I.i.41, 'ever-drizling rain upon the loft'.

XVI

'Waste balm and feverfew' (line 4) are herbs used for pain and the reduction of fever; here they grow 'vague in the walks' as weeds, without the sisters (Gertrude and Gulielma, of the previous sonnet) to harvest them. 'Black' (line 2) was originally 'dark' in the manuscript and in the 1860 edition of *Poems*.

XVIII

The sonnet's vision of the ancient forest employs the native name 'Quonecktacut' (line 8) for the Connecticut River, which runs through Tuckerman's hometown of Greenfield, Massachusetts. Tuckerman probably pronounced 'vase' (line 11) with a long 'a'.

XIX

The 'Hessian' (line 6) were mercenary soldiers from Hesse, Germany, in the employ of the British during the American Revolution. Lines 12–14 describe sources of fear and strife in Massachusetts history. A 'Tory' (line 12) is a supporter of the British cause during the Revolution. 'The Shay's-man' (line 13) is a follower of Daniel Shays, a Massachusetts man and Revolutionary veteran who led the insurrectionary militia in 'Shays' Rebellion' of 1786. The Shays'-men fought a state army who sought to enforce the widespread, court-ordered foreclosure of farms in western Massachusetts that followed the economic depression of 1785. A 'sagamore' (line 14) is a chief among the American Indians of New England, some of whom fought against the American colonists in the French and Indian Wars of 1754–63. 'Shaug' and 'Wassahoale' (line 14) are obscure; 'Wassahoale' also appears in line 70 of Tuckerman's 'The School-Girl'.

XX

'Deep' and 'deeper' (line 2) were originally 'dark' and 'darker' in the 1860 edition of *Poems*. Tuckerman pencilled in the change in his copy of 1860, and it was retained in the 1863 and subsequent editions. The 'dark' of the 1860 edition itself had already been changed; in the manuscript the word was originally 'dim', which was crossed out and replaced with 'dark'. 'Brooding' (line 11) was 'darkly' in the 1860 edition. The change appears in the 1863 edition, though there is no pencilled change evident in the 'author's copy' of the 1860 edition in the collection of Tuckerman's papers at Harvard University. We may assume that Tuckerman ordered the change through some other communication, now lost.

XXI

'Knowledge must bring relief' (line 7), is a reversal of Ecclesiastes 1:18, 'he that increaseth knowledge increaseth sorrow'. See *Sonnets, Part I*, XVII and XXVIII for other connections to Ecclesiastes. Lines 2–4 recall Tennyson's 'Morte d'Arthur' (1842), lines 321–2, 'till the hull / Look'd one black dot against the verge of dawn'. Arthur's boat is described as a 'bark' at line 344 of Tennyson's poem.

XXIII

'Asterisms' (line 10) are constellations. 'Sirius' (line 13) is the Dog Star, the brightest star in the sky, which is visible in the winter half of the year. It 'lingers on till light return' (line 12) not only in the sense that it shines through the night until dawn, but also in that it shines brightly through the winter until the spring, when the greater quantity of light returns to the northern hemisphere. In the summer, the Dog Star rises with the sun, bringing in the 'dog days' of great heat.

XXVI

'Wisdom sucked from out the fingers' end' (line 14) is an alteration of the idiom 'like a bear sucking its paws', said of someone who appears busy but accomplishes nothing. It comes from the belief that a bear deprived of food (such as during hibernation) could obtain nourishment by sucking on its paws.

XXVII

To 'exheredate' (line 8) is to disinherit. 'Exheredated' is the normal adjectival form; the rhythm of the line required Tuckerman to use 'exheredate' as the adjective. Compare lines 12–14 with Longfellow's 'A Psalm of Life' (1838), lines 25–8:

> Lives of great men all remind us
> We can make our lives sublime,
> And, departing, leave behind us
> Footprints on the sands of time.

XXVIII

'Respectant' (line 1) means looking backward. The alexandrine (iambic hexameter) in the poem's final line recalls the stanzaic form of Spenser's *The Faerie Queene*, and it is also seen in Keats's 'The Eve of St Agnes'.

XXIX

Though this sonnet suggests that it was somewhat feigned during his schoolboy years, Tuckerman did suffer from 'o'erwrought sight' (line 3). His son Frederick believed it to be the reason that Tuckerman left Harvard University after his first year of study. (See Bynner, pp. 24–5.)

XXX

Line 9 has a (barely legible) footnote in the 1854 manuscript: 'Anybody who has once heard this sound can never forget it.'

XXXII

The first two lines of this sonnet were used as the epitaph on Tuckerman's gravestone in Greenfield, Massachusetts.

XXXIV

'Esdras' (line 13) who 'fed / On flowers' (lines 13–14) is the prophet
Ezra, the author of the apocryphal books of Esdras. In 2 Esdras 9:24–
6, an angel commands Ezra to go into a field and eat nothing but wild
flowers for seven days. After doing this, Ezra sees a vision of a weeping
woman who reveals that she is mourning the death of her son. Ezra
urges her to lay aside her sorrow and trust God to grant her peace.
Because of his faith in God as the answer to grief, the 'glory' (line 14)
of the future Jerusalem is then suddenly revealed to Ezra. In a letter of
24 April 1861, the poet (and Tuckerman's former teacher at Harvard)
Jones Very wrote: 'The concluding sonnets of the 2nd part 34th, 35th,
and 36th are beautifully expressed, and call forth my deepest sympathy
with your loss, and with the faith that sustains you.'

XXXV

'Happiness too deep for joy' (line 5) recalls the final line of Words-
worth's 'Ode: Intimations of Immortality' (1807), 'Thoughts that do
often lie too deep for tears.'

XXXVI

'Earthy' (line 4) was mistakenly changed to 'earthly' in the 1863 and
subsequent editions of *Poems*. The errata slip in the 1864 edition noted
the correct word as 'earthy', but the 1869 mistakenly retained it as
'earthly'. Tuckerman uses the word in the biblical sense (compare
1 Corinthians 15:47, meaning of the earth or worldly). Compare line
7, 'Oh! round that mould which all thy mortal hath', with Milton's
Comus, lines 244–5, 'Can any mortal mixture of earth's mould /
Breathe such divine enchanting ravishment?'

'As Eponina brought, to move the king'

Momaday (p. xxvii) notes that Plutarch describes 'Eponina' (line 1) as
the wife of Julius Sabinus, a Gallic leader of the Rhine rebellion against
the Roman leadership in AD 70. After the failure of the rebellion,
Sabinus took refuge in a cave for nine years (the 'tomb' of line 2).
During his hiding Eponina bore Sabinus two sons, who were apparently
kept hidden in the cave as well. She brought the boys to 'the king' (line
1) 'To plead a father's cause' (line 4) in an effort to secure a pardon
for their father. After 'nine long years' (line 14) the family was executed.

Sonnets, Part III

The third sequence (totalling fifteen sonnets, of which three are here printed) was discovered after Tuckerman's death (along with the fourth and fifth sequences) in a notebook dated December 1872.

I

A pencil draft of this sonnet appears in an earlier notebook (Harvard MS Am1349 [3]) where it is numbered 'I'; however, no sonnet follows there. Edmund Wilson (*Patriotic Gore*, New York, 1962, p. 493) thought 'Dagoraus Whear' (line 14) an invention of Tuckerman, but Degory Wheare (1573–1647) was a Professor of History at Oxford. 'His Method' (line 5) is Wheare's *De Ratione et Methodo Legendi Historias* (The Method and Order of Reading Histories), published (in Latin) in 1625. Tuckerman's spelling, 'Dagoraus', is closest to that on the title-page of Edmund Bohun's English translation in 1685: 'Degoraeus Wheare'. The fact that Wilson disbelieved Wheare's real existence bears up Tuckerman's description of Wheare as 'a forgotten sage' (line 2).

Sonnets, Part IV

The fourth sequence (totalling ten sonnets, of which eight are here printed) was discovered after Tuckerman's death (along with the third and fifth sequences) in a notebook dated December 1872.

I

The sonnet's opening image of the soul as 'a City, seated on a height' recalls Jesus' Sermon on the Mount in Matthew 5:14: 'A city that is set on an hill cannot be hid.' The 'shafts', 'stone' and 'bolt' of lines 8–9 are the projectiles of the bow, catapult and crossbow respectively. Bynner and Momaday read 'And views' in line 13, but the words are 'God views'.

II

A pencil draft of this sonnet (like *Sonnets, Part III*, I above) appears in an earlier notebook (Harvard MS Am 1349 [3]). The pencil draft has 'dark' for 'gloom' at line 4, showing that Tuckerman himself made changes involving the word 'dark'. An 'embrasure' (line 3) is an opening in a wall, through which arrows are fired. In *Webster's Dictionary* (1828), it is pronounced with the main stress on the last syllable. Bynner and Momaday read 'archer' in line 1, but the word is 'warder'.

III

Momaday reads 'thronged' in line 9, but the word is 'throned'. Bynner reads 'Of life be touched' in line 12, but the words are 'Of life we touch'.

IV

The 'Floralia' (line 8) were ancient Roman springtime celebrations honouring Flora, the goddess of flowers. Here Tuckerman uses them as an example of pagan dissipation. The 'Conqueror' (line 13) was Alexander the Great, who invaded Thebes in 335 BC. 'Antigenidas' (line 14) was a famous musician in ancient Thebes. Bynner and Momaday read 'Beside' in line 10, but the word is 'Besides'.

V

Bynner and Momaday both have trouble reading line 8 in the manuscript. The correct phrase, 'If ill enureth', has a pencilled caret below the line and between the words 'ill' and 'enureth'. Bynner reads 'enureth' as 'sneereth', taking the caret to indicate Tuckerman's dissatisfaction with the word 'ill'. Bynner introduces the word 'evil', which completes the syllable count that was shortened by the misreading of 'enureth' as 'sneereth'. Momaday follows Bynner: 'If evil sneereth'. Tuckerman's word 'enureth' is based on an archaic spelling of 'inure', which survived in legal documents and which Tuckerman would have seen during his training as a lawyer. Bynner alters line 9 to read 'And even could we look where the white ones wait'. Also, Bynner adds a question mark at the end of the final line.

VIII

'Blood-flecked like hæmatite' (line 4) refers to the red mineral iron oxide, whose name means literally 'blood stone'; Bynner and Momaday misread it as 'hamatite'. 'D'Acunha's isle' (line 10) is the small, remote island of Tristan da Cunha in the South Atlantic.

IX

A 'sagamore' (line 14) is an American Indian chieftain; 'George' (line 14) was Tuckerman's close friend George D. Wells, with whom the poet often wandered and explored the woods around their hometown of Greenfield. Wells, a US Army colonel, was killed in the Civil War in October 1864.

X

The 'Prophet's miracle' (line 1) occurred in Exodus 7, when Moses and Aaron go before Pharaoh with the message that the Lord will bring the people of Israel out of slavery in Egypt. When Pharaoh demands a miracle as proof of God's power, Aaron throws down his staff and it turns into a snake. Line 1 describes a reversal of this, in the cryptic behaviour of certain caterpillars which become rigid and twig-like when hiding from predators. The barberry flower's 'spermal odour' (line 5) is reminiscent of spermaceti oil, which was produced from the sperm whale and was used to make candles and perfumes.

Sonnets, Part V

The fifth sequence (totalling sixteen sonnets, of which twelve are here printed) was discovered after Tuckerman's death (along with the third and fourth sequences) in a notebook dated December 1872.

I

Although this sequence of sonnets is clearly differentiated from the preceding sequence (by a blank space and by its beginning over with a sonnet number 1), this sonnet continues the thought from the end of the previous sequence. The 'much that we in manifest behold' (line 3) that is 'faint to some' (line 4) can be taken to refer to 'Nature's secrecies' (line 11) in Sonnets, Part IV, X. 'In manifest' (line 3) means clearly. 'Ortive' (line 11) is an astronomical term that means rising. Tuckerman was an amateur astronomer. Bynner alters line 5 to 'that to our sense are veiled and furled'.

II

Bynner has 'for the mind itself' in line 9, but the words are 'from the mind itself'. Momaday misreads line 13, 'the night-heron wading in the swamp', as 'the night-heron waking in the swamp'.

VI

A 'Sybil' (line 3) is a female prophet of ancient Greece, inspired by Apollo. Usually the Sibyl would write her prophecies on leaves which she left at the entrance of her cave or 'Grot' (line 3). 'Copernick' (line 4) is Nicolaus Copernicus (1473–1543), the Polish astronomer whose theory of heliocentrism revolutionized astronomy. The 'Licentiate of the schools' (line 1), who claims that the stars move, shows himself to be ignorant of Copernican theory.

VIII

A 'holm tree' (line 14) is a holly tree. Golden (p. 90) reports that 'ople tree' (line 14) is an archaic name for the witch-hazel. 'Sycamine' (line 14) appears in the New Testament, probably referring to the black mulberry.

IX

'Ule' (line 7) is apparently an invention. Golden (p. 91) identifies it with a Norwegian village named 'Ula', but if this is Tuckerman's actual reference it makes little difference to the sonnet.

X

Bynner and Momaday misread lines 1-2, 'Love must lend / An ear to Reason' as 'love must lend / Answer to reason'.

XI

Momaday misreads 'earthy' (line 4) as 'earthly'. The 'whirling Pillar' (line 12) describes a tornado at sea, also known as a water spout. This image connects the lovers with Dante's Paolo and Francesca (see note to Tuckerman's 'Paulo to Francesca', above), who were sentenced to spend eternity in hell, spinning together inside a whirlwind.

XII

'Phædimus and Tantalus' (line 14) were the sons of Niobe, who grew so proud that she demanded to be worshipped instead of Leto, the mother (by Zeus) of Apollo and Diana. Leto complained to Apollo, who punished Niobe by shooting her children with arrows. Phædimus and Tantalus were engaged in a wrestling match when one of Apollo's arrows pierced them both. Tuckerman's source was probably Ovid, *Metamorphoses*, VI.239 ff. Momaday misreads 'whither' (line 6) as 'whether'.

XIII

'Shives' (line 13) are splinters or pieces of chaff that fall from plants as they decompose in the autumn.

XIV

Bynner and Momaday misread 'cluster' (line 6) as 'clusters'. A 'corymb' (line 6) is a cluster of flowers where the lower flower-stalks are proportionally longer, so that the flowers are nearly on a level. The alexandrine (iambic hexameter) in the poem's final line recalls the stanzaic form of Spenser's *The Faerie Queene*, and it is also seen in Keats's 'The Eve of St Agnes'.

XV

Compare the use of 'darkling' in line 7 with Arnold's 'Dover Beach', line 35: 'And we are here as on a darkling plain'. Although 'Dover Beach' was not published until 1867, it is possible that Tuckerman had read the poem in manuscript. (See note to 'Twilight' above.) 'The peace that passeth understanding' (line 14) comes from Philippians 4:7.

XVI

This sonnet, with the two or three that precede it (coming as they do so late in Tuckerman's life), comprise Tuckerman's farewell to his life as a poet.

The Cricket

Composed after 1860; published 1950. Compare line 7 with Abraham Cowley's 'The Wish' (1647), lines 6–8: 'Who for it can endure the stings, / The crowd, and buz, and murmurings / Of this great hive, the city.' Eugene England (*Beyond Romanticism*, Provo, 1990, p. 283) notes that there is evidence of Tuckerman's having read Cowley. Lines 17–18, 'Or in a garden bower / Trellis'd and trammel'd with deep drapery', recall Tennyson's 'Ode to Memory', lines 105–6, 'Or a garden bower'd close / With plaited alleys of the trailing rose'. 'Winrows' (line 33) is an archaic spelling for windrows, which are rows in which mown grass or hay is laid to expose it to the wind for drying before it is gathered up. Compare line 67 with Virgil's *Eclogues*, VII.12: 'Here Mincius fringes his green banks with tender reeds'. Compare lines 90–91, 'That twittering tongue, / Ancient as light, returning like the years', with Keats's 'Ode to a Nightingale', lines 63–4, 'The voice I hear this passing night was heard / In ancient days by emperor and clown.' Compare lines 109–12, where the sound of the crickets seems 'Naught in innumerable numerousness', with Hawthorne's *The Old Manse* (1846):

I have forgotten whether the song of the cricket be not as early a token of autumn's approach, as any other; – that song, which may be called an audible stillness; for, though very loud and heard afar, yet the mind does not take note of it as a sound; so completely is its individual existence merged among the accompanying characteristics of the season.

Line 129 echoes the end of Tennyson's 'The Two Voices' (1833), 'Rejoice! Rejoice!'. Keats's 'Ode to a Nightingale' (1819) is a major influence on the poem. Tennyson's 'Ode to Memory' (1830) was probably the model for the form, with its free alternation of two, three, four and five stress lines. Another probable influence is Tennyson's 'The Grasshopper' (1830). England (p. 294) points out that 'dorcynium' (line 85) is a misspelling of 'dorycnium,' a southern European plant. (Tuckerman's spelling is here retained.) 'Cayster' (line 67) was a river in Asia Minor that entered the Aegean near Ephesus. It appears in Ovid's *Metamorphoses*, V.386-7: 'Not Cayster on its gliding waters hears more songs of swans than does this pool.' The *Iliad*, II.461 ff., also describes it as a favourite place of swans, which were supposed to retain the souls of poets (see note to *Sonnets, Part I*, I). 'Reedy Eurotas' (line 71) was a river near Sparta; according to Lemprière's *Classical Dictionary*, 'laurels, reeds, myrtles, and olives grew on its banks in great abundance'. Laurels were sacred to Apollo, the god of music, and the reed was used to make the Pan-pipe, an early musical instrument. 'Psammathe' (line 76) was a nereid or sea-nymph who appears in the *Metamorphoses*, XI.346-406. 'Pan' (line 78) was the Greek god of pastures and forests who made his home in Arcadia or 'Arcady' (line 81).

EDWIN ARLINGTON ROBINSON

The following abbreviations are used in this section of the Notes:

Avon's Harvest Avon's Harvest, Etc. (New York, 1921)
Brower *Letters Edwin Arlington Robinson's Letters to Edith Brower*, ed. Richard Cary (Cambridge, Mass., 1968)
Children of the Night The Children of the Night (New York, 1897)
Dionysus Dionysus in Doubt (New York, 1925)
Man Against the Sky The Man Against the Sky (New York, 1916)
Three Taverns The Three Taverns (New York, 1920)
Torrent The Torrent and the Night Before (New York, 1896)
Town Down the River The Town Down the River (New York, 1910)
Untriangulated Stars Untriangulated Stars: Letters of Edwin Arlington Robinson to Harry De Forest Smith, 1890-1905, ed. Denham Sutcliffe (Cambridge, Mass., 1947)
Winters Winters, Yvor, *Edwin Arlington Robinson* (Norfolk, Conn., 1946)

The Torrent

Published November 1896 in *Torrent*. 'The Torrent' was first submitted to a magazine editor who offered to print it on the condition that Robinson alter the last two lines, which the editor regarded as nonsensical. The poet refused, and instead the poem made its appearance as the opening to Robinson's first book of poetry, *The Torrent and the Night Before*, which was published (after several rejections from publishing houses) at his own expense.

Aaron Stark

Written by January 1895; published November 1896 in *Torrent*. The description of the 'loveless exile moving with a staff' (line 11) suggests an ironic comparison to the Old Testament figure of Aaron, the brother of Moses. In Numbers 17, the high priest Aaron's stick miraculously blossoms to show that the tribe of Levi is marked as the priestly élite among the Israelites. The stick is later used to cause water to flow from a rock when the Israelites are encamped in the desert.

Dear Friends

Published November 1896 in *Torrent*. In a letter to Harry Smith on 1 October 1893, Robinson wrote, 'I am afraid that my "dear friends" here in Gardiner will be disappointed in me if I don't do something before long, but somehow I don't care half as much about the matter as I ought' (*Untriangulated Stars*, p. 107). Line 9 alludes to Matthew 24:15, 'whoso readeth, let him understand'.

Sonnet ('When we can all so excellently give')

Published November 1896 in *Torrent*. In Daniel 5, 'Belshazzar' (line 13) is the decadent last king of Babylon, who is warned of his downfall and death by a disembodied hand that writes in an unknown language on the wall of the banquet hall. Unable to read the writing, Belshazzar summons the Hebrew prophet Daniel, who interprets it as a judgement from God that the arrogant Belshazzar must die and the kingdom be divided between the Medes and the Persians (perhaps the 'partnership' of line 14). Lines 10 and 11 show a Wordsworthian influence: for example, from 'Mark the concentrated hazels that enclose' (1815), line 5, 'seldom free to touch the moss that grows', and also the final lines of the 'Ode: Intimations of Immortality' (1807), lines 203–4, 'To me the meanest flower that blows can give / Thoughts that do often lie too deep for tears.'

Her Eyes

Published November 1896 in *Torrent*.

George Crabbe

Published November 1896 in *Torrent*. George Crabbe (1754–1832) was an English clergyman and poet who continued the tradition of the heroic couplet verse form into the 19th century, after it had become unfashionable. With descriptive verse tales that resisted romantic sentimentality about country life, Crabbe tried, as he put it in 'The Village' (1783), lines 53–4, to 'paint the Cot / As Truth will paint it, and as Bards will not'. Crabbe and Robinson share an affinity for realistic 'type' or 'character' poems (not mere stock characters). Cf. Crabbe's 'Peter Grimes' (*The Borough*, 1810) or 'The Gentleman Farmer' (*Tales*, 1812) and Robinson's 'Aaron Stark' or 'The Clerks', though Robinson's characterizations lead less directly to moral conclusions than do Crabbe's. The sonnet admits that Crabbe has fallen from favour with modern readers, while it affirms that the truth of poetry withstands the vicissitudes of poetic fashion.

Sonnet ('Oh, for a poet – for a beacon bright')

Published in the New York periodical the *Critic*, 24 November 1894; reprinted (with minor changes) November 1896 in *Torrent*. Lines 5 and 6 echo Tennyson's 'In Memoriam' (1850), v.5–8:

> But, for the unquiet heart and brain,
> A use in measured language lies;
> The sad mechanic exercise,
> Like dull narcotics, numbing pain.

'Parnassus' (line 4) was a mountain in Greece sacred to the Muses. On 9 May 1897 Robinson complained, 'I am getting sick of surface praise, and very sick of the sight of "Oh! for a Poet." If that is the best thing I have done, the sooner I stop the better' (Brower *Letters*, p. 43).

Luke Havergal

Written by 14 December 1895; published November 1896 in *Torrent*. In a letter to Harry Smith on 14 December 1895, Robinson referred to 'Luke Havergal' as 'a piece of deliberate degeneration', probably in a joking reference to Max Nordau's *Degeneration* (1895), which attacked the decadence of the Symbolist movement. President Theodore Roosevelt, who secured Robinson a job as a Treasury Agent in 1905, wrote an article on *The Children of the Night* for the *Outlook* magazine, 12 August 1905, which read in part, 'I am not sure that I understand "Luke Havergal," but I am entirely sure I like it.' The command 'Go to the western gate' (line 1) perhaps alludes to Horace Greeley's famous injunction, 'Go West, young man, and grow up with the country', which was Greeley's expansion of the phrase 'Go West, young man' that appeared in an article in the Terre Haute *Express* in 1851. For his *Collected Poems* in 1921, Robinson revised lines 4–6 from the original version in *Torrent*, which read:

> The wind will moan, the leaves will whisper some –
> Whisper of her, and strike you as they fall;
> But go, and if you trust her she will call, –

According to Edith Brower, Robinson had decided that the use of 'some' in line 4, meaning 'somewhat' or 'a little', was too 'provincial' (Brower *Letters*, p. 208). Line 13 echoes Tennyson's 'The Vision of Sin' (1842), line 50: 'God made Himself an awful rose of dawn.'

The Chorus of Old Men in 'Ægeus'

Early version written by 12 January 1895; published November 1896 in *Torrent*. Although Euripides and Sophocles are recorded to have written plays about Aegeus, no known texts survive. Robinson planned an *Ægeus* of his own, but it was never finished and only this chorus remains. In Greek mythology, Ægeus was king of Athens and father (by the princess Aethra) of the mythic hero Theseus. To save his city from the ravages of plague, Aegeus was required by the Oracle at Delphi to send victims in tribute to the Cretans. Theseus volunteered to go and slay the Minotaur, a bull-headed monster to whom King Minos of Crete was sacrificing the young Athenians. King Aegeus commanded that Theseus, if successful, should change his ship's black sail to a white one on the return voyage. When the triumphant Theseus

forgot to do this, Aegeus saw the black sail and jumped, grieving, off
the Acropolis and into the sea.

Horace to Leuconoë

Published November 1896 in *Torrent*. Robinson had written an earlier
version of this translation of Horace's famous 'Carpe diem' ode (Odes
I.11) by 21 May 1891. By 14 December 1895, he had reworked the
opening lines into the form given here. The Chaldeans (line 4) were an
ancient people of Babylonia, famous for their skills in astrology and
fortune-telling.

Reuben Bright

Written by 7 September 1897; published December 1897 in *Children
of the Night*. On 7 September 1897, Robinson wrote, 'It can't be you
are squeamish after all. If you are, don't read "Reuben Bright" or he
will knock you down' (Brower *Letters*, p. 56). In the first edition of
Collected Poems (1921) there appeared what Robinson called 'one of
those diabolical errors that make a sort of sense' (Brower *Letters*,
p. 180). In the final line, the phrase 'and tore down the slaughter house'
appeared as 'and tore down to the slaughter house'.

The Ballade of Dead Friends

Written by 25 November 1894; published November 1896 in *Torrent*.
The *ballade* was a form of French lyric poetry popular in the 14th
and 15th centuries, most famously in the work of François Villon
(1431–after 1463). The *ubi sunt* motif, found in Villon's famous line
from 'Ballade des dames du temps jadis' ('*Mais ou sont les neiges
d'antan?*', 'But where are the snows of yesteryear?' [trans. D. G.
Rossetti]), is seen here. Robinson's poem follows the *ballade* form's
traditional pattern of rhymes and line repetitions. In former times, the
envoi would often address a lofty patron; here it is 'we all' (line 25).

Thomas Hood

An early version was composed by 8 December 1891; published Febru-
ary 1896 in the New York periodical *The Globe*; reprinted (with minor
changes) November 1896 in *Torrent*. Thomas Hood (1799–1845) was
an English poet whose poverty and lack of success in selling his serious
poetry led him to concentrate on humorous writing. Hood's puns, as

Robinson's poem notes, are often blended with bitterness, such as in 'Faithless Nelly Gray' (1826):

> Ben Battle was a soldier bold,
>   And used to war's alarms:
> But a cannon-ball took off his legs,
>   So he laid down his arms!

The 'branded man of Lynn' (line 5) refers to *The Dream of Eugene Aram* (1829), which is set in Lynn. The usher Eugene Aram is branded because of the murder he has committed, like Cain with the Lord's mark upon him (Genesis 4:15). 'Ines' (line 14) comes from Hood's *Fair Ines* (1823), lines 1–2: 'Oh saw ye not fair Ines? / She's gone into the West'.

For a Book by Thomas Hardy

Written by 14 April 1895; published 23 November 1895 in the *Critic*; reprinted November 1896 in *Torrent*. When this poem appeared in the *Critic*, the editors saw fit to add a note, 'Written before the appearance of *Hearts Insurgent*.' Thomas Hardy's novel *Hearts Insurgent* (at first called *The Simpletons*, later changed to *Jude the Obscure*) was serialized in *Harper's New Monthly Magazine* from December 1894 to November 1895. For the magazine, Hardy consented to alter some sections that might offend tender readers; these sections were restored and the novel published in August 1895, meeting with outcry against its 'indecency'. When the sonnet was composed in April 1895, Robinson had only seen up to part 3 of Hardy's novel (in the expurgated magazine form). 'Wessex' (line 14) is a fictional region in south-western England where Hardy's novels are set.

Supremacy

Written in April 1892; an early version was published 16 June 1892 in the *Harvard Advocate*; reprinted (in the form given here) November 1896 in *Torrent*. In a letter to his friend Harry Smith on 1 October 1893 (*Untriangulated Stars*, p. 108), Robinson referred to this poem as 'the "hell" sonnet', and he wrote:

I have brought out the idea of the occasional realization of the questionable supremacy of ourselves over those we most despise . . . There is poetry in all types of humanity . . . and I have tried to find a little for the poor fellows in my hell, which is an exceedingly worldly and transitory one, before they soar above me in my ignorance of what is, to sing in the sun.

'Lorn' (line 4) means abandoned and wretched, with an archaic sense of being doomed to destruction.

Three Quatrains ('As long as Fame's imperious music rings')

Published November 1896 in *Torrent*. A slightly different version of the first quatrain (with 'imperial' rather than 'imperious' in line 1) was composed by 9 December 1894. In a letter to his friend Edith Brower on 29 December 1897, Robinson expressed dismay at 'scholarly people' who saw 'no connection between the first and second parts of the quatrain "Drink to the splendor, etc." . . . Such criticisms as these make me wonder what kind of stuff I have been writing and if it is worth while for me to keep on' (Brower *Letters*, p. 68). 'Lucullus' (line 7) was a wealthy Roman general whose gluttony became a byword. 'Nero' (line 8) was the infamous Roman Emperor who played the lyre as he watched Rome burn. The 'Fates' (line 10) were the Greek and Roman goddesses whose spinning of the thread of life determined the course of human existence. To 'coax the Fates for us to quarrel' (line 10) would be to cause them to fight among themselves, thereby allowing the thread to run longer and extend our lives unnaturally.

John Evereldown

Written by 14 December 1895; published November 1896 in *Torrent*. This poem is in modified traditional English ballad form, which usually consists of quatrains of alternating four and three stress lines. For example, the traditional ballad 'Sir Patrick Spens':

> To Noroway, to Noroway,
>   To Noroway o'er the faem;
> The king's daughter o' Noroway,
>   'Tis thou must bring her hame.

'Tilbury Town' (line 4) is Robinson's fictional name for his hometown of Gardiner, Maine. In a letter to his friend, the Gardiner native Harry Smith, on 14 December 1895 (*Untriangulated Stars*, p. 238), Robinson made the earliest known reference to Tilbury Town in describing the fictional title character of this poem: 'old John Evereldown who had all the women of Tilbury Town under his wing, or thought he had'.

The Clerks

Published 4 June 1896 in the *Boston Evening Transcript*; reprinted (with minor changes) November 1896 in *Torrent*. 'Tiering' (line 13) means to arrange or pile in tiers. 'Alnage' (line 14) is an archaism meaning measurement by the ell, a unit about 45 inches in length, used especially in the preparation of woollen cloth for sale.

Verlaine

Written by 22 May 1896; published 28 July 1896 in the *Boston Evening Transcript*; reprinted (with minor changes) November 1896 in *Torrent*. Paul Verlaine (1844–96) was a French poet whose infamous debauchery threatened to eclipse the fame of his poetry. The 'star that shines on Paris now' (line 14) refers to the ancient belief that great heroes were borne to the heavens after death to become stars and constellations.

Walt Whitman

Published November 1896 in *Torrent*. Walt Whitman died on 26 March 1892, widely revered as 'the poet of democracy'. In line 8, 'the song that was the man' refers to Whitman's 'Song of Myself', the masterpiece which he continually revised right up until his death. In a letter to his friend Chauncey Giles Hubbell, on 16 December 1896, Robinson mentioned that Emanuel Swedenborg's philosophy influenced the final section of 'Walt Whitman'. Swedenborgianism was a popular trend among 19th-century Christians, emphasizing an ideal correspondence of earthly things to the eternal spiritual world. Compare the final lines with Keats's self-authored epitaph, 'Here lies one whose name was writ in water', and Longfellow's 'A Psalm of Life' (1838), lines 25–8: see note to Tuckerman, *Sonnets, Part II, XXVII*, above.

Boston

Published 8 October 1896 in the *Boston Evening Transcript*; reprinted (with minor changes) November 1896 in *Torrent*. Robinson removed the sestet of this sonnet for the 1905 edition of *Children of the Night*, leaving it as an eight-line poem in all subsequent collections. The poem is a memory of Robinson's September 1891 journey from his boyhood home in Gardiner, Maine, to Harvard University, where he studied from 1891 to May 1893, leaving without a degree.

Richard Cory

Written by July 1897; published December 1897 in *Children of the Night*. In a letter to Harry Smith on 24 April 1897, Robinson reported the death (apparently suicide by shotgun) of Frank Avery, a local Gardiner man. The regal connotations of the name Richard Cory stem from the name of Richard Coeur de Lion, the 'lion-hearted' crusader and king of England. Winters (p. 52) writes, 'the poem builds up deliberately to a very cheap surprise ending; but all surprise endings are cheap in poetry . . . for poetry is written to be read not once but many times.'

Amaryllis

Published 2 August 1897 in the *Boston Evening Transcript*; reprinted December 1897 in *Children of the Night*. In the pastoral tradition of Virgil's *Eclogues*, and in later poetry (such as Milton's 'Lycidas'), Amaryllis is a traditional name for a beautiful shepherdess. Here, it can also be taken as a symbol for the pastoral tradition itself. The final line expresses sadness not because Amaryllis had died, but because she 'had grown old'; in pastoral poetry the beloved nymphs and shepherdesses are forever young.

Cliff Klingenhagen

Published December 1897 in *Children of the Night*. 'Wormwood' (line 5) is a bitter herb which, according to legend, first grew out of the tracks left by the Serpent as it was driven out of Eden. The poem contrasts it with wine, which is used in Christian liturgy as a symbol for the blood of Christ. Robinson plays with this salvatory symbolism by including the phrase 'what the deuce' (line 9), which is a euphemism for 'what the devil'.

Octaves

Written 1897; published December 1897 in *Children of the Night*. 'Octave V' was first published in the New York periodical the *Globe* in June 1897. In a letter to his friend and literary confidante Edith Brower on 10 April 1897, Robinson said that he had written forty octaves, and planned to end with about sixty. When *Children of the Night* appeared, it contained a pared-down total of twenty-five octaves. The first and third of those twenty-five were dropped by Robinson for *Collected Poems* (1921). The twenty-three octaves printed above follow the poet's choice. The 'All-Soul' (line 47) perhaps echoes 'The Over-Soul' (1841) by Emerson, in whom Robinson took a keen interest in late 1896. But Winters (p. 50) denies that the philosophy is necessarily Emersonian. Discussing Robinson's use of 'language applied in these poems to the evidence for a belief in God', like 'spirit-gleams of Wisdom' (lines 62–3), he writes:

[It] would perhaps appear to indicate a belief in the discovery of God through pure intuition and lend some support to those who find a strong trace of Emerson in Robinson; but there is not sufficient evidence in the poems to prove that the intuition is Emersonian intuition or that the God is Emerson's God . . .

The Growth of 'Lorraine'

Written by 5 July 1900; published August 1902 in *Captain Craig*.

The Corridor

Published February 1899 in the *Harvard Monthly*; reprinted (with several changes) October 1902 in *Captain Craig*.

Pasa Thalassa Thalassa, 'The sea is everywhere the sea'

Published February 1910 in *Scribner's Magazine*; reprinted October 1910 in *Town Down the River*. The 'sea-faring friend' (line 1) was probably Captain Israel Jordan, whose family lived near the Robinsons in Gardiner, Maine. After years of returning from sea with adventurous tales to tell, Captain Jordan disappeared while on a voyage. The poem's dactylic hexameter recalls the rhythm of the Greek and Roman epics, perhaps suggesting a comparison between the poem's subject and Odysseus, who eventually returned from sea.

Momus

Published October 1910 in *Town Down the River*. Momus was the Greek god of carping and ridicule, and he once complained that humans ought to have been made with doors or windows over their hearts so that their true feelings could be plainly seen. 'King Kronos' (lines 4–5) was a Titan in Greek mythology who castrated his father Uranus and swallowed all his own children except Zeus. Momus' dismissal of the poets is nested in poetic allusions. Line 9 alludes to Alexander Pope's

'Epistle to Dr Arbuthnot' (1735), line 1, 'Shut, shut the door, good John!' (i.e., against the crowds of bad poets). The reference to Byron (line 8) probably alludes to Byron's own use of Momus:

> All – all suspected me; and why? because
> I am the worst clothed, and least named amongst them;
> Although, were Momus' lattice in our breasts,
> My soul might brook to open it more widely
> Than theirs . . . (*Werner*, III.i.31–5)

'What's become of / Browning?' (lines 12–13) alludes to Robert Browning's *Waring* (1843), lines 1–2: 'What's become of Waring / Since he gave us all the slip?'

Uncle Ananias

Published August 1905 in *The Century Magazine*; reprinted October 1910 in *Town Down the River*. In the Acts of the Apostles, there are two men named Ananias who relate to the Uncle of the poem. In Acts 5, there is the Ananias who sold his land to give the money to the Apostles of Jesus, but secretly kept a portion of the proceeds for himself: perhaps this is the 'authoritative liar' of line 5. The other Ananias, in Acts 22:12–16, is given power by Jesus to return sight to Saul, who then converts and becomes the Apostle Paul; hence the 'fairer visions to our eyes' (line 22). 'Benedight' (line 9) is an archaic word meaning blessed. 'Birds of paradise' (line 24) are ornate, colourful birds found in New Guinea.

How Annandale Went Out

Published May 1910 in *Scribner's Magazine*; reprinted October 1910 in *Town Down the River*. The speaker is describing an act of euthanasia. In September 1899, Robinson's brother Horace Dean Robinson, a physician whose practice had been destroyed by his addiction to morphine, died of a self-administered overdose. The 'slight kind of engine' (line 13) is a hypodermic syringe. Robinson has perhaps separated his brother into two personalities: the wrecked addict and the merciful physician who ends his (own) suffering.

Miniver Cheevy

Published March 1907 in *Scribner's Magazine*; reprinted October 1910 in *Town Down the River*. The word 'miniver' means the fur of a grey and white animal used as trim in the clothing of the Middle Ages, the era which elicits Miniver's nostalgia. The allusion in the phrase 'rested from his labors' (line 10) makes an ironic contrast with Genesis 2:2–3, when God 'rested from all his work' on the seventh day of the Creation. For Romance to be 'on the town' (line 15) means that it has become so poor in modern times it has gone on welfare. 'Priam' (line 12) was king of Troy during the siege by the Greeks, who were encamped near the city so long that they might have come to seem like neighbours. The 'Medici' (line 17) were a notorious family who ruled in Florence during the 15th and 16th centuries. As great patrons of the arts, the Medici would indeed be loved by Miniver, who despairs at 'Art, a vagrant' (line 16).

For a Dead Lady

Published September 1909 in *Scribner's Magazine*; reprinted October 1910 in *Town Down the River*. On 15 March 1914 Robinson wrote, 'As for the obscure line in the "Dead Lady", I never thought of meaning or indicating anything more than her way of presuming on her attractions and "guying" those who admired her' (Brower *Letters*, p. 155). 'Guying' means laughing at someone. 'Saturn' (line 14) was the ruler of the gods during the Golden Age of ancient Greece.

Eros Turannos

Published March 1914 in Harriet Monroe's magazine *Poetry*; reprinted February 1916 in *Man Against the Sky*. 'Eros Turannos' means 'Love, the Tyrant', referring to Eros, the Greek god of love. Winters (p. 32) calls this poem 'a universal tragedy in a Maine setting'.

Theophilus

Published January 1915 in the periodical the *Trend*; reprinted (with minor changes) February 1916 in *Man Against the Sky*. The name 'Theophilus' comes from the Greek for 'lover of God', so it is an ironic one for the man described in the poem. 'Belial' (line 9) is a devil, of whom Milton writes in *Paradise Lost*, I.490–92: 'a spirit more lewd / Fell not from heaven, or more gross to love / Vice for itself'. The

'Cyclops' (line 3) refers to a mythic race of savage one-eyed monsters like the one named Polyphemus whom Odysseus encountered in *Odyssey*, IX. 'Caligula' (line 19) was a notoriously cruel and decadent emperor of Rome; 'Caliban' (line 19) is the monstrous servant of Prospero in Shakespeare's *The Tempest*; and 'Cain' (line 20) slew his brother Abel and became the world's first murderer (Genesis 4:8).

Veteran Sirens

Published February 1916 in *Man Against the Sky*. The Sirens (*Odyssey*, XII) were mythical bird-women whose song could enchant men and lure them to their deaths. The term is also applied to any alluring woman, as here. 'Ninon' (line 1) refers to the French courtesan Ninon de l'Enclos (*c.* 1620–1705), who was admired by the nobility as much for her wit and style as for her looks, which she retained to an advanced age.

Another Dark Lady

Published February 1916 in *Man Against the Sky*. 'Lilith' (line 7) is a female demon of Jewish folklore, held to be Adam's first wife who refused his dominion and flew away to haunt the night.

Bewick Finzer

Published February 1916 in *Man Against the Sky*. The 'six per cent' (line 2) is the rate of interest that Finzer's money was earning (before he lost it). Compare with Pope's 'Of the Use of Riches' from the 'Epistle To Lord Bathurst' (1732), lines 369–72:

> The tempter saw his time: the work he plied
> Stocks and subscriptions pour on every side,
> Till all the demon makes his full descent
> In one abundant shower of cent per cent.

The Man Against the Sky

Published February 1916 in *Man Against the Sky*. In a letter to Edith Brower on 1 March 1916 (Brower *Letters*, p. 167), Robinson wrote:

I am particularly glad that you like my 'Man.' I suppose, as you say, that superficial readers will call it "pessimistic," that being one of the easiest words to toss about. For instance, it has the great advantage of not meaning anything.

Compare line 34, 'The bread that every man must eat alone', with Matthew 4:4, 'Man shall not live by bread alone'. Lines 40–46 refer to Daniel 3–4, where the 'three in Dura' (line 42), Shadrach, Meshach and Abednego, were put into a furnace by the 'king of Babylon' (line 44), Nebuchadnezzar. Through the power of the Lord they walked out unharmed. 'Gules' (line 140) is a term from heraldry meaning red. 'A grave that holds a clown' (line 168) recalls *Hamlet*, V.i. The 'great grasshoppers' (line 177) appear in Nahum 3:17, 'when the sun ariseth they flee away, and their place is not known where they are'. Compare line 212, 'A manifest end of ashes and eternal night', with Herrick's 'Corinna's Going a-Maying', line 68, 'drowned with us in endless night'. Lines 275–6, 'The Word itself, the living word / That none alive has ever heard', allude to 1 John 1:1, 'That which was from the beginning, which we have heard . . . the Word of life.' Line 281 refers to the Angel of Death.

The Flying Dutchman

Published 9 November 1918 in the *Nation*; reprinted (with minor changes) September 1920 in *Three Taverns*. 'The Flying Dutchman' was a legendary ghost ship that haunted the waters around the Cape of Good Hope, its appearance foreboding disaster to sailors. Its blasphemous captain, Vanderdecken, was condemned to round the Cape for ever, with all ports closed to him. As a devotee of opera, Robinson was probably familiar with the version of this legend contained in Wagner's *Der fliegende Holländer* (1843). Compare lines 13–16 with Tennyson's 'Tithonus' (1860), lines 68–71:

> when the steam
> Floats up from those dim fields about the homes
> Of happy men that have the power to die,
> And grassy barrows of the happier dead.

The poem's first readers would have seen it against the backdrop of World War I, which ended on 11 November 1918. In 1915, the Germans had warned that they would destroy any allied ship entering the waters adjacent to the British Isles ('the shore from which we came' of line 6). British and American merchant and passenger ships (such as the *Lusitania*) defied the German submarines throughout the war, though many were sunk.

Firelight

Published October 1918 in the periodical *Youth: Poetry of Today*; reprinted (with minor changes) September 1920 in *Three Taverns*. The 'snake' and 'sword' (line 7) are two famous impediments to love: the first in the Garden of Eden and the second in the legend of Tristram and Iseult, where a sword lying between the two lovers keeps them separated while they sleep.

Mr Flood's Party

Published 24 November 1920 in the *Nation*; reprinted March 1921 in *Avon's Harvest*. The name 'Eben Flood' suggests the phrase 'ebb and flood', referring to the fall and rise of the tides, or of fortune. Line 11 alludes to Edward FitzGerald's *The Rubáiyát of Omar Khayyám* (1859), lines 27–8: 'The Bird of Time has but a little way / To fly – and Lo! the Bird is on the Wing.' 'Roland's ghost winding a silent horn' (line 20) is a reversal of the 8th-century knight Roland who warned the Emperor Charlemagne with an extremely loud blast upon an ivory horn when the defeat of Roland and the rest of Charlemagne's paladins at Roncesvalles was imminent. The story is recounted in the 11th-century *Song of Roland*. Compare with Milton's 'Lycidas', line 28: 'What time the greyfly winds her sultry horn'. Lines 35–6, 'since last it was / We had a drop together', and lines 42 ff. recall Robert Burns's song 'Auld Lang Syne' (literally, *old long since*, i.e. old long-ago times; 1796). 'Lifted up his voice' (line 46) is a common biblical phrase meaning sung.

The Tree in Pamela's Garden

Published 24 November 1920 in the *New Republic*; reprinted March 1921 in *Avon's Harvest*. The title alludes to the tree of knowledge of good and evil in the Garden of Eden (Genesis 2–3). The name 'Pamela' is most famous in literature as the title character in Samuel Richardson's novel *Pamela, or Virtue Rewarded* (1740), in which a servant girl's long resistance to her master's seductive overtures results in his proposal of marriage. That the Pamela of the poem tells the truth only to her roses makes a pun on the Latin phrase *sub rosa* (literally, 'under the rose'), which means in strict confidence. 'Apollo's avatar' (line 3) would be a perfect man, the earthly incarnation of the Greek god.

Lost Anchors

Published 2 February 1921 in the *Nation*; reprinted March 1921 in *Avon's Harvest*. The anchor is a symbol of hope in Christian symbology, as in Hebrews 6:19: 'hope we have as an anchor of the soul'.

Monadnock Through the Trees

Published 5 January 1921 in the *Outlook* (New York); reprinted March 1921 in *Avon's Harvest*. Monadnock is a mountain in southern New Hampshire that was popular with artists and writers (such as Thoreau) in the 19th century. It was visible to Robinson from his studio in the MacDowell artist colony in Peterborough, where he worked every summer from 1912 until his death in 1935. In summer 1934 he remarked to Mrs MacDowell, 'I rather think the old fellow [Monadnock] will miss me a bit when I'm gone' (Hermann Hagedorn, *Edwin Arlington Robinson: A Biography*, p. 371). In a letter of 15 March 1897, Robinson quoted Ralph Waldo Emerson's poem *Monadnoc* (1847), which, like Robinson's poem, contrasts the permanence of the mountain with the transience of its human admirers.

Many Are Called

Published 3 November 1920 in the *New Republic*; reprinted (with minor changes) March 1921 in *Avon's Harvest*. The title refers to the parable told by Jesus (Matthew 22:1–14) comparing the kingdom of heaven with a wedding to which 'many are called, but few are chosen'.

The Sheaves

Published 15 December 1923 in the *Literary Review: New York Evening Post*; reprinted (with minor changes) March 1925 in *Dionysus*.

Silver Street

Published December 1923 in the London periodical the *Bermondsey Book*; reprinted (with minor changes) March 1925 in *Dionysus*. In April 1923, Robinson journeyed to London, where the American poet John Gould Fletcher took him on a tour of Shakespearean sites. Christopher Mountjoy (line 4) had a house at the corner of Silver and Monkwell Streets, and Shakespeare is believed to have lodged there around 1604. Near this site, at the corner of Silver and Wood Streets, is the cemetery which (as Robinson rightly draws it) Shakespeare would have passed on his way home from the Mermaid Tavern in Cheapside, where he sometimes met with his friends and fellow dramatists.

A Man in Our Town

Published February 1924 in the *Dial* (New York); reprinted March 1925 in *Dionysus*. 'Nemesis' (line 2) was the Greek goddess of retribution and the personification of resentment.

Why He Was There

Published 2 July 1924 in the *New Republic*; reprinted March 1925 in *Dionysus*.

Glass Houses

Published July 1924 in the *Yale Review*; reprinted (with minor changes) March 1925 in *Dionysus*. The title stems from the proverbial saying, 'Those who live in glass houses shouldn't throw stones'. This saying is perhaps an alteration of the warning given by Jesus against judging one's fellow men in John 8:7, 'He that is without sin among you, let him first cast a stone.'

New England

Published 3 November 1923 in the *Outlook* (London); reprinted (with several changes) March 1925 in *Dionysus*. In its first published version, the third line began with the word 'Intolerance' rather than 'Wonder'. It set off a severe reaction against Robinson by those who interpreted the poem as an attack on his native region. In a letter to the editor of the *Gardiner Journal* (his hometown newspaper), Robinson explained that 'intolerance' had been intended ironically. Read in this way, the poem contains 'an oblique attack upon all those who are forever throwing dead cats at New England for its alleged emotional and moral frigidity' (Robinson, quoted in Charles Beecher Hogan, *A Bibliography of Edwin Arlington Robinson*, p. 180; via (ed.) Lawrance Thompson, *Tilbury Town: Selected Poems of Edwin Arlington Robinson*, p. 142). When the poem appeared in *Dionysus*, 'Intolerance' had been changed to 'Wonder'. Compare the use of personifications such as Love and Passion with those used in Elizabethan sonnets, for example Michael

Drayton's 'The Parting', lines 9–10: 'Now at the last gasp of Love's latest breath, / When, his pulse failing, Passion speechless lies.' 'Soilure' (line 9) means soiling, staining. The final line refers to the proverb 'Care killed the cat', which means that even nine lives won't last long when burdened with an excess of worry.

Reunion

Published 7 November 1923 in the *Nation*; reprinted March 1925 in *Dionysus*.

Young Gideon (Judges 6)

Published 20 September 1932 in *Nicodemus*. In Judges 6, Gideon is the least important member of the weakest clan in the Israelite tribe of Manasseh. The 'Voice' (line 20) is that of God, who encourages Gideon to lead an insurrection to free the Israelites from their rulers, the Midianites. Two days before the attack on the Midianites, the doubting Gideon asks God for a sign: if Gideon is to rescue Israel, morning dew will appear on a piece of wool but not on the ground beside it. On the 'second morning' (line 43), the sign is to be the opposite if Gideon is the chosen one: dew on the ground but not on the fleece. Lines 15–16 recall Horace's *Odes*, IV.ix.50, '[He] . . . who fears dishonour worse than death'.

Index of Titles and First Lines

HERMAN MELVILLE

FREDERICK GODDARD TUCKERMAN

EDWIN ARLINGTON ROBINSON

PENGUIN ⓟ CLASSICS

The Classics Publisher

'Penguin Classics, one of the world's greatest series' JOHN KEEGAN

'I have never been disappointed with the Penguin Classics. All I have read is a model of academic seriousness and provides the essential information to fully enjoy the master works that appear in its catalogue' MARIO VARGAS LLOSA

'Penguin and Classics are words that go together like horse and carriage or Mercedes and Benz. When I was a university teacher I always prescribed Penguin editions of classic novels for my courses: they have the best introductions, the most reliable notes, and the most carefully edited texts' DAVID LODGE

'Growing up in Bombay, expensive hardback books were beyond my means, but I could indulge my passion for reading at the roadside bookstalls that were well stocked with all the Penguin paperbacks ... Sometimes I would choose a book just because I was attracted by the cover, but so reliable was the Penguin imprimatur that I was never once disappointed by the contents.

Such access certainly broadened the scope of my reading, and perhaps it's no coincidence that so many Merchant Ivory films have been adapted from great novels, or that those novels are published by Penguin' ISMAIL MERCHANT

'You can't write, read, or live fully in the present without knowing the literature of the past. Penguin Classics opens the door to a treasure house of pure pleasure, books that have never been bettered, which are read again and again with increased delight' JOHN MORTIMER

CLICK ON A CLASSIC
www.penguinclassics.com

The world's greatest literature at your fingertips

Constantly updated information on over 1600 titles, from Icelandic sagas to ancient Indian epics, Russian drama to Italian romance, American greats to African masterpieces

•

The latest news on recent additions to the list, updated editions and specially commissioned translations

•

Original scholarly essays by leading writers: Elaine Showalter on Zola, Laurie R. King on Arthur Conan Doyle, Frank Kermode on Shakespeare, Lisa Appignanesi on Tolstoy

•

A wealth of background material, including biographies of every classic author from Aristotle to Zamyatin, plot synopses, readers' and teachers' guides, useful web links

•

Online desk and examination copy assistance for academics

•

Trivia quizzes, competitions, giveaways, news on forthcoming screen adaptations

•

eBooks available to download

TOLSTOY
Anna Karenina

'Everything is finished ... I have nothing but you.
Remember that'

Anna Karenina seems to have everything, but she feels that her life is empty until the moment she encounters the impetuous officer Count Vronsky. Their subsequent affair scandalizes society and family alike, and soon brings jealousy and bitterness in its wake. Contrasting with this tale of love and self-destruction is the vividly observed story of Levin, who strives to find contentment and a meaning to his life – and also a self-portrait of Tolstoy himself.

This new translation has been acclaimed as the definitive English version. The volume contains an introduction by Richard Pevear and a preface by John Bayley.

'Pevear and Volokhonsky are at once scrupulous translators and vivid stylists of English, and their superb rendering allows us, as perhaps never before, to grasp the palpability of Tolstoy's "characters, acts, situations"' JAMES WOOD, *New Yorker*

Translated by RICHARD PEVEAR *and*
LARISSA VOLOKHONSKY
With a preface by JOHN BAYLEY

TOCQUEVILLE

Democracy in America
and Two Essays on America

*'A new political science is needed for a totally
new world'*

In 1831 Alexis de Tocqueville made a nine-month journey
through eastern America. The result was *Democracy in
America*, a monumental study of the strengths and weaknesses
of the nation's evolving politics and institutions. Tocqueville
looked to the flourishing democratic system in America as a
possible model for post-revolutionary France, believing that the
egalitarian ideals it enshrined reflected the spirit of the age –
even that they were the will of God. His insightful work has
become one of the most influential political texts ever written on
America and an indispensable authority for anyone interested in
the future of democracy. This volume includes the rarely trans-
lated 'Two Weeks in the Wilderness', an evocative account of
Tocqueville's travels in Michigan among the Iroquois and
Chippeway, and 'Excursion to Lake Oneida'.

This is the only edition that contains all Tocqueville's writings
on America, and it includes a chronology, further reading and
explanatory notes. Isaac Kramnick's introduction discusses
Tocqueville's life and times, and the enduring significance of
Democracy in America.

Translated by GERALD BEVAN
With an introduction and notes by ISAAC KRAMNICK

MADISON, HAMILTON AND JAY

The Federalist Papers

'The establishment of a Constitution, in a time of profound peace, by the voluntary consent of a whole people, is a PRODIGY'

Written at a time when furious arguments were raging about the best way to govern America, *The Federalist Papers* had the immediate practical aim of persuading New Yorkers to accept the newly drafted constitution in 1787. In this they were supremely successful, but their influence also transcended contemporary debate to win them a lasting place in discussions of American political theory. Acclaimed by Thomas Jefferson as 'the best commentary on the principles of government which ever was written', *The Federalist Papers* make a powerful case for power-sharing between state and federal authorities and for a constitution that has endured largely unchanged for more than two hundred years.

In his brilliantly detailed introduction, Isaac Kramnick sets the *Papers* in their historical and political context. This edition also contains the American constitution as an appendix.

'The introduction is an outstanding piece of work ... I am strongly recommending its reading' WARREN BURGER, former Chief Justice, Supreme Court of the United States

Edited with an introduction by ISAAC KRAMNICK

EDGAR ALLEN POE

The Fall of the House of Usher and Other Writings

*'And much of Madness and more of Sin
And Horror the Soul of the Plot'*

This selection of Poe's critical writings, short fiction and poetry demonstrates his intense interest in aesthetic issues, and the astonishing power and imagination with which he probed the darkest corners of the human mind. 'The Fall of the House of Usher' describes the final hours of a family tormented by tragedy and the legacy of the past. In 'The Tell Tale Heart', a murderer's insane delusions threaten to betray him, while stories such as 'The Pit and the Pendulum' and 'The Cask of Amontillado' explore extreme states of decadence, fear and hate. These works display Poe's startling ability to build suspense with almost nightmarish intensity.

David Galloway's introduction re-examines the myths surrounding Poe's life and reputation. This edition includes a new chronology and further reading.

**'The most original genius that America has produced'
ALFRED, LORD TENNYSON**

'Poe has entered our popular consciousness as no other American writer' *The New York Times Book Review*

Edited with an introduction by DAVID GALLOWAY